Praise for
To Rescue the Republic

"Bret Baier's *To Rescue the Republic* is narrative history at its absolute finest. With great verve and a fair and balanced ethic, Baier brilliantly recounts the heroic life of Ulysses S. Grant—as Civil War general, US president, Reconstruction era leader, and beloved national icon. His dramatic retelling of the election of 1876, which pitted Samuel J. Tilden against Rutherford B. Hayes, is stupendous. A fast-paced, thrilling, and enormously important book. Highly recommended."

—Douglas Brinkley, Katherine Tsanoff Brown
Chair in Humanities and professor of history at Rice
University and author of *American Moonshot*

"With *To Rescue the Republic*, Bret Baier, the nation's leading reporter of history, has written a veritable tour de force. This remarkable book is history as it should be: magnificently composed, meticulously researched, and brimming with lessons for today's divided political arena. Baier has brought to life the riveting but too often forgotten story of how U. S. Grant preserved the Republic at one of its moments of greatest peril. This is not just a tale for our age, but an absorbing tale for the ages. It belongs on the bookshelf of every lover of history."

—Jay Winik, *New York Times* bestselling
author of *April 1865* and *1944*

"Yes, history can help light the way. Bret Baier's absorbing book shows us why Ulysses Grant was a far more important president than later generations gave him credit for, and how the crises of civil war, Reconstruction, and the deadlock of 1876 resemble the turbulent period we are living through now."

—Michael Beschloss, author of *Presidents of War*

"A thoroughly researched account of the Civil War general's life and work. Baier grippingly portrays the crisis Grant faced at the end of his presidency, when the election produced no clear successor, and the painful compromise that settled it—a historical moment ripe for examination today."

—*New York Post*

"Until recently, historians have tended to focus on the rampant corruption that took place during the administration of Ulysses S. Grant. . . . Baier . . . surveys Grant's life from his Midwestern origins through his undistinguished West Point education, his military successes leading Union forces, and his 1868 elevation to the presidency. . . . Baier finds parallels to contemporary politics in this, which makes his account all the more compelling."

—*Booklist*

"Throughout history, great men have stepped forward at just the right moment to save America at its most critical times. In *To Rescue the Republic*, Bret Baier brilliantly chronicles how Ulysses S. Grant was that great man multiple times. Perhaps you think you know the story, but Bret brings you back to the 1870s in a way I didn't think possible. A must-read!"

—Brian Kilmeade, #1 *New York Times* bestselling author

"Bret Baier once again brings his wonderful journalistic storytelling skills to the task of examining a significant moment in American history. *To Rescue the Republic* is the richly detailed and often suspenseful story of Ulysses S. Grant, our eighteenth president. In particular Bret focuses on those dramatic moments when Grant rescues the Republic—first during the Civil War, then making peace after the war, and finally in the bitterly contested election of 1876, when he devised a grand bargain to save the presidency and the nation. The parallels with modern times are striking, and the lessons Bret raises are worth serious attention: The future of the Republic isn't a given. We must fight for it in every era."

—Mark Levin, #1 *New York Times* bestselling author

"A brilliant character study of a great American. In *To Rescue the Republic*, Bret Baier brings Ulysses S. Grant—war hero, president, and author—to life in a vivid, gripping style that speaks to the issues of our time."

—James L. Swanson, *New York Times* bestselling author
of *Manhunt: The 12-Day Chase for Lincoln's Killer*

"As the United States suffers through turbulent times, news anchor Bret Baier reaches back to earlier years of heroism, when the nation, then and now, experienced an earlier example of woe. This is a book that, when carefully read, provides insight into a difficult era."

—John F. Marszalek, executive director of the
Ulysses S. Grant Presidential Library

"Bret Baier has provided a valuable public service by showing why Ulysses S. Grant deserves much more public acclaim for his presidential years than he has traditionally been given. If you enjoy reading about American history, you will love Bret Baier's fresh look at the man most responsible for the outcome of the Civil War and for the peaceful resolution of the contested presidential election of 1876. I highly recommend this book on one of America's most important leaders."

—David Rubenstein, chairman of the Council on Foreign Relations

"In *To Rescue the Republic*, Bret Baier combines the journalist's instinct for timeliness and a great story with the historian's ability to document and chronicle in ways that stand the test of time. *To Rescue the Republic* doubles as a political and military portrait of U. S. Grant and as a definitive account of Grant's ability to broker a settlement of the contentious election of 1876. This success marked the culmination of Grant's efforts as general and president to win and end the American Civil War. A key message of this book—in this time of discord and racial conflict—is that the American republic is a land of opportunity. Talent rises to the top. And because of this, no problem confronting Americans is ultimately beyond resolution. This book is as inspiring as it is readable, and it is easily my favorite book of 2021."

—David Eisenhower, director of the Institute for Public Service, Annenberg School for Communication, University of Pennsylvania, and author of *Eisenhower: At War, 1943–1945*

"A terrific account of the famous Civil War general turned eighteenth president. . . . Bret Baier has done it again, producing another presidential history that will last as long as there are presidential history books."

—*The American Spectator*

"Baier succeeds in humanizing Grant and clarifying the complex factors behind his decision-making. This is an accessible and nuanced introduction to an oft-misunderstood figure of American history."

—*Publishers Weekly*

TO RESCUE
THE REPUBLIC

ALSO BY BRET BAIER

Special Heart
Three Days in January
Three Days in Moscow
Three Days at the Brink

TO RESCUE THE REPUBLIC

ULYSSES S. GRANT,
THE FRAGILE UNION, AND THE CRISIS OF 1876

BRET BAIER

WITH CATHERINE WHITNEY

MARINER BOOKS

New York   Boston

HarperCollins books may be purchased for educational, business, or sales promotional use. For information, please email the Special Markets Department at SPsales@harpercollins.com.

A hardcover edition of this book was published in 2021 by Custom House, an imprint of William Morrow.

FIRST MARINER BOOKS PAPERBACK EDITION PUBLISHED 2022.

Designed by Leah Carlson-Stanisic
Title page art by Georgios Kollidas/AdobeStock

Library of Congress Cataloging-in-Publication Data

Names: Baier, Bret, author. | Whitney, Catherine,
Title: To rescue the republic : Ulysses S. Grant, the fragile Union, and
   the crisis of 1876 / Bret Baier, with Catherine Whitney.
Other titles: Ulysses S. Grant, the fragile Union, and the crisis of 1876
Description: First edition. | New York, NY : Custom House, [2021] |
   Includes bibliographical references and index.
Identifiers: LCCN 2021023681 (print) | LCCN 2021023682 (ebook) | ISBN
   9780063039544 (hardcover) | ISBN 9780063039568 (trade paperback) | ISBN
   9780063117877 | ISBN 9780063039551 (ebook)
Subjects: LCSH: Grant, Ulysses S. (Ulysses Simpson), 1822-1885. |
   Presidents—United States—Biography. | United States—Politics and
   government—1869-1877. | Presidents—United States—Election—1876. |
   Generals—United States—Biography.
Classification: LCC E672 .B35 2021 (print) | LCC E672 (ebook) | DDC
   973.8/2092 [B]—dc23
LC record available at https://lccn.loc.gov/2021023681
LC ebook record available at https://lccn.loc.gov/2021023682

ISBN 978-0-06-303956-8

22 23 24 25 26 LSC 10 9 8 7 6 5 4 3 2 1

To all those who try every day to bring the country together in tense and partisan times. Those efforts, like Grant's, will hopefully lay the groundwork for a bright future for generations to come.

CONTENTS

PART FOUR: A GRAND BARGAIN

PART FIVE: THE FINAL BATTLE

INTRODUCTION

Ulysses Grant in Living History

The engineer adjusted the lights in my home studio as I got ready to go live. I put in my earpiece and patted some makeup on my nose and forehead. During the global Covid-19 pandemic, most anchors broadcast from studios like this, plugging in from home in order to limit personal interaction as much as possible. This day, January 6, 2021, was to mark the official certification of the electoral college vote on Capitol Hill.

President Donald Trump was wrapping up a speech on the National Mall challenging the election results and firing up the crowd. "Our country has had enough; we will not take it anymore! That's what this is all about. And to use a favorite term that all of you people really came up with. We will 'stop the steal,'" the president said as the crowd chanted in unison, "Stop the steal! Stop the steal!"

I explained on air that the reality was different than the president's speech had indicated to the crowd now marching to the Capitol. There was zero chance that his vice president, Mike Pence, could overturn the results of the election during this certification process in Congress, and while several senators would rise to object to the vote in several different states, they wouldn't have the votes to change the outcome.

Then the sights and sounds outside the Capitol Building changed. Amid the chanting and waving of Trump flags, some people in the crowd started pushing the barricades on the west front of the Capitol Building. Screams from the Capitol Police of "Pull them this way!" and "Get back" rang out as the police tried to hold the line—all these images and sounds playing out on live TV. I got on the phone with lawmakers and others inside the Capitol to get a sense of what they were seeing and hearing.

On the Senate floor, Senator James Lankford of Oklahoma rose to object to the vote count in Arizona.

"My challenge today is not about the good people of Arizona—" Then the sound of the gavel interrupted Lankford. Moments earlier, Vice President Pence had been whisked from the chamber. Presiding in the chair, Iowa senator Chuck Grassley, the Senate president pro tempore, nervously said, "The Senate will stand in recess until the call of the chair!" Stunned, senators started filing out of the chamber.

The crowd outside had swelled and the barricades had been breached. I waved to the camera, signaling to the control room that I had new information. Dana Perino was anchoring, and she came to me right away. "Our chief political anchor, Bret Baier, I understand you have some new details?"

"Protesters, Dana, have made their way inside the Capitol. You're seeing the police presence increase on the outside, but there are people inside the actual Capitol Building, just outside the Senate chamber. And both the House and Senate have now adjourned or paused this entire process because of the security concerns."

What was supposed to have been an orderly, even ceremonial,

electoral college certification process had been suspended and was devolving into chaos inside the Capitol Building. I stayed in the chair commenting on the horrific images as they came in. We wouldn't get a true sense of the scope of the breach until a few hours later, when cell-phone videos and other images started to surface. January 6, 2021, was a moment that will be in the history books—a sad chapter for our country.

At the time, I happened to be putting the finishing touches on this book, about another unsettling chapter of our country's history. *To Rescue the Republic* is the story of Ulysses S. Grant's resolve and heroism in times of unparalleled turmoil for our nation. Grant was perhaps best known as the commanding general of the Union armies during the Civil War. But he also showed his strength as a leader on Reconstruction after the war and during his presidency. In his final days as president he rose to the challenge of preserving the Republic during the contested election of 1876, when violence threatened to once again overwhelm the nation to the point of war. As president, he led the effort to craft a resolution that would be accepted by both sides and head off a potential second civil war. It so happened that this nineteenth-century election drama was the centerpiece of my book.

Now here I was, watching the violence unfold on Capitol Hill in reaction to the 2020 election, while writing about President Grant's actions after the election of 1876. Two defining moments in history brought together on January 6, 2021.

The heartbeat of our Republic is the electoral process, in which the people declare their choice of president, freely and fairly. But what happens when the fairness of an election is in doubt, when the freedom of the people is constrained, and when the divisions on the public square strangle the process? This was the case in 1876 as the growing toll of the war and Reconstruction on the South began to undermine progress in several key states. Those states issued two sets of electoral votes—one for the Republican, Rutherford B. Hayes, and one for the Democrat, Samuel Tilden. Having won the war that almost destroyed the United States and cost over six hundred thousand lives, shattered the economy, and left four million freed slaves to an uncertain fate, Grant now faced the mission of healing the deep wounds in the body politic, which was in jeopardy.

I was drawn to the clear parallels between Grant's time and our own, and in particular to the final drama of his presidency: at the one-hundred-year mark of our nation's life, the fate of the United States was once again at stake, not on the bloody fields of war, where Grant had served so valiantly, but in the constitutional crisis of a disputed election.

In the midst of a real constitutional crisis in 2021, the story of Grant and 1876 took on new meaning. I could see across the landscape of our history that there had been those crucial times when everything we stood for was at risk—when divisions were so deep that there were two separate realities being experienced by the citizenry. What did we do in the past to survive such a moment? And what do we do now?

Since the publication of my first presidential biography, *Three Days in January: Dwight Eisenhower's Final Mission*, I've been writing about American presidents at defining moments in our nation's history. These presidential lives have been fully recorded by historians, and I've never tried to compete with their works. I like to say that I am a reporter of history, not a historian. I try to bring a fresh reporter's perspective to the lives and times of US presidents—not only to look through a soda straw into singular events that changed history but also to find a parallel in our own times. In this way, I hope I've been able to give new meaning to what are considered familiar tales. As a reporter, I'm an observer of living history who believes that presidents long dead are not relics to observe from a distance, but ever-present in the lives of Americans.

My fascination with Grant began with reading his own writing. In the final years of his life, he penned his war memoir, which would be published by Mark Twain. Not only is it a riveting and elaborately detailed biography, but it also provides a rare inside view of a man's character. It is so well written that many people at the time thought Twain had penned it himself. Grant was a stellar writer. After reading his memoir, along with the colorful memoir of his wife, the works of historians, and a rich library of documents (many in the recently opened Ulysses S. Grant Presidential Library at Mississippi State University), I knew Grant was the next presidential figure to explore—especially in today's context.

Like Dwight Eisenhower, Ronald Reagan, and Franklin D. Roosevelt, the presidents I wrote about in the *Three Days* series, Grant was a complicated man, both more and less than what he seemed. A brilliant general who despised the battlefield, a controversial president who has often scored low in historians' presidential rankings, a man of great self-control and vision who nonetheless stumbled—in many ways Grant reflected both the conflicts and aspirations of America itself after the war.

It is just the kind of story I love to tell—especially at a time when people are asking whether some wounds are too deep to heal. We are a nation divided, in part, by issues similar to those that plagued Grant's era. If his story is in some respects our story, what can we learn from the healing mission of our eighteenth president that might show us a path toward union?

On January 6, 2021, the director counted me down to the end of the commercial break: "Three, two, one, cue." I was ending my show, *Special Report*, on one of the darkest days on Capitol Hill in more than one hundred years. I had our staff put together a montage of all the compelling video clips and still photos we had collected through the day with the accompanying audio to end the show. "Now we take a look back at the sights and sounds of an historic day, a horrible day on Capitol Hill. But we're a strong country, we're a resilient country. We can get through this. That's it for *Special Report*. 'Fair, balanced, and still unafraid.'"

TO RESCUE
THE REPUBLIC

PROLOGUE

A Dark Night in Philadelphia

In Philadelphia on the evening of November 8, 1876, President Ulysses S. Grant was comfortably settled in the elegant Walnut Street home of publisher George W. Childs, awaiting the results of a contentious election held the previous day. He was smoking a cigar in his customary calm manner, which he'd mastered in wartime, but inwardly he was churning. Never before had an electoral tally been so close and so uncertain. Whispers of irregularities had haunted this high-stakes election, which pitted the Republican Rutherford B. Hayes against the Democrat Samuel J. Tilden.

This was a moment with the same gravity as Grant had felt back when success and failure were meted out through cannon fire. For nearly twelve years, since the end of the terrible Civil War, he had made it his mission to heal the breach and to bring the nation together—North and South, white and Black. For a time, it had felt as though that goal was possible. He'd believed that his election to the presidency in 1868 had been a mandate for Reconstruction, and he'd seen the same optimism expressed in his easy reelection in 1872. But since 1874, the battle had resumed. Blood was being spilled in racial violence throughout the South, and he'd sent federal troops to restore order and protect the rights of Black citizens. Ultimately, however, sending in troops was an unsustainable solution. How could the Union survive if peace could only be maintained at gunpoint?

These days being a champion of Reconstruction was a lonely place. Even the Republicans who had been so dedicated to the cause were growing tired. Yet, while he was not certain that Hayes would be a faithful shepherd of the task of reunification, Grant was sure that the Democrat Tilden would not be. He shared the view of most Republican Northerners that it was too soon to turn the White House over to the party of the Confederacy.

Despite being troubled by the uncertainty, Grant was relieved to be out of the running. Many of his supporters had urged him to seek a third term and complete the unfinished business of his presidency. Leading the chorus was his wife, Julia. Julia had loved every minute of being in the White House. She would have happily accepted another four years. Knowing this, Grant didn't tell her right away when he decided not to run. He quietly arranged a meeting with his cabinet and shared the news. Then he sat down and wrote a letter to the Republican Party chairman, informing him of his decision.

Julia didn't miss a trick. Suspecting that something was up, she confronted Grant. "I want to know what is happening. I am sure there is something, and I must know."

Grant sighed. He promised to speak to her as soon as he lit his cigar. That done, he confessed, "You know what a to-do the papers have been making about a third term. Well, I have never until now had any opportunity to answer." Then he told her he had sent a letter to the head of the Republican Party informing him that he would not run.

Julia was upset. "Bring it and read it to me now," she demanded.

He smiled apologetically. "No, it is already posted."

"Oh, Ulys, was that kind to me?" she raged. "Was it just to me?"

Grant felt for his wife, but he knew his heart. "Well, I do not want to be here another four years. I do not think I could stand it," he told her. He begged Julia to let it go, but for a while, she was inconsolable. He hated disappointing his wife, but he assured her that it was for the best. He was tired. He felt he hadn't rested for a moment since the first shot had been fired at Fort Sumter at the beginning of the war in 1861. Now more than fifteen years had passed, and he'd pledged every one of them to the survival of the nation. It was time for another man to step up.

As he sat with Childs, puffing on his cigar, Grant felt himself relaxing. He'd always found that easy to do with his friend by his side. The two men had become close after the war, and Childs had helped the Grants purchase their Philadelphia house. In the first year of his presidency, when Grant had complained to Childs about the miserable Washington heat, Childs had intervened again, urging them to come to the beautiful beach in Long Branch, New Jersey, near his own family house, where they could escape Washington. The Grants' two-story chalet, fronting the ocean, became known as the Ulysses S. Grant Cottage, or the Summer White House. Grant and Childs would spend every day of their vacations together, sitting on their porches playing cards, eating, or just talking. Childs held the unique position of being Grant's only close friend who wasn't a military associate. Grant could relate to this man of humble beginnings who had made something of himself, and he especially appreciated Childs's generosity and self-effacing charm.

Childs brought out qualities in Grant that he hadn't known he had—in particular, a creative spirit, which he would later express in his *Memoirs*. They shared a basic philosophy, including the principle that one needn't be mean to be successful. It was fitting that Grant was spending this transitional election aftermath with his friend.

The early returns seemed to be predicting a Tilden victory. Having won the popular vote, he had won 184 of the 185 electoral votes needed, according to the initial count. The problem was that three states—South Carolina, Louisiana, and Florida—had yet to announce their results. In those states, both sides were claiming victory.

No one was surprised by that. The presidential campaign season in those states had looked a lot like warfare, as the anger and suspicion spilled over into the electoral process. All three states were led by Republican governors, who controlled the election boards and had pulled out all the stops to press for Hayes's success. The other side believed that election fraud was possible, even probable, but it wasn't just Democrats who were suspicious of Republicans. Republicans, too, made many claims of fraud, particularly around the suppression of the Black vote.

Grant's allies were hopeful that Hayes would eke out a victory in the electoral college. As he examined the electoral map, Grant did not share their optimism, and he went to bed that night believing that Tilden would be elected. However, at daybreak, there was still no certainty about the outcome. Childs invited Grant to continue the vigil at his newspaper office. The men around him were optimistic that Hayes would prevail, but after watching for a time, Grant quietly observed, "It looks to me as if Mr. Tilden has been elected."

However, the election was far from settled. South Carolina, Louisiana, and Florida had finally submitted disputed tallies, one from the Republican boards and another from self-appointed Democratic counters. "Everything now depends on a fair count," Grant told reporters as he prepared to return to Washington.

No one could have predicted that the count would drag on for four months—or that a fair count seemed so maddeningly beyond reach. Grant, who had expected to symbolically pass the torch with the election, found himself facing an unexpected final act that involved once again rescuing the national promise he had won on the battlefield.

A man of common roots, a reluctant but heroic warrior, a flawed but resolute president, Grant lived his life by a moral code of respect for the worth of every individual. His habit in the heat of battle, be it bloody or bureaucratic, was to envelop himself in a cloak of calm, even while those around him panicked.

As news came that Southern militia were planning to march on Washington and forcibly install Tilden in the presidency, and as the two parties wrangled in Congress over the electoral count, Grant was faced with a choice about whether to insinuate himself into the drama. As president, he had no direct role in the election—that was Congress's purview. But he had influence, and he decided to use it to expedite a fair result—even if that result required sacrificing his own achievements.

Grant had always been a conciliator. He knew when to hold firm and when to strike a bargain. Now, finally, he sensed that a grand bargain was called for, one that would shape the coming era with equal measures of pain and promise. He wondered if the two sides had the courage to strike that deal.

In the closing days of his presidency, Grant was called upon to summon the character and courage that had long been his hallmark. He had rescued the Republic once before, when it was endangered on the bloody fields of war. Now he had to rescue it again, on its troubled path to peace. His whole life had been preparing him for this moment.

PART ONE

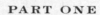

SEASONED BY STRUGGLE

THE MAKING OF GRANT

We might envision him on a steed, tall and erect in the saddle—the classic portrait of a military leader. His uniform is sharply pressed, his beard flowing, his boots catching the light with their high polish. His eyes are shaded and his face is still, as if carved in granite. He is the greatest general in American history, save for George Washington.

But Ulysses S. Grant never looked the part. Ironically, the image just described better suits a different man, Grant's Civil War nemesis Robert E. Lee. In Grant's case, we have to look beyond the ideal to see the real man, whose bearing was a little rough around the edges.

Grant was a man of average height—five-foot-eight—and is always described as slightly stooped. At the peak of his wartime fame he weighed only 135 pounds. The snapshots of Grant at war show his slender frame, his rumpled uniform and muddy boots, his unthreatening demeanor, his dark, melancholy eyes.

He was, wrote biographer William S. McFeely, an "ordinary man," which made him interesting. "I liked the way he looked,"

McFeely wrote, "the picture of the mild, rather small person slouched comfortably in front of a tent suggested neither the fierce killing warrior nor the bumbling and perhaps crooked politician that I had often read about." McFeely's prose was not always so flattering to Grant, but he could find little fault with him for his ordinariness. In many respects, Grant symbolized a particularly American characteristic—the ability of ordinary people to accomplish the extraordinary.

Historians concur that Grant is an enigma. It's hard to paint a portrait of a man so inner-focused. It's challenging to stitch together the contradictory elements of his character to form a complete picture. Inevitably, the confusion leads to inaccuracies born of ill will and supposition.

Ron Chernow, whose important biography, *Grant*, captures Grant's complex character as few have, tried valiantly to clear through the muck of a century and a half of false narratives. "Grant has been subjected to pernicious stereotypes that grossly impede our understanding of the man," Chernow writes in his more satisfying reconstruction of the truth about Grant.

No doubt much of the confusion is due to Grant's failure to conform to what we think is the nature of powerful men. Union Army commander George Meade, who was no great fan of Grant, described him as "ill at ease," especially around strangers, a man who "has never mixed with the world." Grant wasn't shy so much as extremely reserved, with a dose of moral rigidity—he despised obscenity and had little patience for any of the vulgarities common among Army men.

Even as he achieved great victories on the battlefield and then attained the highest office in the land, Grant was consistent in his demeanor. When asked by a reporter if his father had changed when he took command of all the armies, Grant's son Fred replied, "No, that was impossible. My father was always the same.

He was always grave. He was always thoughtful. He was always gentle. He was always extraordinarily considerate of the feelings of others."

His wartime correspondence with his beloved Julia reveals a romantic streak that would not have been apparent in his public behavior. His deepest feelings were reserved for private moments. Even those who knew him best had trouble divining his inner thoughts. His brother-in-arms, the great general William Tecumseh Sherman, said, "To me he is a mystery, and I believe he is a mystery to himself."

Some of Grant's Civil War opponents accused him of being a butcher, a characterization that is debated to this day. Yet, although he was unwavering in his strategic vision, he was kind in victory, heartsick about losses on both sides, and quick to forgive his enemies. His devoted military secretary, Adam Badeau, wrote that, after the war, "Grant was the most popular man in America"—in the North "because he had been victorious," and in the South "because he had been magnanimous."

A reluctant politician, Grant was prone to political stumbles while in the White House, yet he pursued the most ambitious campaign imaginable—Reconstruction of the South.

Through it all he was humble. "It is certain that nothing was farther from my father's mind than thought of pomp or power," wrote his son Jesse. Ulysses Grant had learned humility from his mother, Hannah, who believed that praise should be given to God alone for allowing humans to achieve. The purpose of life was not to gain personal glory, she preached to her children. It was, rather, to simply do one's best. Because Hannah Grant had no concept of "pomp or power," she never visited her son in the White House. On the day of his first inauguration, she was observed by a neighbor calmly sweeping her porch.

We often search for clues to the character of our heroes in the forces that shaped them. In his contemporaneous biography of Grant, written in 1885, the Honorable J. T. Headley noted that people look for the origins of the greatness of notable figures in their childhoods and, in the absence of early evidence, tend to invent romantic childhood tales about them. He cited Napoleon and Washington as examples. "But the truth is," he concluded, "circumstances make men."

That's partly and maybe even largely true. But Grant's character stands out, and the sheer unlikelihood of his rise adds a special dimension to his story. Had his father not secured a place for him at West Point without his knowledge, he might never have thought of being a soldier. He rose up in the ranks through skill and industry but never had the qualities often associated with great military leaders—brazenness, a dominating physical presence, an outsized ego, or an authoritarian nature. In light of that, his success on the battlefield is worthy of attention.

And so, this unremarkable man became America's surprising hero. Because he wrote a war memoir and letters expressing his deepest thoughts, we are fortunate to have an inside view of his character and journey. Before the twentieth century, it was rare for a president to write an autobiography. But we can know Grant, not only through the recollections of others but through his own words. And it's quite a story.

The one-level white frame cottage in Point Pleasant, Ohio, was square and squat, comprised of one large room measuring sixteen and a half feet by nineteen feet, which served as living room, bedroom, and kitchen. A fireplace was at the center. It was tight quarters. But it had the advantage of overlooking the Ohio River, a floating highway with its steady traffic and the promise of grand vistas beyond. Newlyweds Jesse and Hannah Grant paid $2 a month in rent for the privilege of a world-class view. In reality, they were chained to the earth. Jesse was the partner in a tannery right next door, and they lived in the billowing stench of its bloody commerce.

They'd been married only a month when Hannah became pregnant, and now their tiny abode would be accommodating a child. In the bloom of early spring, on April 27, 1822, Hannah went into labor and Jesse called for the doctor, a stern-faced abolitionist who dispatched the nervous father-to-be to the outdoors. As Jesse paced nervously, wearing a track in the dirt (they had no porch), he heard his son's voice for the first time and was overcome with joy. Five more children later, he would never forget the feeling that at last his life had come to its fulfillment.

Within days the relatives had descended—specifically Hannah's family—to convene a dramatic naming conference. Only the most majestic name would do for this precious offspring! Hannah's father favored Hiram, the Old Testament king. Her mother and Jesse preferred Ulysses, a romantic name from their reading of the classics. Hannah liked Theodore. Her aunt favored Albert. The proposed names were put in a hat, leaving the decision to chance. Hannah reached in and drew the name. Ulysses.

She paused. Hannah saw the delight of her mother and husband, but she felt compelled to please her father. She announced that the child would be named Hiram Ulysses. But he was called Ulysses.

It was a big name, but he was a big boy, weighing in at ten and three-quarters pounds, with healthy pink cheeks, blue eyes, and reddish hair. During the long days of spring and summer, after the chores were completed, Hannah would sit with her son and watch the river. It wasn't in her nature to whisper to him of the adventures he might have one day. She never dreamed of another life. But when Ulysses's blue eyes lit up at the sight of tall steamers making their way east, he might have been imprinted with the sense of a quest.

If one were to choose a quality that most characterized Ulysses's upbringing, it would be independence. And with that independence came a physical courage that was evident even in his earliest years.

In this he modeled his father, who nurtured his favorite son's spirit. Jesse's own youth had been one of great hardship and then abandonment. After his mother died when he was eleven, his father, Noah, an unstable wanderlust and sometime drunk, pulled up stakes and moved with his other two children to live with his older son Peter in Maysville, Kentucky. Jesse was left to his own devices. Noah, who had served in the Continental Army and fought in the Battle of Bunker Hill, could have been a sterling example to his impressionable son. Instead, he abandoned him.

Small and alone, Jesse worked as a hired hand at various farms until he was taken in by the family of Judge George Tod in Youngstown, Ohio. There he received room and board in exchange for helping Mrs. Tod with her five children while her husband was away on his circuit. Jesse was provided with a good home and the first formal schooling he'd ever received. He came to love Mrs. Tod, whom he found quite beautiful and kind. Missing his mother, he was comforted by her care. He was also determined not to become his father. Having had a taste of love and stability, he vowed to make it his pursuit. He set a plan for himself—to marry by age twenty-five and retire rich at sixty.

Mrs. Tod encouraged him to pursue a career as a tanner, and he decided to move to Maysville, where his half-brother Peter owned a tannery. There he became an apprentice. After his apprenticeship, Jesse returned to Ohio and got a job with a tanner named Owen Brown, who was an abolitionist. Jesse lived with the Browns, and under their influence he developed a passion for the antislavery cause.

Brown's son John was as devoted to abolition as his father, but he chose a violent path. John Brown would become famous for his ultimate protest—an assault on the armory in Harper's Ferry, Virginia, in 1859, for which he was hanged.

When Ulysses was a child, Jesse spoke admiringly of the Browns and their antislavery virtues, and he continued to do so even after John Brown's death. "I have often heard my father speak of John Brown, particularly since the events at Harper's Ferry," Ulysses would later write. "Brown was a boy when they lived in the same house, but he knew him afterwards, and regarded him as a man of great purity of character, of high moral and physical courage, but a fanatic and extremist in whatever he advocated. It was certainly the act of an insane man to attempt the invasion of the South, and the overthrow of slavery, with less than twenty men." In any case, Jesse would never flag in his devotion to the cause of abolition, which began in those early days at Owen Brown's fireside.

As Jesse Grant approached his twenty-fifth year, he became a partner in a Ravenna tannery and felt truly on his way. It was time to carry out the second part of his plan—finding a wife.

He thought about the women he knew of in the area and concluded that none of them struck his fancy. But he had learned, he said, "that if I ever got a mate I must hunt her, for she would not hunt me." On his birthday, his landlady saw him pacing and asked, "What are you thinking about so seriously?"

"About looking for a wife," he replied honestly.

"Where are you going to look?"

"Well, I don't know," he said. "Somewhere where there are girls."

But before he could fulfill his goal, he became deathly ill with malaria. Sickness and bad luck sidetracked him for a year and a half, but he righted himself, as he always had before, and secured a partnership in a tannery in Point Pleasant. And then he once again went looking for a wife.

He found Hannah Simpson, the daughter of a well-established farmer in the area. She was a slim, attractive twenty-three-year-old woman of medium height, with soft brown hair and rosy cheeks. His description of her seems to be a cool review and not very romantic, but for him it was the highest praise: "I discovered she was a person of good sense, neat in person, industrious in her habits, amiable in disposition, and quite handsome without the slightest appearance of vanity."

For his part, Jesse brought the promise of stability to the union. Tanning was a respectable profession, if one did not mind the smell of dried blood, animal flesh remnants, and sulfuric acid that permeated everything. The labor was hard, but it allowed Jesse to rise above his troubled youth and stand out in the rugged frontier towns of the era by actually making a good and steady living. Were it not for this prospect of his solvency, Hannah's parents would hardly have looked twice at Jesse as a mate for their daughter. He was poorly educated—something that mattered to her family—and his family connections were sketchy. He was entirely on his own. A tall, sober man who out-talked everybody in a room, he wasn't handsome either—just average in looks. But the Simpsons respected his seriousness and admired his genuine desire for a wife and children. He also liked Hannah's parents very much, and they bonded over their mutual love of books. The many occasions on which they would sit by the fire and talk about books revealed Jesse's more thoughtful side and his desire to transcend his limited formal education.

Jesse was very much a product of his time, and what a time it was. Ohio was like the center of the universe, the gateway to the West in a nation that now stretched from sea to shining sea. In the years following the purchase of the Louisiana Territory, which doubled the landmass of the country, pioneers were on the move. Lured by the promise of opportunity and the wide-open expanses in the far West, they traveled by horse and covered wagon, passing through Ohio and continuing on. For Jesse, Ohio was far enough west and unsettled enough that a man could make his own way there.

The sounds of Ulysses's early childhood were the mellow hum of his mother's voice and the strident certainty of his father's. Neighbors preferred Hannah's quiet manner to Jesse's bombast. He was a man of very strong opinions, which he didn't hesitate to share at high volume. Drawn to controversy, especially when politics was involved, he was an outspoken member of the Whig Party.

In demeanor, Ulysses was more his mother's child. Quiet and self-contained, he seemed much older than his years, like a small adult. According to the journalist and author Albert Deane Richardson, a contemporary of Grant's, "Ulysses inherited many of his best traits from his mother. . . . She was amiable, serene, even-tempered, thoroughly self-forgetful, kind and considerate to all, and speaking ill of none." Hannah adored her children but would not stand for boasting. A reporter who interviewed her noted that when Ulysses became a very famous and revered man, she couldn't bear to hear people speak glowingly of him, "for it seems akin to hearing self-praise, which she regards with unmitigated horror."

The rod was spared in the Grant household. In fact, as Grant remembered it, there was "never any scolding or punishing by my parents." Even at a very young age, he was allowed remarkable freedom. As Jesse Grant prospered, more opportunities opened up to expand his horizons.

By the fall of 1823, Jesse had saved enough money to buy his own tannery in Georgetown, Ohio. He built a lovely two-story brick house down the street, and it became the family home for the remainder of Ulysses's childhood. Over the years, as more children came, Jesse built additions onto the house, including a full kitchen. In this bucolic environment, Ulysses thrived.

In addition to the tannery, Jesse had an area of farmland, and this was Ulysses's playground. He enjoyed farm work, and by the age of eight he was happily hauling chopped wood felled on the forest land and plowing the field with horse-drawn plows to plant and harvest corn and potatoes. And when the hard work was completed, Ulysses was free to go fishing or swimming and even to ride a horse to visit his grandparents fifteen miles away.

His true love was horses. Ulysses had his first encounter with the marvelous beasts when he was only two. A circus came to town, and he was delighted by the sight of a trained pony. He begged to ride it, and Jesse indulgently lifted him up and held on to him as the pony pranced around the ring. Ulysses was full of joy, and from then on horses were his obsession. He lived in his own quiet world with them and was content with the solitude.

He had a way with the animals that was a clue to his character. Calm, firm, and quiet, he could settle the most fractious beast. Once mounted, he could ride like the wind. Later, during his military service, Grant's speed, dexterity, and fearlessness in the saddle would be his secret weapon.

Jesse was bursting with pride as he watched his son's brave antics. At only five years old, the boy would mount a steed and balance himself on its bare back. His skill developed rapidly. "At eight or nine he would ride them at the top of their speed," Jesse recalled, "he standing upon one foot and balancing himself by the bridle reins. . . . He always broke his own horses. I never knew one to balk with him."

Eight-year-old Ulysses was obsessed with owning his own colt, and he set his sights on one owned by a Mr. Ralston in a nearby village. He begged his father to buy the horse for him, and Jesse indulgently agreed. However, the negotiation did not go well. Jesse offered $20, but Ralston asked for $25. They haggled back and forth and were unable to reach a deal.

Heartbroken, Ulysses pleaded with Jesse to reconsider. Jesse softened and agreed to let the boy approach Ralston himself. He instructed him this way: the pony was worth only $20 and he should offer that. If Ralston rejected the price, he should offer $22.50, and if that failed, finally he could offer $25. So Ulysses hopped on his horse and rode to Ralston's house, where he announced innocently, "Papa says I may offer you twenty dollars for the colt, but if you won't take that, I am to offer twenty-two and a half, and if you won't take that, to give you twenty-five." Twenty-five it was. This, according to Grant, was his father's version of the story and only "nearly true." But in the aftermath, he was subjected to ribbing by the other boys. "Boys enjoy the misery of their companions, at least village boys in that day did," Grant wrote of the incident, adding that "in later life I have found that all adults are not free of the peculiarity."

Ulysses may have been quiet like his mother, but he was very popular with his peers. His classmate James M. Sanderson recalled late in life, "Ulysses Grant was one of the quietest boys I ever knew, and yet he was liked by every boy in Georgetown who knew him, and that is saying a good deal, because we Western boys used to be as noisy and rollicking a lot of fellows as there ever was."

Schools at the time were mostly by subscription, with children of all ages crammed together receiving the most rudimentary education. Jesse was quite passionate about his son's studies. In spite of his own lack of formal education, he had what Ulysses called a "thirst for education." Jesse read every book he could get his hands on and read the newspaper every day of his life until he died at eighty. This love of learning was behind his insistence that his son get a good education.

At the subscription school in Georgetown, Ulysses wasn't a particularly impressive student, but Sanderson did cite one skill: "I remember that he especially liked problems in mental arithmetic. The teachers used to give us a lot of them, one after another, every other day during the term. Most of us hated them and would make all kinds of excuses to get out of the exercise, while young Grant was anxious to have the teacher fire them at him. His mind seemed exactly fitted for solving such problems on a moment's notice."

However, according to one of his teachers, Thomas Upham, Ulysses had no taste for spelling, grammar, or geography, and he hated writing essays. Public speaking was also a wash. Upham recalled him making a complete mess of a recitation of part of George Washington's Farewell Address.

Over time Jesse became dissatisfied with the mediocrity of the subscription school. He was also offended by a practice that was never followed in the Grant home: the frequent use of a switch to whip kids into shape. "I can see John D. White—the teacher—now, with his long beech switch always in his hand," he later wrote. "It was not always the same one, either. Switches were brought in bundles, from a beech wood near the school house, by the boys for whose benefit they were intended."

Jesse wanted more for his son, and in 1836, when Ulysses was fourteen, he was sent to Maysville, Kentucky, where he attended the Maysville Academy run by W. W. Richeson and Jacob W. Rand, two prominent scholars. He lived with his uncle Peter's widow. Overall, Ulysses was less than impressed with his new schooling. He wrote that most of the time was spent "going over the same old arithmetic which I knew every word of before, and repeating: 'A noun is the name of a thing,' which I had also heard my Georgetown teachers repeat, until I had come to believe it."

After one winter at the school, Ulysses returned home for a year before attending a second private school in Ripley, Ohio. The Presbyterian Academy was run by Jon Rankin, a prominent abolitionist. There Grant made little impression and felt that he hadn't made "progress enough to compensate for the outlay of board and tuition."

Over the years, Ulysses had plenty of time alone on his horse to dream about the future, but there is little evidence of where those dreams took him. Perhaps he hoped to be a farmer surrounded by horses, or perhaps to work in the river trade, or to get an education. Being a soldier wasn't on the list.

Neither was working in a tannery. Ulysses *despised* the tannery. He detested the sickening stench and ugliness of the tanning process. When he was sixteen, Ulysses informed Jesse, quite respectfully, that he would not be joining him in the family business, although he offered his services until he turned twenty-one.

Jesse, who loved his son above all and was quite aware of his distaste for tanning, replied, "My son, I don't want you to work at it now if you don't like it and don't mean to stick it out. I want you to work at whatever you like and intend to follow." Needless to say, seeking self-fulfillment in work was not common fatherly advice for that day. And Jesse did not exactly follow through. He wanted his son to have a good education, but lacking the funds to send him to college, he set his sights on the West Point Military Academy, a fine institution that had the added advantage of being tuition-free.

Set above the Hudson River, some fifty miles north of New York City, the setting had served as a military fortress during the Revolutionary War. Afterward, George Washington had the idea of creating an elite military training academy, but it wasn't until 1802 that President Thomas Jefferson established the West Point Military Academy by law.

Having a West Point cadet in the family was a source of pride for the whole family and community, and Jesse believed that West Point would provide an excellent start for his son. There was only one stumbling block. Admission to West Point required the recommendation of a US senator or congressman from one's state. When Jesse first wrote to his friend, Ohio senator Thomas Morris, no appointments to the academy were available. Then, in a stroke of luck (from Jesse's perspective), a neighbor's son, who was a friend of Ulysses's, left West Point, opening up a slot.

Jesse quickly contacted his congressman, Thomas Hamer, a Democrat. The two men had once been very close friends, but Jesse had ended the friendship over a political dispute between Democrat and Whig. After that they never spoke again, as neither was willing to make the first move toward reconciliation. Now Hamer was the ticket to his son's future, and Jesse decided to end the grudge. Graciously, Hamer, who was due to retire, agreed to nominate Ulysses as one of his last acts in office. From then on, he and Jesse were friends again.

Apart from George Washington, Grant would become the most celebrated military leader in American history. But when his father informed him that he had secured a place at West Point through an appeal to the local congressman, Ulysses was distraught. The conversation took place while he was home from Ripley for Christmas.

"Ulysses, I believe you are going to receive an appointment," Jesse told him.

"What appointment?" Ulysses had no clue what he was talking about.

"To West Point. I have applied for it."

"But I won't go!"

His protests were short-lived. "He said he thought I would, and I thought so, too, if he did," Grant wrote in his memoir. In other words, Jesse wanted him to follow his dream, but first he wanted him to follow *Jesse's* dream, and there would be no argument about it.

His appointment disturbed some of the elite of the district, who felt that places at West Point should be reserved for those with social standing, not for a "short, stubby boy" (as one put it) who might embarrass the community.

A Philadelphia journalist who had known Ulysses as a youth recalled the common sentiment that he might not have the making of a soldier. "We well remember the stir created by the appointment of the tanner's son to a cadetship at West Point. The surprise among the sons of our doctors, lawyers and storekeepers was something wonderful. Indeed, none of us boys, high or low, rich or poor, could clearly imagine how Uncle Sam's schoolmasters were going to transform our somewhat *outre*-looking comrade into our *beau ideal* of dandyism—a West Pointer."

Ulysses did not remember the riverfront view of his infancy, but the Ohio River always held power in his imagination. Now, aboard a steamer that would carry him east, he thrilled to the journey, even as he worried about what awaited him on the other side. As he stared dreamily at the water bubbling up in the steamer's wake, he fantasized about an accident—not a serious one, just bad enough to injure him a little bit and force him to return home. That didn't happen, and eventually he relaxed and enjoyed the adventure. In Harrisburg he boarded a train—the first railroad he had ever seen. He called the train, which traveled at twelve to eighteen miles an hour, "the perfection of rapid transit." Lingering for a few days in Philadelphia, where he saw every sight, and then in New York City, he finally arrived at West Point at the end of May.

As he approached the entrance to the grand academy, Ulysses felt some dread over the unknown challenges he would face, but little excitement. "A military life had no charms for me," he wrote of his feelings at the time. His main goal was to get through the training without humiliating himself and his family. He had no romantic visions of standing in fields of battle. He understood nothing of the companionship of fellow soldiers who would be friends for life—much less that these companions would come from all parts of the growing nation. He couldn't have realized that the discipline, once learned, would become his constant companion. Or that this was the first moment of the great adventure of his adult life.

When Ulysses showed up to register, he discovered that Congressman Hamer had submitted his name as Ulysses S. Grant, not Hiram Ulysses Grant, perhaps assuming in his rush that Grant's middle name was his mother's maiden name, Simpson. Grant protested and asked that the record be corrected. To his astonishment, he was told this was impossible. West Point could only admit the person by the name registered in his nomination. So he became Ulysses S. Grant from that point on. His classmates teasingly called him "Uncle Sam" and "Sam."

The seventeen-year-old Grant was not built to impress at only five-foot-one and 117 pounds. In the coming years, he would gain seven inches, but he was never a towering figure physically. Yet he was determined to make a decent showing. West Point was unlike any place he had ever been, and he was especially taken by the breathtaking setting. In a letter to his cousin Mc-

Kinstrey Griffith, Grant was poetic in his description of West Point, though his spelling (as always) was poor:

> I have put asaid [*sic*] my Algebra and French and am going to tell you a long story about this prettiest of places West Point. So far as it regards natural attractions it is decidedly the most beautiful place that I have ever seen; here are hills and dales, rocks and river; all pleasant to look upon. From the window near I can see the Hudson; that far famed, that beautiful river with its bosom studded with hundreds of snow [struck: white] sails. Again if I look another way I can see Fort Putnam frowning far above: a stern monument of a sterner age, which seems placed there on purpose to tell us of the glorious deeds of our fathers. and to bid us remember their sufferings—to follow their examples.

Those "fathers" were the nation's first army, the soldiers who fought in the Revolutionary War—men such as the fort's namesake Rufus Putnam, who was instrumental in the settlement and development of Ohio after the war.

But if Ulysses found the setting heavenly, daily life at West Point was another matter. Far from his benevolent household, Grant now learned a harsher way—rigorous physical and mental work and hard punishment for "crimes" of misconduct.

As biographer Lloyd Lewis described it, "From five o'clock in the morning until ten o'clock at night the drums were rolling, drumming Ulysses awake, drumming him to bed, to roll call, to inspection, to drill, to meals, to class, to study and to the sunset parade. And the drums were hard for Ulysses' feet to follow—his small feet—small like his hands."

Despite an aptitude for math and his impressive horsemanship, he was not gifted in military skills or discipline and would graduate twenty-first in a class of thirty-nine. He was notorious for the frequency of his demerits—fifty-nine in his first year, sixty-seven in his second, and sixty-six in his third. Adding to this lackluster performance was his tone-deafness, which caused him to hate both church music and military bands.

Even so, he managed. On a visit home in his final year, his mother observed approvingly, "You've grown much straighter and taller."

"Yes, mother," he said, "they teach us to be erect at West Point."

Grant was popular at West Point and had a solid reputation. But as Richardson pointed out, "neither classmates nor professors fancied that he was born great, or going to achieve greatness, or likely to have greatness thrust upon him."

Once again, he was noticed for his horsemanship. His fellow cadet James Longstreet called him "the most daring horseman at the Academy." He proved his skill with a particularly wild dark bay named York. Only Grant was capable of taming him, and he amazed his classmates with a graduation demonstration involving a record-setting bar jump. Sailing high in the air, with seeming ease and calm, his slender body pressed to York's flanks, he wowed the graduation crowd, who turned to each other in awe, wondering who that young man was.

Among Grant's fellow cadets was one named William Tecumseh Sherman. Neither boy could have guessed the significance of their later relationship. Nor could they have known that the scribes of history would retrieve the story of their unimpressive West Point careers—perhaps as a lesson to the young that redemption is never out of reach. In an article that appeared in the *Army and Navy Journal* at the end of the Civil War, the two West Point grads were savaged in a critique of their time at West Point, neither achieving the status of "good boys" of the institute. Sherman was ranked 124th in the order of good behavior and Grant 147th—"So near the bottom, that he must at times have had visions of falling out altogether." Neither distinguished himself in scholarship either.

Sherman took the critique in stride, and he wasn't above poking at Grant's inadequacies, telling a reporter later in life, "A more unpromising boy never entered the Military Academy. Let this be a lesson to all of us. Looks are deceiving."

And yet, some saw the promise in Grant's unusual qualities. Brigadier General Rufus Ingalls, who was in Grant's West Point class, noted, "Grant was such a quiet, unassuming fellow when a cadet that nobody would have picked him out as one who was destined to occupy a place in history; and yet he had certain qualities which attracted attention and commanded the respect of all those in the corps with him. He was always frank, generous and manly. . . . He had enough marked characteristics to prevent him from being considered commonplace, and everyone associated with him was sure to remember him and retain a high regard for him."

Grant was the first to say he wasn't cut out for the military. "I had not the faintest idea of staying in the army even if I should be graduated, which I did not expect." But he was loyal and responsible, so by the time he graduated, he'd decided he owed Uncle Sam at least a short service. What began as a brief bow to obligation became the work of his life. He found he had a talent for it.

CHAPTER 2

CONFLICTED WARRIOR

It was lonely at the St. Louis Jefferson Barracks, where Grant was cooling his heels as a newly minted brevet second lieutenant to the Fourth US Infantry awaiting an assignment. (The designation brevet was meant as an honorary rank higher than the one actually held, given to those who had distinguished themselves in some special way. In Grant's case, likely his graduation from West Point.) He was saved from going stir-crazy by his West Point roommate Frederick Dent, who was from the area. Although Dent was headed west, he thought his friend would be less lonely if he could occasionally visit his large family. One day they rode out into the country to the Dent estate.

The large farmhouse, named White Haven, was not exactly a plantation in the expansive sense of the term, but a working farm with about thirty slaves, overseen by Frederick and Ellen Wrenshall Dent, who had eight children. As his roommate predicted, Grant felt right at home there. Dent's favorite sister, Julia, was away at boarding school, but his two younger sisters—Nellie, sixteen, and Emma, eight—took to Grant instantly. They thought he was very handsome and very kind, and soon Grant was visiting the family on a weekly basis.

He first set eyes on Julia Dent after he had already become a regular at family dinners. One day he showed up at the farm and immediately sensed a different vibration. Its cause was soon apparent. Julia had returned from school. Ulysses was momentarily speechless in the presence of this petite wonder. Julia was not classically beautiful, but striking, with rich dark hair; lively, curious eyes; and a pleasant disposition. Better still, she loved to ride, and they began to ride often together—he on his dark horse Fashion, and she on her Arabian chestnut Psyche.

Julia had been coddled as a girl—as she herself admitted in her memoir, "Coming as I did to the family after the fourth great boy, I was necessarily something of a pet." She was especially catered to by the household slaves. While Grant's family was staunchly antislavery, the Dents were of the mind that a benevolent form of slavery was possible. They believed that freedom was little more than a technicality for slaves like theirs because they were so kindly treated and personally valued. Julia called the family's male slaves "uncle," and she described playing with the young females. She and Nellie "always had a dusky train of from eight to ten little colored girls of all hues, and these little colored girls were allowed to accompany us if they were very neat."

However, as much as Julia enjoyed her playmates, it was inescapable that stark differences existed. While she was sent to boarding schools and educated, her playmates were trained in service—as Julia put it, they "attained the dignity of white aprons," as if dignity could be found in slavery if one were neatly dressed. It's notable that in her memoir, which was written late in her life, after being at her husband's side through the Civil

War and during his presidency, Julia still held this romantic notion of her family slaves, especially her personal slaves, who she insisted were more like friends to her. The closest of these, also named Julia and called Jule, escaped when she had an opportunity during the Civil War. Julia did not begrudge Jule her freedom at that point, although she had never made a move to offer it.

Besotted, Grant was willing to let this detail go. After only two months in Julia's company, as he was preparing to go home to Ohio on leave, Grant sat with her and shyly asked if she would wear his class ring—an overture he equated with engagement.

Julia deflected. "Oh, no, Mama would not approve of my accepting a gift from a gentleman," she told her deflated suitor. Grant was disappointed, and he left for Ohio with a heavy heart. At that point Julia did not view him romantically. "I, child that I was, never for a moment thought of him as a lover," she wrote of her feelings at the time.

But in the absence of Grant, Julia began to realize how much she missed him, and how lonely she suddenly felt. By the time he returned from leave, she was beginning to see him with new eyes, and Grant, perhaps sensing it, felt emboldened by the strength of his feelings.

Later in life, Julia was asked if it was love at first sight. "I suppose you could call it that." She laughed, but then demurred.

I am a romantic at heart, but I am not one to believe in love at first sight in most cases. I think it would be called attraction and not love, for love is something that should grow and be fostered. But I can safely say that I was enamored of him from his first visits. He was handsome, kind, honest, brave—he was scarcely real to a little girl like myself. When he would leave the house,

my mother would look at him fondly and say, "There goes a very fine young man."

Julia loved showing Ulysses off to her friends, and they all found him quite appealing. "A few of them set their cap for him," she said, "but he was mine and they did not succeed in landing him."

Julia was maddening in her flirtatiousness, but always managed to stay just out of reach. One day Ulysses accompanied her to a wedding in St. Louis. Julia noticed that he was unusually quiet and thoughtful as they rode. She wondered if he was worried about the weather, because as they crossed a small bridge, the waters were rising dangerously. When he told her that he wasn't concerned, she blurted out, "Now, if anything happens, remember, I shall cling to you no matter what you say to the contrary!"

Surely, the thought of Julia clinging to him was pleasant, but they rode on without incident. They attended the wedding, and on the way home the reason for Grant's distracted demeanor became clear: he wanted to ask Julia to marry him. Her response was a tease. She wasn't sure about marriage, but perhaps they could be engaged.

Grant barreled ahead, asking Colonel Dent for his daughter's hand. Dent, portly and imperious, regarded the eager young man with a hint of distaste. This was certainly not the match he had in mind for his beautiful, pampered daughter. She had no idea what she was toying with. The life of a soldier's wife would be full of hardships she could not imagine. Dent bluntly told Grant that he could not give his blessing for such a match. He was unconvinced when Grant assured him that he did not foresee a military career and in fact had applied to be a professor of mathematics after his service. Dent was certain he could make a more prosperous match for his popular daughter.

Soon after, Grant's regiment was ordered to Louisiana, where the army was staging in preparation for a potential conflict with Mexico over the proposed US annexation of Texas. He would see Julia only one time during the next four years but would write to her frequently—long letters with details of his life mixed with modest vows of love, carefully phrased in case of prying eyes.

Camp Salubrity in western Louisiana, near the town of Natchitoches, was a revelation to Grant. "Aligators [sic] and other revolting looking things occupy the swamps in thousands," he wrote Julia, adding that the troops were plagued by nighttime visitors, particularly tiny lizardlike creatures that wriggled into beds.

The mission was vague. Officially, their presence on the western border of Louisiana was unrelated to the potential annexation of Texas, but Grant and his fellow soldiers all figured that's what it was about. Texas had been a battleground off and on for many years. Once a part of Mexico, it had fought for independence, and a great deal of blood was spilled in the effort. The Battle of the Alamo in 1836 was already the stuff of legend. Two hundred Texas volunteer soldiers had occupied a former Franciscan monastery in south-central Texas (near what is now San Antonio), turning it into a fort. Within two months, thousands of Mexican troops had amassed, preparing for an assault. When they attacked on February 23, the fighting was brutal, and the Texans were vastly outnumbered. Even so, they bravely held out for thirteen days before being slaughtered.

The terrible defeat after the men had shown so much courage made the Alamo a symbol of the grit and determination of Texans: "Remember the Alamo!" was the rallying cry on April 21 when the Texans' brave commander Sam Houston carried them to victory in the next battle at San Jacinto. Texas had declared its independence before that battle, and the win made it official.

Since 1836, Texas had been independent, but it wasn't out of the danger zone. Unprotected from further aggression, Texas had to decide whether it would remain an independent state and try to fight its own battles or join the Union. After a vigorous debate, it decided to join the Union, and those negotiations were under way.

Underlying the Texas annexation conflict was a broader mission on the part of leading Democrats in the United States to vastly expand the US territory and also increase the number of slave states. This led to a rancorous election year debate in 1844, which pitted Democrat James Polk against Whig Henry Clay. They held drastically different views of the future. Polk favored annexation of Texas and expansion of US territories, including a full claim to the Oregon territory. Clay viewed expansion as an effort to increase the number of slave states and therefore was opposed.

The concept of expansion that Polk promoted would come to be known as "Manifest Destiny," a belief in American exceptionalism that allowed the spread of territory and influence, not just by treaty but by force. It was widely supported by the Democratic Party in the belief that a larger America was necessary for the good of civilization.

Polk won the election narrowly, and before he took office in early 1845, Congress passed a bill on March 1, 1845, approving the Texas annexation, which was signed by President John Tyler. Grant's regiment waited in Louisiana for word of what would happen next.

By that point it was clear that the annexation issue didn't just involve the free state of Texas. The United States was intent on taking other borderland as well, in a move that would vastly expand its territories.

Grant was a lowly soldier following orders. He had no voice in the matter, but the idea of war-for-land dismayed him greatly. He would later write, "For myself, I was bitterly opposed to the measure, and to this day regard the war, which resulted, as one of the most unjust ever waged by a stronger against a weaker nation." In Grant's view, the aggression was no different than a European monarchy asserting imperial control. He called it "a conspiracy to acquire territory out of which slave states might be formed for the American Union."

When no move had been made by spring, Grant requested a thirty-five-day leave so he could travel to St. Louis and once more press his case with Julia's father. This time Dent gave his consent for their marriage, perhaps because his financial situation had suffered and he could no longer afford to be so picky about his daughter's suitor. But above that consideration, he had little choice because it was what Julia wanted, and he usually gave her what she wanted. This time she accepted Grant's class ring and agreed to marry him.

Grant was overjoyed, but the visit was far too brief. Riding with Julia before he departed, he promised to return as soon as possible. They would not see each other again for three years.

Returning to Louisiana, Grant found his restless comrades still waiting for word of their fate. By summer, war was imminent. President Polk ordered the army, under the command of General Zachary Taylor, to decamp for Corpus Christi. Taylor, nicknamed "Old Rough and Ready," was a seasoned leader who had fought with distinction in the War of 1812 and in the war with the Seminole Indians in 1837.

He would become Grant's military role model. "No soldier

could face either danger or responsibility more calmly than he," Grant wrote of Taylor. "These are qualities more rarely found than genius or physical courage. General Taylor never made any great show or parade, either of uniform or retinue. In dress he was possibly too plain, rarely wearing anything in the field to indicate his rank, or even that he was an officer; but he was known to every soldier in his army and was respected by all."

It is easy to see the signature of Taylor's leadership in Grant's own use of authority in the Civil War. And Taylor saw great promise in the young soldier: he promoted Grant to full second lieutenant before the fighting had even begun.

Grant was intrigued by the Texas terrain, and he loved riding across the flat, dusty plains. Assigned to escort Taylor's supply trains, which were headed to San Antonio, Grant had plenty of time in the saddle. "The journey was hazardous on account of Indians," Grant recalled, adding that, likewise, "there were white men in Texas whom I would not have cared to meet in a secluded place." Along the way, officers would set out to shoot venison and wild turkeys to feed the camp.

One day Grant and his Army friend Calvin Benjamin took off for a nearby creek to shoot turkeys. Standing there, Grant heard a flutter of wings and saw two or three turkeys rise above them, soon followed by a large flock of twenty or thirty roaring overhead. In awe of the sight, Grant stood there with his rifle on his shoulder, watching them leave. He was so captivated by the sight that it didn't occur to him to raise his gun. "I came to the conclusion that as a sportsman I was a failure," he wrote. He returned to the camp, and Benjamin stayed behind to shoot as many turkeys as he could.

On another occasion when Grant was out with Benjamin, they heard "the most unearthly howling of wolves, directly in our front." Unable to see through the high prairie grass, they huddled in silent trepidation. "To my ear it appeared that there must have been enough of them to devour our party, horses and all, at a single meal," Grant wrote.

Benjamin asked, "Grant, how many wolves do you think there are in the pack?"

"Oh, about twenty," Grant replied, swallowing his panic. He actually believed there were many more.

Bravely, they rode forward and soon came upon the dreaded predators—two lone wolves seated on their haunches, their heads together, hardly poised for attack.

In Corpus Christi, the waiting game continued. There was a hope that the presence of the army might lead Mexico to attack, but this was not happening. "We were sent to provoke a fight," Grant wrote about the sense at the time, "but it was essential that Mexico should commence it. It was very doubtful whether Congress would declare war; but if Mexico should attack our troops, the Executive could announce, 'Whereas, war exists by the acts of, etc.,' and prosecute the contest with vigor. Once initiated there were but few public men who would have the courage to oppose it."

But so far, Mexico wasn't taking the bait, and war had not been declared. Wanting to give them a better opportunity, Polk ordered Taylor to move his forces toward the Rio Grande, two hundred miles away. The destination was a spot across the river from Matamoras, Mexico.

Moving such a large force with all of its equipment was a massive effort, months in the making. Surely the Mexicans knew they were coming, but would it be the provocation needed to force them to act first?

On May 8, 1846, US troops approached an area north of the Rio Grande—Palo Alto, meaning "tall trees" or "timber"—where a high line of trees guided them to their destination. There they encountered an army of far greater numbers than their own. "Their bayonets and spearheads glistened in the sunlight formidably," Grant wrote. Taylor halted his men just out of range, and they stood in the tall grass as he formed their lines of battle.

Grant barely had time to think of what he was about to experience when the enemy was upon them. The jolt of gunfire briefly stunned him. He had never before heard a "hostile gun," and he was filled with dread. His first thought was to regret having enlisted. This was his initiation into the violent world of the soldier, and it shook him up. But he quickly got past it and fought determinedly. "There is no great sport in having bullets flying about one in every direction," he wrote Julia, "but I find they have less horror when among them than when in anticipation."

However, the start of this first battle seemed lackluster. The Mexicans, under the command of General Mariano Arista, out numbered the Americans, but they were not as well trained, and their weapons were poor. There was so little force behind their cannonball launches that the cannonballs bounced slowly across the field and were easily avoided by Taylor's men.

They fought throughout the day, and as dusk fell Taylor's forces made a last approach. This time the enemy hit its mark. On the field, Grant watched in horror as a cannonball whizzed by him: "It took off the head of an enlisted man, and the under jaw of Captain Page of my regiment, while the splinters from the musket of the killed soldier, and his brains and bones, knocked down two or three others." It was a terrifying sight.

In two days of battle, the Americans would be victorious, but they were subdued by the intensity of the fight. Many years later, after he had seen much of war, Grant would reflect upon the emotional reality of facing an actual battlefield: "A great many men, when they smell battle afar, chafe to get into the fray. When they say so themselves they generally fail to convince their hearers that they are as anxious as they would like to make believe, and as they approach battle they become more subdued."

The battles gave the American government the opening it had been looking for. President Polk sent a request to Congress for a declaration of war, and Congress complied on May 11, 1846.

Volunteers began to arrive to supplement the forces as Taylor set off with most of the army toward the Mexican city of Monterrey. This would be the first battle on Mexican soil.

General Taylor was taking note of Grant. Recognizing his unflappability, orderly mind, and gift for quiet leadership, Taylor gave him a new assignment: quartermaster and commissary officer, in charge of supplies and logistics. Grant was deeply unhappy with this assignment, which he thought would take him out of the field of battle. He made a formal protest, but his request was denied. In the end, he proved his aptitude for administration, and the assignment taught him valuable skills in warfare that would benefit him greatly in the future—for war is about more than the act of fighting.

Grant's new job was grueling. On the arduous march to Monterrey, each morning began with an ordeal that took hours: lashing cooking pots, utensils, tent poles, and other items to the backs of recalcitrant mules.

By the time we were ready, some of the mules first loaded would be tired of standing so long with loads on their backs. Sometimes one would start to run, kicking up until he scattered his load; others would lie down and roll over; others with tent-poles for part of their loads would manage to run a tent-pole on one side of a sapling while they would take the other. I am not aware of ever having used a profane expletive in my life; but I would have the charity to excuse those who may have done so, if they were in charge of a train of Mexican pack mules at the time.

Clearly Grant was frustrated.

As Taylor's army advanced toward the fight in Monterrey, Grant was ordered to stay behind at camp and perform his duties as quartermaster. But as the first day's battle went on, with the sound of great fury, he grew restless. "My curiosity got the better of my judgment, and I mounted a horse and rode to the front to see what was going on. I had been there but a short time when an order to charge was given, and lacking the moral courage to return to camp—where I had been ordered to stay—I charged with the regiment."

It was the most brutal conflict of the war so far, lasting three days. At one point, they ran low on ammunition, and Grant offered to go back and arrange for reinforcements. His horsemanship came in handy as he sped, riding side-saddle to block himself from enemy view, along the narrow streets behind houses. His journey was halted when he came upon a house packed with wounded Americans. He promised to report their situation, but it was too late. They fell into enemy hands and died.

The American army won at Monterrey, but the toll was high—531 killed, wounded, or missing.

Although Grant relished battle as an exercise in skill and fortitude, he despaired of its result and was deeply affected by the sight of the fallen—not only his brethren but the Mexicans as well. All were unlucky victims of bloodshed in a war whose cause he felt was misguided at best and corrupt at worst.

"My pity was aroused by the sight of the Mexican garrison on Monterey marching out of town as prisoners," he wrote, "and no doubt the same feeling was experienced by most of our army who witnessed it. Many of the prisoners were cavalry, armed with lances, and mounted on miserable little half-starved horses that did not look as if they could carry their riders out of town. The men looked in but little better condition. I thought how little interest the men before me had in the results of the war, and how little knowledge they had of 'what it was all about.'"

General Taylor was a fair and considerate leader who ordered his troops to protect the rights of all individuals and property during occupation. That meant no plundering of local resources. The American soldiers paid locals for goods sold at the market, and as a result the local economy thrived while the US Army was in residence.

"The Mexican War was a political war, and the administration conducting it desired to make party capital out of it." This was Grant's reflection as the war dragged on, going deeper into Mexico. President Polk was becoming increasingly concerned about the adulation of General Taylor in the press and his growing popularity back home. As a Whig often spoken of as a presidential candidate in the 1848 election, Taylor was becoming a threat to the entire Democratic Party. Even though Polk had vowed not to seek a second term himself, he didn't like Taylor and certainly didn't want him to become a public hero and potential president. Polk decided he had to be replaced.

Winfield Scott, Taylor's superior and a likely candidate, was no favorite of Polk's either. However, he couldn't come up with anyone else he deemed to be a fit replacement. In the end, Polk chose Scott to lead and Taylor to take a secondary role, swallowing his concern that Scott was a Whig too. Never mind that Scott was a brilliant military tactician and an imposing leader. Grant still remembered Scott's visit to West Point and his impressions of the general: "With his commanding figure, his quite colossal size and showy uniform, I thought him the finest specimen of manhood my eyes had ever beheld, and the most to be envied."

Scott's mission was to take Vera Cruz and then move on to capture the capital, Mexico City. He took most of Taylor's forces—including Grant—and left him with a smaller contingent of mostly volunteers to hold the line at the Rio Grande. Unfortunately, just as Scott was getting up to speed, the president started fiddling with his authority. He even tried to appoint a civilian to have command over Scott, an effort that failed only because Congress wouldn't hear of it. So, as Scott and his army proceeded, he was weakened by his own commander-in-chief. In addition, while Polk had promised greater forces to supplement Scott's modest army of twelve thousand, these reinforcements never arrived. It appeared that Scott would go into the final surge of the war with far fewer numbers than the Mexican army.

However, Scott's method—rapid movement and attack—scored a quick victory in Vera Cruz, leading to a dominating surge of US forces toward Mexico City. Although still outnumbered, the US Army under Scott's leadership was revealing itself to be highly skilled. Among his most talented commanders was one named Robert E. Lee, whom Scott greatly admired. "I tell you," he once said, "that if I were on my death bed tomorrow, and the President of the United States would tell me that a great battle was to be fought for the liberty or slavery of the country, and asked my judgment as to the ability of a commander, I would say with my dying breath, 'Let it be Robert E. Lee!'"

By late summer of 1847, with Scott's forces approaching Mexico City, a pause for negotiations carried new hopes that a treaty could be reached without further bloodshed. But the Mexican government was outraged by the terms—a complete surrender of Texas and New Mexico and California given up for a sum yet to be named. Negotiations collapsed on September 4.

The siege of Mexico City and the surrounding area lasted a week. As they approached Molino del Rey, southwest of the city, US Army forces found a grouping of stone buildings known as the King's Mill, which was once the site of flour and gunpowder mills. They thought them deserted, but as they neared, hidden Mexican forces opened fire on them. An intense battle ensued, and when Grant advanced toward the mill, he was horrified to stumble across Fred Dent, his old West Point roommate and Julia's brother. Fred was lying wounded, blood pouring from his thigh. Grant stopped his advance and, with gunfire around him, pulled Fred out of the line of attack and saved his life.

After a couple of hours of fighting, the US troops took the King's Mill and headed toward the gates of Mexico City, which were protected by a military academy called Chapultepec.

As they advanced under heavy fire at this critical juncture, they were greatly outnumbered. Grant searched for a way to find an advantage. He spotted a church with a high belfry and had an idea. Instructing his men to take apart their large howitzer and carry it in pieces, he then led them stealthily toward the church, knowing there were enemy forces around them. Grant knocked on the door, and when a priest appeared, he asked politely to enter. The priest refused to let him in.

Grant quietly explained to the priest, in halting fragments of Spanish, that if he opened the door and let them in, he might save the church from destruction and save himself from being captured. "And besides," Grant recalled, "I intended to go in whether he consented or not. He began to see his duty in the same light that I did and opened the door."

Grant and his men carried in the howitzer pieces, reassembled them in the belfry, and then began firing on the enemy with great success. If Grant ever regretted using a house of God in this way, he didn't say so.

Scott's army had one victory after another in the areas surrounding Mexico City, and by the time they arrived at the center of the city it was deserted and silent, except for an intermittent smattering of gunshots. The fight was all over but for setting the terms of the treaty.

For Grant, Scott's strategy was an inspiration—and he'd later use similar strategic moves during the Civil War. "General Scott's successes are an answer to all criticism," he wrote. "He invaded a populous country, penetrating two hundred and sixty miles into the interior, with a force at no times equal to one-half of that opposed to him; he was without a base; the enemy was always intrenched, always on the defensive; yet he won every battle, he captured the capital, and conquered the government. Credit is due to the troops engaged, it is true, but the plans and the strategy were the general's."

In the coming months, negotiations would lead to an agreement that was a tremendous breakthrough for expansion-minded Americans. The Treaty of Peace, Friendship, Limits, and Settlement between the United States of America and the Mexican Republic was signed on February 2, 1848, in the Mexico City neighborhood of Villa de Guadalupe Hidalgo. In exchange for $15 million, plus $3 million to settle American suits against Mexico, not only did Mexico give up its claim to Texas, but the United States added more than five hundred square miles of land in the areas that would become California, New Mexico, Nevada, Utah, and Arizona, along with parts of present-day Colorado, Kansas, and Wyoming.

Elated by the victory and not taking too much time to consider the complexities and domestic battles still to be fought over all of this new territory, American voters went to the polls in November and elected Zachary Taylor president in a victory for the Whig Party.

After the treaty was made, Grant had only one thought: how quickly he could get back home to marry Julia. "I at least hope dear Julia that it will not be long before I can see you again," he wrote. "It is too bad aint it? Just think we have been engaged almost four years and have met but once in that time, that was three years ago."

As it turned out, he had to stick around for a few months and help oversee the transition. He came to love Mexico, but he loved Julia more. He couldn't wait to remedy the unbearable distance.

CHAPTER 3

THE LOST YEARS

The hot summer air and the sweet scent of bougainvillea accompanied Grant as he rode his gray steed toward the Dent farm on a July day in 1848. After securing a four-month leave, he'd made the long journey to St. Louis by steamer from Mississippi, where his regiment was stationed, and had now nearly reached the destination he had dreamed of for so long.

Longing was not the only emotion that filled him. There was also fear.

In the manner of a man who worried that his beloved was well above his status and perhaps beyond his reach, he went over in his mind the evidence that Julia might reject him.

During Grant's long absence, Julia had proved to be an unreliable correspondent. Her letters were so erratic and unsatisfying that Grant often chided her for failing to write, while he, even in the midst of battle, managed lengthy letters every couple of weeks. Writing soothed him and cleared his mind. He loved recounting the human drama of battles and encampments, even if some of the details might have gone over Julia's head. A letter from her was a precious thing indeed. Once he'd been so excited to receive a letter that he'd torn it open without thought. It happened to be a windy day, and the dried rose petals Julia had placed inside were carried away by a heavy gust.

Grant also tormented himself with memories of Julia's popularity. He had seen for himself at the Jefferson Barracks that Julia was the light of every social occasion, her winning personality and saucy nature putting everyone at ease. She was naturally flirtatious. Could such a girl remain alone for long, especially with her father quietly lobbying against the union? Had a better prospect for her affections emerged?

He needn't have been worried about what he'd find there. When he rode up on his horse that fateful July day in 1848, Julia was overjoyed to see him. She immediately said that a wait of four years for marriage had been quite enough. She wanted to be married soon! They quickly set a date for August 22, and Grant was filled with relief that all the hopes and dreams of four years were finally coming to pass.

If Grant saw only that Julia was as delightful as ever, Julia and her sisters noticed the change in him. He was the same quiet, affectionate man, but they saw a new maturity, a battle-hardening, which they found attractive. Julia liked the way the experience of war sat on Grant's brow. In the long separation, he had become a man.

Before the wedding, Grant traveled to Ohio to visit his family. They were happy to see him, but his father at least was disappointed to learn that he still intended to marry into the slaveholding Dent family. Jesse, who had become increasingly outspoken as an abolitionist, refused to attend the wedding and prevented other family members from going. Grant returned alone to St. Louis. His thoughts about slavery were not well formed at the time, but on principle he despised it. Yet somehow his own standard failed to apply to the Dents. Blinded by love, he showed little sign of being a man who would essentially make the emancipation of slaves and the well-being of freedmen his life's work.

Despite the pretense of being a wealthy plantation family, the Dents had fallen on more difficult times, and Julia wasn't anticipating a lavish wedding. Then her friend Caroline O'Fallon arrived with a beautiful box containing a glamorous wedding dress from Paris. Julia was dazzled and so grateful. The dress was "rich, soft, white, watered silk," accompanied by a white tulle veil. Her bouquet was of white cape jessamines—Southern gardenias—with their heady fragrance. She also wove them into her veil piece.

On the morning of their wedding, Grant broke with tradition when he arrived at her home to see Julia. She later said she didn't mind at all when "Lieutenant Grant—he was just a poor Lieutenant then—called to see me on the morning of the day we were to be married. And never shall I forget how the family, especially the girls, teased me about it. 'Oh, it isn't proper for you to see her now,' they said. 'No one must see her today, not even the bridegroom. You must wait until tonight.'

"He didn't, however," Julia said, laughing at the memory. "No, indeed!"

At 8:00 P.M., Julia descended the staircase as a lone fiddler played. Grant waited at the foot of the stairs, serious and upright in his military uniform.

"Never shall I forget when I came down the staircase that hot August evening in my wedding gown," Julia recalled to an interviewer in her later years. "And I felt just as happy at that moment as if I had been married in church, as girls are now, with a great crowd of people to see me. It wasn't the fashion then, by the way, for girls to be married in church. They were always married from their own houses, and in what would be thought now, I suppose, rather too informal a way."

Julia was accompanied by three bridesmaids—her sister Nellie, cousin Julia Bogg, and friend Sally Walker. In her memoir, Julia mentioned three military officers standing up for Grant as grooms-men, but their identities have never been fully confirmed. James Longstreet has often been mentioned as Grant's groomsman, and some biographies convey that as fact, but it doesn't seem likely. Longstreet himself told the *New York Times* that he was only a guest. The story of the man who would become one of the most important generals of the Confederate Army being a groomsman for the man who would become the most important general of the Union Army was probably just an irresistible fiction.

The couple said their vows before the Reverend J. H. Linn, and the ceremony was followed by a reception where friends were received throughout the evening. A table was set up in the parlor, serving ices, fruits, and other foods, along with a wedding cake. A heavy rain had left an atmosphere of steaming heat, and windows and doors were flung open to provide cooling relief. By all accounts, everyone was in high spirits and had a wonderful time, with the possible exception of Colonel Dent.

After the wedding, the Grants set off on a three-month honeymoon trip, going first by boat to Ohio, where Julia would be introduced to Ulysses's family. As they took off up the Mississippi—Julia's first boat trip—their wedding guests threw bouquets of flowers as the newlyweds beamed and waved.

"Our honeymoon was a delight," Julia remembered. "We had waited four long years for this event and we adjusted to one another like hand to glove. The Lieutenant was always lovely to me when I was unjust or childish. I was still a little girl who had never spread her wings, yet he had been widely traveled. We saw everything through rose colored glasses." Julia was twenty-two by then, not quite a "little girl." But Grant loved playing the role of the worldly protector.

Julia was nervous about meeting the imposing in-laws who had refused to attend her wedding, but the Grants seemed to embrace her warmly from the start. Struck by Hannah's gentle manner, Julia found her mother-in-law affectionate, self-sacrificing, and kind. Grant's father, Julia noted, was much taller than his son and very warm: "The Captain's father met me cordially, I might say." Left unnoted was the stark difference in manner between Grant's mother and his wife. Perhaps Julia, with her immense emotional capacity, lively personality, and worshipful devotion to her husband (which never wavered during their entire lives), fulfilled a craving in Grant to be loved openly and unconditionally.

At the end of their honeymoon, it was back to the reality of military life. Grant had never meant to stay in the Army, yet here he was, seasoned by four years in uniform on top of his West Point training, and he wasn't ready to give it up. Little was said of what motivated him to stay. It was certainly not money: the pay was $1,000 a year. Maybe it was simply the awareness, growing in him during the long days and nights of war, that this was something he was good at. He had the nerves for it, the temperament.

He was scheduled to report for duty in Detroit, accompanied by his new wife. But as they prepared to depart, Julia collapsed in tears at the thought of leaving her family for a life of conditions unknown. "I could not . . . think of it without bursting into a flood of tears and weeping and sobbing, as if my heart would break."

Unnerved to see his beloved daughter so distraught, Colonel Dent made a proposal. "Grant, I can arrange it all for you. You join your regiment and leave Julia with us. You can get a leave of absence once or twice a year and run on here and spend a week or two with us. I always knew [Julia] could not live in the army."

Grant froze. Could this be happening? After all the waiting and longing over the previous four years, would his great romance end this way, with the mere pretense of a marriage?

He held Julia close, and whispered, "Would you like this, Julia? Would you like to remain with your father and let me go alone?"

Julia pressed into him. "No, no, no, Ulys. I could not, would not think of that for a moment."

Grant smiled. "Then dry your tears and do not weep again. It makes me unhappy."

There were surprises ahead. Upon arriving in Detroit with his bride, Grant was immediately reassigned to the Madison Barracks in Sackets Harbor, New York, a distant outpost on Lake Ontario at the Canadian border. Grant protested the order, but while his reassignment was being considered, the Grants made the long, hard trip north.

Although Sackets Harbor was a bitterly cold and isolated setting, the Grants were happy there. Julia, not accustomed to being without her closest slave, Jule, embraced it as an adventure in the unfamiliar art of homemaking. When she asked Grant to provide her with an allowance, so that she wouldn't have to constantly ask him for necessities, he agreed. He didn't begrudge her spending, even when it was over the limit. If Julia's accounts didn't add up, he shrugged it off. "I cannot make out your mathematical conundrums," he said cheerfully. "Do not bother anymore. Come and let us have a ride."

Julia tried her best to lighten their lives with entertaining. Once she organized a Mardi Gras masquerade party, which was a great success, although Grant insisted on wearing his military uniform. With little to do, however, Grant often felt restless and would ride his horse Cicotte down to the tavern in nearby Watertown to play checkers. While at Sackets Harbor, Grant joined the Sons of Tem-

perance, the first reference to his drinking and perhaps the aware-
ness of a problem.

In the spring of 1849, Grant was transferred back to Detroit,
where he and Julia would finally have what felt like a semiperma-
nent home. They bought a small house, and Julia recalled it as the
happiest time of their early marriage. "I look back with especial
fondness to our years in Detroit," she told an interviewer. "All my
soldier had to offer me was a frame vine-covered cottage near the
barracks. Those are some of my dearest memories."

In her memoir, Julia vividly recalled "the pleasant people we
met, the gay parties and dinners, the *fetes champetres*, the delightful boat rides on the gallant Captain Willoughby's magnificent lake steamer." And best of all was the birth of their first
son. In May 1850, Julia left Detroit for St. Louis and gave birth
at White Haven on the thirtieth, surrounded by the comforts of
family and the attentions of slaves. She named the child Frederick
Dent Grant, after her father.

Soon after, the family returned to Sackets Harbor, where they
spent a very happy year until the spring of 1852, when the Fourth
Infantry was assigned to the Pacific Coast. Among other challenges, it was tasked with maintaining order in the chaos of what
came to be known as the California Gold Rush. After gold was
discovered in 1848, hundreds of thousands of prospectors had
headed west, seeking their fortunes. They totally overwhelmed the
fledgling towns, displaced the native populations, spread disease,
and brought lawlessness. In light of the long, dangerous journey
and the circumstances that awaited him, Grant told Julia—who
was pregnant with their second child—she must stay behind for
the time being. She disagreed. "Of course I was indignant at this
and said I would go, I would, I would; for him to hush. . . . And
of course I shed tears."

Grant could never bear to see his wife cry. She knew this and kept it as a primary weapon in her arsenal. "You know how loath I am to leave you," he argued, "but crossing Panama is an undertaking for one in robust health, and then my salary is so small, how could you and my little boy have even the common necessities of life."

In the end, Grant told Julia that if she insisted, he would agree, but eventually she saw reason and remained behind, living in comfort with her family. The plan all along was for her to join Grant later, after their second child was born. This never came to fruition, but not for lack of desire. The conditions out west were terrible, and the journey to get there was brutal. Grant's own journey west was very unpleasant: there was a cholera outbreak aboard his steamer headed for Panama, followed by an arduous trip by land along the rugged coast.

Every time Grant contemplated sending for Julia, he had to face reality. He was gone for so long and was so far away that he sometimes seemed to be lost to her. When their second son was born, he was pleased when she named him Ulysses. But her friends joked that she should have named the child Telemachus after Ulysses's son in Homer's *Odyssey*, whose mission was to find and bring back his father.

San Francisco in 1852 was a land booming with the promise if not yet the reality of prosperity. Gold diggers had flooded to the area, bringing with them a vibrant and dangerous nightlife. Grant quickly saw through the ruse and delivered a scathing verdict. "All thought that fortunes were to be picked up, without effort, in the gold fields on the Pacific," he wrote. "Some realized more than their most sanguine expectations; but for one such there were hundreds disappointed, many of whom now fill unknown graves; others died wrecks of their former selves, and many, without a vicious instinct, became criminals and outcasts."

Grant became a close observer of the spectacle of the prospectors and noted how many of them came from the privileged classes of the East, "who had never done a day's manual labor in their lives" but had come west seeking an easy fortune.

In the fall of 1852, Grant was assigned away from the bustling urban area to Fort Vancouver in the Oregon territory, on the Columbia River, which was the dividing line to the Washington territory. At the time the Hudson Bay Company's trading posts—one of which was located at Fort Vancouver—made it the de facto "establishment." Grant was impressed by the friendly and helpful treatment of the Indians in the area. They had been taught farming techniques and were well compensated for their labor. During Grant's time at Fort Vancouver, there was no trouble with the Indians, and he came to respect them as peaceful, good people.

Grant was able to observe the life of native tribes firsthand. Even though there was peace, the Indians were plagued by illnesses brought by outsiders, especially measles and smallpox. Until then, the natives had not been exposed to these illnesses, and they had no immunity to them. Grant noted that until the white man came on the scene, the Indians' chief ailments were dietary, and these were soothed by the steam bath. He was intrigued by this inventive cure and wrote in detail about it:

Something like a bake-oven was built, large enough to admit a man lying down. Rushes were stuck in the ground in two rows, about six feet long and some two or three feet apart; other bushes connected the rows at one end. The tops of the bushes were drawn together to interlace, and confined in that position; the whole was then plastered over with wet clay until every opening was filled. Just inside the open end of the oven the floor was scooped out so as to make a hole that would hold a bucket or two of water. These ovens were always built on the banks of a stream, a big spring, or pool of water. When a patient required a bath, a fire was built near the oven and a pile of stones put upon it. The cavity at the front was then filled with water. When the stones were sufficiently heated, the patient would draw himself into the oven; a blanket would be thrown, over the open end, and hot stones put into the water until the patient could stand it no longer. He was then withdrawn from his steam bath and doused into the cold stream near by. This treatment may have answered with the early ailments of the Indians. With the measles or small-pox it would kill every time.

At Fort Vancouver, Grant was immediately struck by the high prices. Food was so expensive that he organized a growing operation on a plot of land, but it failed dramatically when the spring thaw flooded the Columbia River, decimating the crop. It was a precursor to his later failure as a farmer.

It was a lonely posting, and Grant often wrote to Julia with promises that he was doing all he could to make things ready for her and the boys. But every time he thought of the rugged journey and the makeshift conditions he now lived in, he could not imagine bringing his lovely, delicate wife and his precious boys to live there.

On July 5, 1853, Grant was promoted to captain and given a new assignment at Humboldt Bay, California. It would be his undoing. Humboldt Bay was an extremely isolated spot in northern California, with a somber fort that sat on an imposing bluff. It was far removed from civilization.

Almost immediately falling into a depression, Grant desperately wrote to Julia: "My dear wife. You do not know how forsaken I feel here."

Bitterly lonely, often bored, and given to bouts of depression, he did what soldiers at ease often did at that time—he drank heavily.

Many historical accounts have mentioned Grant's drinking, some calling him an alcoholic. But it's possible that Grant drank no more than any other soldier. His biggest mistake was being careless about when and where he drank. When his unforgiving commander found him drunk one day, he ordered Grant to resign or face court-martial. Grant's friends at the time urged him to stand trial and were confident of his acquittal, but, actuated by a noble spirit, he said he would not for all the world have his wife know that he had been tried on such a charge. He therefore resigned his commission and returned to civilian life.

In his memoir, Grant did not comment on the subject of his drinking, but those close to him had explanations that put the situation in a fairer light. The most common was that Grant was not a big drinker but could not hold his liquor very well. However, the label of being a drunk followed him throughout his career. Unfairly, every time he showed the slightest weakness or uncertainty, the ever-present chorus was there to raise suspicions of drunkenness.

At first Grant felt only relief to be headed back to Julia. Grant's longing for his family was so great that it was all he could think of. The shameful end to his military career receded in the distance as he neared home. Back at White Haven with Julia, he was reintroduced to young Fred and met his second son Ulysses (nicknamed "Buck") for the first time. They lived for a while at Wish-ton-Wish, Julia's brother's house on the property. But Grant chafed at being dependent on his in-laws and insisted on building a house of their own and farming the one-hundred-acre plot of White Haven land that Julia had received as a gift from her father. He built a log house by hand and named it Hardscrabble, which seemed like a dig at the Dents and the pretentious names they gave their properties. Julia preferred the relatively deluxe accommodations at Wish-ton-Wish and the main house, to which she returned often, especially after her mother died. The Grants' two youngest children were born there—Nellie in 1855, and Jesse in 1858.

Grant was determined to make a life of it on their Hardscrabble farm. He loved the work and relished the daily labor, which seemed so much more meaningful than the restless, idle period he'd spent out west. Needing help, he hired two Black men for pay, while Julia's father gave him the gift of a slave named William Jones to work on the farm. According to the writer Hamlin Garland, who interviewed the farm's neighbors, Grant felt shame at using slave labor, as "he was not a slavery man." He soon freed William, filling out all the paperwork.

The experience haunted Grant. He had always chosen to ignore his wife's dependence on her house slaves and her father's use of farm slaves, even as his father railed against the Dents, but now he had been complicit. Despite the protestations of the Dents that they were the kindest of masters, he realized that the defining truth of master and slave made kindness an impossibility.

After all of Grant's efforts to hold it together, the farm failed. It wasn't entirely his fault. Plagued by terrible weather and a depressed economy, and struck ill by malaria, he abandoned the idea of farming in 1858. Colonel Dent quickly sold the Hardscrabble property along with hundreds of additional acres, but the Grants saw little if any money from the sale; Dent's "gift" to Julia had not included an official deed.

These hard times went unnoticed by the children. The oldest, Fred, recalled only happiness on the farm and remembered his father as doing well. "He raised crops successfully and spent his evenings with his family. I, being the oldest, was permitted to accompany him about the farm, and he began to teach me, at an early age, to ride and to swim. I can see myself now, a chubby little chap, sitting on the back of one of the farm horses and holding on for dear life, my father urging me to be brave. He would not tolerate timidity in his small boy, and a display of it meant an unhappy hour for him, and me also." Recalling his own delight at engaging in physical exploits in the great outdoors, Grant wanted his son to experience all the wonders he had enjoyed. And the lessons stuck. Fred became a spirited, adventurous boy.

Feeling panicked by his financial failure, Grant pawned his gold watch and chain and wrote humbly to his father, offering—at last—to go into business with him. But his father did not respond, the reason being evident: as long as his son lived with the slaveholders, Jesse Grant wanted nothing to do with him.

Out of options, Grant accepted help from the Dents. Colonel Dent's nephew, Harry Boggs, owned a real estate firm in St. Louis, and he offered Grant a position there, collecting the rents. It was a poor professional fit for a man as shy as Grant, and it meant leaving his family behind, but he gave it his best. He lived with the Boggs family while Julia and the children remained at White Haven. It was a lonely existence, only appeased by a weekly twelve-mile walk to visit his family.

His spirit seemed to be ebbing away. Others noted his slouching demeanor, the grubby state of his dress, the far-off set of his eyes. At thirty-seven, he seemed a decade or more older. Lloyd Lewis described him as "the ghost of a soldier."

One day his old friend James Longstreet met him on a street in St. Louis. Longstreet thought Grant looked terrible, really down on his luck. Grant immediately pressed a five-dollar gold piece into Longstreet's hand, citing a debt from fifteen years earlier. Longstreet tried to refuse it, but Grant insisted. "You must take it," he said. "I cannot live with anything in my possession which is not mine." Finally, Longstreet accepted, "to save him mortification." He was sad when they parted, never imagining that their next meeting would be on opposite sides in the field of war.

A brief glimmer of hope came when a job opened for county engineer. Grant thought he was well suited for the job, and the annual salary of $1,900 was quite appealing. He gathered letters of recommendation from an impressive collection of men—Grant always knew how to hold on to his friendships. But he didn't get the job. The committee making the decision was weighted on the side of abolition, and they held it against Grant that he was associated with the Dents.

In 1860, with a string of failures behind him and poverty staring him down, Grant swallowed his pride and once again sought a job from his father. This time Jesse agreed to hire his son in his wholesale and retail leather business in Galena, Illinois. At least at that store he would not be involved in the stinking, bloody side of the trade that had so revolted him as a boy. The Galena operation was managed by Grant's brother Simpson, who was not in good health. Later, his brother Orvil would also arrive to work in the store.

Grant did not make a great impression upon his arrival. Galenians who were asked about it later, after Grant had achieved fame, described him as seeming depressed, and they frequently mentioned his shabby clothes—a faded blue overcoat and slouch hat.

His life was stable, but it was not a good time for him. Soon after his arrival, a local man observed him entering a tavern, where the city lawyers were gathered around the fire, drinking and talking. One of the lawyers noticed Grant. "Stranger here?" he asked.

Grant said yes.

"Traveled far?"

"Far enough."

"Looks as though you might have traveled through hell," the lawyer joked.

"I have."

"Well, how did you find things down there?"

"Oh, much the same as in Galena," Grant deadpanned. "Lawyers nearest the fire."

Grant settled into the leather business and the restoration of family life. He believed this was his fate now, like it or not.

Three-year-old Jesse was delighted to have his father around as a playmate. At the end of each day he waited eagerly for the sight of Grant coming home from the store. As he walked up the steps, Jesse would cry, "Mister, do you want to fight?"

Grant pretended to be offended. "I am a man of peace; but I will not be hectored by a person of your size."

At that point they would fall on one another and tussle, before Grant gave in and declared himself beat.

In his memoir, Jesse wrote glowingly of his siblings and their many kindnesses to him. His fearless oldest brother Fred was his personal hero; his brother Buck was most like their father in temperament, though broader in physique; and Nellie, their sister, had a "rare and fine personality."

They were a loving, demonstrative family. Grant was a warm and lenient father. Fred recalled that his punishments were rare— "His usual method of correction was to show disapproval of our actions [with] his manner and quiet words. This was more effective with us than scolding or whippings would have been. We all felt consternation and distress when he looked with disapproval upon what we had done."

Grant's children even teased him about his soft touch. After

Buck appeared late for breakfast one morning, his father gently chided him, "When I was your age, I had to get up, feed four or five horses, cut wood for the family, take breakfast and be off to school by eight o'clock." His son smiled at him and replied, "Oh, yes, but you did not have such a papa as I have, you see."

It was left to Julia to be the disciplinarian. "The General had no idea of the government of the children," she explained to an interviewer. "He would have allowed them to do pretty much as they pleased. . . . Whenever they were inclined to disobey or question my authority, I would ask the General to speak to them. He would, smiling at me, and say to them, '. . . you must not quarrel with Mama. She knows what is best for you and you must always obey her.'

"He was always the same, whether he was a humble Lieutenant or the President of the United States," Julia said. "He had very simple needs and wants. He never was a great eater, he was not fussy, though he expected people to be prompt in their appointments. He wasn't a scolder or cross, he was a gentle and affectionate father and so deeply generous to me and my faults. Even before our marriage we found it easy to get along with each other and talk to each other, it was a comfortable, pleasing match, always."

If Julia had any complaint, it was the way her husband hid his light from others. Responding to the assertion that Grant was unable to speak articulately, she exclaimed,

The nonsense of this! I shall tell you the truth of the matter, the General was a very good talker and exceedingly interesting. He was always an enthusiastic talker when he was in a circle he knew. When I first knew him, he was initially shy with family friends who came on calls. I had told some of them of a young soldier that I was interested in and they came specially to see him. My Lieutenant would be on the porch, with me proudly at his side, talking and chatting with such absorbing interest. Then the people that I wished to impress would call and Ulysses would be quiet as a mouse. When they left he would start chatting again.

I finally said, "Ulys! I told these people you were a fascinating and wonderful conversationalist. I think they have gone away disappointed. Why can't you be as interesting to them as you are to me?" My Lieutenant just smiled at me. He said nothing.

Many others among Grant's friends in civilian life and the military expressed frustration with his enigmatic ways. But they also spoke of the times they were rewarded with an illuminating conversation that showed Grant's thoughtful and passionate side.

From Galena, Grant watched the development of a national crisis, as though tracking the rapid movement of a prairie storm. He grimly recalled the first spark of secession spirit he had witnessed before the Mexican war, when the topic of slave state expansion had been on the table. Now it was a growing conflict that was enveloping the entire nation.

Talk of secession enraged him: "It made my blood run cold to hear friends of mine—Southern men, as many of my friends were—deliberately discuss the dissolution of the Union as though it were a tariff bill. I could not endure it. The very thought of it was a pain. I wanted to leave the country if disunion was accomplished."

Most Northerners at the time, though opposed to the institution of slavery in the South, believed that those states had the right to their slave system—as long as the practice did not spread. But with expansionism, the question of spread was now urgent. Keeping the secessionist passions at bay was becoming more difficult.

In the 1856 presidential election, Grant had made a calculated political decision in voting for the Democrat James Buchanan. The vying parties were in chaos. The Whigs had ceased to exist. The spanking-new Republican Party was untried and barely functioning. Grant figured the goal should be to buy some time to subdue the passions for secession, and Buchanan seemed fit for the task.

"With a Democrat elected by the unanimous vote of the Slave States, there could be no pretext for secession for four years," he wrote. "I very much hoped that the passions of the people would subside in that time, and the catastrophe be averted altogether."

Buchanan, a wealthy bachelor from Pennsylvania, won the election and proved to be a disappointing steward of the nation. Already sixty-five when he took office, he was unable to hold the nation together—and he hardly tried. To this day scholars consider Buchanan one of the worst American presidents, if not the worst. He made the fateful choice of downplaying the crisis and abdicating federal responsibility.

The stage was set for disaster from the moment of Buchanan's inauguration. At the time the Supreme Court was deliberating a case expected to shed light on whether slavery should be allowed or restricted in the territories. The debate had been raging for years, even before Texas statehood. The issue was whether the new territories seeking admittance as states would be allowed to be slave states if they so chose, and therefore whether new settlers heading west could bring their slaves without fear of being challenged.

The Supreme Court case, *Dred Scott v. Sanford*, involved the plea for freedom by a slave whose master had moved with him to free states over the years. Dred Scott and his wife, Harriet, were slaves whose owners moved from Missouri, a slave state, to Illinois, a free state, and then to the Wisconsin territories. When their owner refused to give them their freedom, they sued for emancipation based on a Missouri statute that any slave taken to a free territory would automatically become free. It wasn't such a simple matter, though, and their case had been making its way through the courts for an entire decade. At one point, they actually won a verdict before it was reversed by the Missouri court. The case had been going on for so long that they no longer "belonged" to their original owners.

In his inaugural address, Buchanan seemed to imply that the matter was settled; possibly he'd received a heads-up from the justices. The question of slavery in the territories, he said, was "happily, a matter of but little practical importance. Besides, it is a judicial question, which legitimately belongs to the Supreme Court of the United States, before whom it is now pending, and will, it is understood, be speedily and finally settled."

Two days later, Supreme Court chief justice Roger B. Taney delivered the seven-to-two decision overturning the Missouri Compromise and declaring that there was no such thing as "free soil": the US Constitution protected the property rights of slave owners. Furthermore, the Scott case had no standing because African Americans could not be US citizens and therefore could not sue in federal court. The opinion read: "There are two clauses in the Constitution which point directly and specifically to the negro race as a separate class of persons, and show clearly that they were not regarded as a portion of the people or citizens of the Government then formed."

The Dred Scott decision would thereafter be recognized as the most scathing rebuke to Black freedom ever formalized. Southerners celebrated, but in the North a severe backlash threatened. In Congress, non-Southern members tried to walk a delicate line, which amounted to decrying slavery but accepting the rights of slave owners and of slave states.

In Illinois, an unknown Republican named Abraham Lincoln, running for the US Senate against two-term Democratic senator Stephen A. Douglas in 1858, made a stir with his nomination acceptance speech when he declared, "A house divided against itself cannot stand . . . this government cannot endure permanently half slave and half free." Douglas accused Lincoln of being a radical abolitionist. Not only was this not true, but Lincoln and Douglas actually weren't so far apart in their views on slavery. Even Lincoln's "house divided" speech called only for national unity, not to end slavery. Lincoln challenged Douglas to a series of seven public debates to examine the issue that was tearing America apart. At the time, senators were chosen by state legislatures, not by popular vote, but in bringing their cases before the people, Douglas and Lincoln hoped to sway the legislators' vote.

The debates, which were each about three hours long, were a stunning intellectual exercise and constitutional tutorial that revealed most of all how difficult it was to simultaneously argue the immorality of slavery and the right of states to practice it.

Douglas won the election, but the debates gave Lincoln a national profile. Ironically, Douglas, far from being a proslavery purist, was often castigated by the Southern wing of his party, who said that he might as well be a Republican.

In 1860, it was once again clear that a Republican victory might set the secession of states in motion. Grant favored Lincoln. He worried about talk of secession but didn't really think it would happen—it was "so plainly suicidal."

In Grant's thinking, secession, which might have once been allowable when the nation was young and the colonies limited, had long ago ceased to be a right. He himself had been part of the expenditure of blood and treasure of the entire nation to bring Texas and other territories into the Union. He reasoned that the prospect of Texas withdrawing from the Union after the extreme sacrifice on its behalf was unthinkable.

The election of 1860 was entirely devoted to this question that had infected the body politic. There was no unity, even within the parties. The Democrats split into the Northern party and the Southern party. Buchanan, who was not running for reelection, backed his vice president, John C. Breckinridge of Kentucky, who was running on the Southern platform. Stephen Douglas represented the Northerners on the Democratic ticket. Abe Lincoln was the Republican candidate. A fourth candidate, John Bell, represented the new Constitutional Union Party, a quasi-libertarian group that seemed to stand for little at all, except its opposition to the others.

It was a fiery campaign season, and much of the heat seemed to surround Lincoln. His striking physique and oratorical gifts made him a standout. And in the North, he represented the one true path. During the campaign, an upstart political organization made up of young men who called themselves the "Wide Awakes" flooded the towns and cities of the North, marching with lit torches and dressed in military-style uniforms. Their cause was the election of Abe Lincoln.

From the sidelines, Grant watched with sober concern, hoping for rational minds to prevail but fearing that the match had been lit on a runaway fire. He doubted that the Constitution's framers had ever predicted such a scenario, but he also believed that, were the issue not so swept up in emotional rhetoric, solutions might be found. Most Southerners, not themselves slaveholders and many of them from the poorer classes, were not necessarily inclined to secession, much less war, which would rob them of their young men and devastate their economies. But the powerful pressure of the elite slaveholders and the excitability of young Southerners pressed them ever closer to conflict.

Ulysses and Julia discussed the matter frequently. Julia's position was complicated by family loyalty and by the belief that slavery could be a benevolent and even an affectionate practice. However, she was horrified by the prospect of secession. Even as her father leaned toward acceptance of a separate confederacy of states, Julia sided with her husband and believed that the Union must be preserved.

"Galena was throbbing with patriotism," Julia recounted, describing the scene that had infected the community as men and women alike organized themselves to support the great national effort. She was standing with the Union, apart from the Dent family.

There is some evidence that Lincoln did not fully appreciate how his election could imperil the Union, nor understand how serious the South was about its threat to secede. He believed that the crisis would pass, telling a journalist on election day that "elections in this country were like 'big boils'—they caused a great deal of pain before they came to a head, but after the trouble was over the body was in better health than before."

November 6 produced the highest voter turnout in American history—over 81 percent of eligible voters. With four candidates, the results were all over the map, and although Lincoln's victory was numerically decisive, the rift was clear. Lincoln was not on the ballot in a single Southern state, and his victory was entirely dependent on the North, which gave him wins in every state but one. Breckinridge won most of the South, with Bell taking Virginia, Kentucky, and Tennessee. Douglas won only Missouri.

With the North and South drawn in clear opposition, there was a sense of dread across the nation. It didn't improve the fraught tenor of the national mood that Lincoln would not take office until March 4, which was four months away. Until then, the lame-duck Buchanan would coexist with the Southern fearmongers and the Northern abolitionists. As was his habit, he turned his back on any effort to address the looming crisis. "It is beyond the power of any president, no matter what may be his own political proclivities, to restore peace and harmony among the states," he said in his final State of the Union address. "Wisely limited and restrained as is his power under our Constitution and laws, he alone can accomplish but little for good or for evil on such a momentous question."

PART TWO

THE MAKING OF
A GENERAL

CHAPTER 4

THE UNION CAUSE

"Sir, if you are as happy in entering the White House as I shall feel on returning to Wheatland, you are a happy man indeed," the aging and weary President James Buchanan told Abraham Lincoln as they began a carriage ride to the Capitol for Lincoln's swearing-in on March 4, 1861. Buchanan's eagerness to be rid of the job was understandable; the state of affairs had been rapidly unraveling since election day.

The months following the election had been devastating as secessionist states unspooled from the Union. On December 20, South Carolina became the first state to formally secede, followed within a month by six additional states: Mississippi, Florida, Alabama, Georgia, Louisiana, and Texas. Even as Lincoln was making his way to Washington, the Confederate States of America was being formally established in Montgomery, Alabama. Jefferson Davis, a Democratic senator from Mississippi, was appointed its first president, pending an election. His goal was to create an army of one hundred thousand volunteers, prepared to fight.

At the leather store, Grant learned of the Confederacy when

an acquaintance sympathetic to the Southern cause burst into the store, excited about the news. Grant glared at him. "Davis and the whole gang of them ought to be hung!" he declared bitterly.

It was this national fever that Lincoln faced when he stood to take his oath of office, after handing his tall stovepipe hat to none other than Stephen Douglas, who was seated close by.

The task of writing the inauguration speech had been difficult, requiring the utmost delicacy. How to inspire without inflaming? How to speak to such different audiences? Each word had to be chosen carefully so as not to trigger more states to secede.

Lincoln's faithful and insightful guide during this process was the New Yorker William Seward. Seward had been the expected Republican nominee until Lincoln defeated him in a convention surprise. But now he was a loyal and indispensable aide. (He would be foremost among Lincoln's "team of rivals"—a term popularized by historian Doris Kearns Goodwin—and would serve as secretary of State.)

Lincoln's initial draft, which he'd written before he left Springfield, Illinois, for Washington, had a warlike tone. For example, he wrote, "In *your* hands, my dissatisfied fellow countrymen, and not in *mine*, is the momentous issue of civil war. . . . With *you*, and not with *me*, is the solemn question of 'Shall it be peace, or a sword?'"

Seward advised a less aggressive tone. He cautioned Lincoln that a blatant threat could lead to the secession of Virginia and Maryland. The final, more conciliatory version was quite different:

> In your hands, my dissatisfied fellow-countrymen, and not in mine, is the momentous issue of civil war. The Government will not assail you. You can have no conflict without being yourselves the aggressors. You have no oath registered in heaven to

destroy the Government, while I shall have the most solemn one to preserve, protect, and defend it.

Seward also urged Lincoln to look for ways to appease the troubled South—to reach out to the citizens in a warm, embracing way. This led to the construction of the "better angels" conclusion—a phrase that is summoned to this day.

I am loath to close. We are not enemies, but friends. We must not be enemies. Though passion may have strained it must not break our bonds of affection. The mystic chords of memory, stretching from every battlefield and patriot grave to every living heart and hearthstone all over this broad land, will yet swell the chorus of the Union, when again touched, as surely they will be, by the better angels of our nature.

Lincoln was determined to try everything in his power to settle the secession upheaval peacefully. But on April 12, barely a month after the inauguration, the Confederacy fired the first shot at Fort Sumter, one of only two federal forts in the South. With Fort Sumter in Confederate hands, the war was officially on. Virginia, Arkansas, Tennessee, and North Carolina joined the Confederacy. Hanging in the balance were Kentucky, Missouri, Maryland, and Delaware.

The population on both sides was up in arms, at least figuratively, but in the North the media tried to make light of the Confederacy's chances. The *New York Times* predicted that the conflict would be over in a month, and other newspapers concurred that it would be a short war. The *Chicago Tribune* boasted, "Illinois can whip the South by herself."

Julia watched the developments with horror. "I was greatly exercised at this time," she wrote. "I was Southern by all rights, born and reared in a Southern state, and being a slaveholder at the beginning of the war, and a very pronounced Democrat, but that came all right, for when I would coaxingly ask the Captain to be a Democrat he would smile and say, 'I cannot, you know when I received my commission at West Point, I took a solemn oath to support the government and the administration, and that is now Republican.'"

For Grant, it was more than loyalty to a party: it was a sense of duty to serve. When President Lincoln sent out a call for seventy-five thousand volunteers, Grant's neighbors, knowing of his military service, asked him to preside over a large meeting in Galena on April 16. The mood was electric and almost festive. Throughout the day crowds of people had poured into town, accompanied by marching bands hopped up on pro-Union fervor.

At the meeting, a young man named John Aaron Rawlins, who was a friend of Grant's and would become instrumental in his service, rose to speak. "I have been a Democrat all my life; but this is no longer a question of politics," he boomed. "It is simply Union or disunion, country or no country. I have favored every honorable compromise, but the day for compromise is past. Only one course is left for us. We will stand by the flag of our country and appeal to the God of Battles!" The packed meeting cheered, and it was decided to organize a rifle company.

Grant was deeply moved by Rawlins's words. Walking home that night with his brother Orvil, he said he thought he should rejoin the Army. At that moment, Grant effectively walked away from his father's business. "I never went into our leather store again," he wrote with pleasure. He volunteered to drill the local company but declined an offer to lead it. Instead, he decided to go to the state capital in Springfield and seek a higher command. He wrote to his father, "Whatever may have been my opinions before, I have but one sentiment now. That is, we have a Government, and laws and a flag and they must all be sustained."

He agreed to accompany the rifle company by train to Springfield, and the day of their departure the whole town turned out to send them off. The Reverend John H. Vincent, pastor of the Methodist Episcopal Church in Galena and a close friend of Grant's, addressed the farewell ceremony. Afterward, the Reverend Vincent paid a visit to Julia, hoping to offer comfort.

"She was brave and hopeful," he recalled. "Whatever other people may have thought, Mrs. Grant knew her husband, and whatever he may have desired, dreamed or resolved, his wife was animated by a noble ambition, and by unbounded faith in his ability."

Soberly, Vincent told Julia that he hoped her husband "might be preserved from all harm and restored to his family."

Julia exclaimed, "Dear me! I hope he will get to be a major-general or something big!"

As to what kind of commander Grant might make, Vincent had no doubt of his suitability. "Grant is often called 'the silent man,'" he wrote. "As a matter of fact he was an interesting and able talker. . . . His reserve arose in part from natural timidity but for the most part from wisdom. He knew when to be silent. And he knew when and how to speak."

With the benefit of hindsight, Grant's wartime aide Adam Badeau listed the rigorous training ground that had prepared Grant for the great cause of his life. Yes, Badeau acknowledged, Grant had known poverty and failure. And yet: "He had learned patience when hope was long deferred, and endurance under heavy and repeated difficulties; he had displayed audacity in emergencies, as well as persistency of resolve and fertility of resource. If one means failed, he tried another; he was not discouraged by ill fortune, nor discontented with little things. . . . The leather merchant of Galena was not without preparation even for the great future which awaited him."

"Our trip was a perfect ovation," Grant wrote to Julia. "At every station the whole population seemed to be out to greet the troops. There is such a feeling aroused through the country now as has not been seen since the Revolution." Even as they traveled, the president was sending out a second call for volunteers, now increased to three hundred thousand, to serve three years or until the end of the war. As the US regular Army had only about sixteen thousand troops, these volunteers would form the majority of the fighters. Experienced soldiers were priceless. So Grant was appointed by Illinois governor Yates as a colonel leading the Twenty-First Volunteer Infantry, known as "Governor Yates's Hellions."

"My regiment was composed in large part of young men of as good social position as any in their section of the State," Grant wrote. "It embraced the sons of farmers, lawyers, physicians, politicians, merchants, bankers and ministers, and some men of maturer years who had filled such positions themselves. . . . I found it very hard work for a few days to bring all the men into anything like subordination; but the great majority favored discipline, and by the application of a little regular army punishment all were reduced to as good discipline as one could ask."

This was the moment Grant became a leader, a quality he had not fully displayed before. While those who loved him had always seen the signs, it was not apparent that the leather shop clerk was fit to lead. But his essential character was lying dormant, ready to emerge. And now, with such an urgent, all-enveloping purpose, he became the man he'd always had it in him to be.

In his new position, Grant found himself thinking of his friend Rawlins, whose fiery speech in Galena had inspired him to rejoin the military. He wrote to Rawlins, citing his need for good men—although Rawlins had no military experience—and offering him a job as aide-de-camp. Rawlins accepted immediately, but before he could leave he had to attend to his wife, who was dying from a long illness. Grieving after her death, Rawlins reluctantly left their three children in the care of relatives and joined Grant.

Rawlins would remain by Grant's side and become his most valuable supporter, defender, and protector. He was a savvy man who did not hesitate to speak his mind, but whose undying loyalty was unquestioned. According to James Harrison Wilson, who served with Rawlins on Grant's staff and later wrote a biography of him, Rawlins "was always the complement and counterpart of his taciturn but kind-hearted Chief, and was enabled to render him most invaluable services throughout the war . . . his highest function was in protecting Grant from himself as well as from others, in stimulating his sense of duty and ambition, and in giving direction and purpose to his military training and aptitudes." Every leader needs such a person.

In Washington, the Union Army was organizing a force of fresh recruits, and the mood was more high-spirited than one might imagine. There was still a strong sense that the war wouldn't amount to much and that the rebels would be easily defeated. So, on July 18, when thirty-five thousand Union volunteers marched into Virginia under the command of Brigadier General Irvin McDowell, there was an atmosphere of sport about it. Washington civilians packed picnic baskets and joined the flow of carriages to the battlefield, eager to have a summer adventure watching the action.

The army's destination was Manassas Junction, twenty-five miles from Washington, where twenty thousand Confederate soldiers under the command of General Pierre Gustave Toutant (P.G.T.) Beauregard were camped near the Bull Run River.

Inexperienced and stiff from the recent comforts of civilian life,

McDowell's army approached Manassas. McDowell himself was nauseated from eating a tin of bad fruit. Still, they were confident, expecting to dispatch the enemy quickly and forcefully.

Near dawn on July 21, the Union forces launched a cannonball through an enemy tent, and the fight was on. The battle was intense throughout the morning. McDowell hadn't expected such a large Confederate force, which had heavy reinforcements arriving throughout the morning. By the time he received reinforcements himself, in the form of Colonel William Tecumseh Sherman and his brigade, McDowell's army had suffered heavy casualties.

Sherman, at forty-one, was the picture of a soldier, although he had never been in combat. Unlike many of his West Point classmates, he hadn't fought in the Mexican-American War. Most of his jobs had been administrative, including a stint as superintendent of a Louisiana military academy before secession. But what Sherman lacked in battlefield experience he made up for in guts and intellect, as would be proven time and again during the war.

Arriving at McDowell's side, Sherman was shocked by the sight. He would recall later that "for the first time I saw the Carnage of battle—men lying in every conceivable shape, and mangled in a horrible way."

Holding out on one flank of the fight was a rebel brigade commanded by Thomas J. Jackson, a savvy fighter and a true and passionate believer in the Confederate cause. As other brigades fell and Jackson stood and waited for reinforcements, someone described him as appearing "like a stone wall." Thus his nickname, Stonewall Jackson. When the reinforcements arrived, Jackson joined the counterattack, calling on his soldiers to "yell like furies." They surged toward Sherman's men, and at that point Sherman made a terrible discovery: "I found that my brigade was almost alone." He realized then that McDowell's army was in retreat. The battle had been lost.

In Sherman's view, it was a shameful showing for the first major battle of the war. He wrote to his wife, Ellen, expressing disgust: "So it seems to be true that the north is after all pure bluster—Washington is in greater danger now than ever. . . . The Proud army characterized as the most extraordinary on earth has turned out the most ordinary."

He felt disgraced by the fleeing soldiers of his army, ashamed of their easy retreat and abandonment of the cause. When he was promoted to brigadier general after the battle, he told President Lincoln that he didn't feel fit for the new responsibility. He was ill, suffering from such a deep depression that it brought on hallucinations. He sought a leave of absence and returned to his home in Lancaster, Ohio, where Ellen could care for him. The man who would become, alongside Grant, one of the great heroes of the war was declared insane in the press. But by the end of 1861, Sherman had returned to duty, and he would never falter again.

While Sherman was experiencing disillusion, Grant was finding a Confederate Army struggling with its own war footing. His Twenty-First Infantry set off on July 3 from Springfield, Illinois, heading south to Missouri. Grant's orders were to confront Confederate colonel Thomas Harris, another Mexican-American War veteran, and his twelve hundred men at a critical juncture in the southern part of the state. Before leaving, he had to take care of a domestic matter. When he'd first gone to Springfield, eleven-year-old Fred had accompanied him, at his mother's urging. Julia saw the whole matter as a boy's adventure—"I considered it a pleasant summer outing for both of them." Now Grant notified Julia that he was ordered to Missouri and was sending Fred home, as "we may have some fighting to do." He bid goodbye to a disappointed Fred, not knowing that his tenacious son would join him many more times during the war.

As they came upon what he was sure was the field of battle

where he would find Colonel Harris and his men, Grant contemplated his new position. For the first time, he would be leading men into a fight against their countrymen, and his new responsibility sat heavily upon him. He felt the weight of the moment:

> As we approached the brow of the hill from which it was expected we could see Harris' camp, and possibly find his men ready formed to meet us, my heart kept getting higher and higher until it felt to me as though it was in my throat. I would have given anything then to have been back in Illinois, but I had not the moral courage to halt and consider what to do; I kept right on.
>
> When we reached a point from which the valley below was in full view I halted. The place where Harris had been encamped a few days before was still there and the marks of a recent encampment were plainly visible, but the troops were gone. My heart resumed its place. It occurred to me at once that Harris had been as much afraid of me as I had been of him. This was a view of the question I had never taken before; but it was one I never forgot afterwards.

Still untested by battle, Grant learned that, after a group of Illinois congressmen had petitioned the president on his behalf, Lincoln promoted him to brigadier general. He now had full command authority. And if he'd been perplexed by Harris's missing army, he'd soon find its counterpart in Belmont, Missouri.

One of the early Union goals of the war was to cut off the Confederates from access to the Mississippi River, which was a massive open highway for troops and supplies. This goal was jeopardized when Confederate troops crossed the river into Belmont. Grant's strategy for reaching them was to hide his troops on ships nearby and launch a surprise attack. On November 6, he sailed down the river with three thousand men, arriving early on the seventh and attacking quickly. It seemed to work. It was a bloody fight, and Grant's horse was shot out from under him. But they drove the enemy back. That was when things collapsed. Grant's men were so excited by their victory that they fell on the deserted enemy camp and began rummaging through the tents, grabbing trophies.

The Confederates, under the command of General Leonidas Polk, had huddled nearby, preparing to surrender. But seeing an opportunity posed by distraction, Polk ordered them to attack once again. Grant's forces soon retreated back to the river. In the final tally, the fallout was about even, with both sides declaring victory. But Grant did not feel like a winner. Embarrassed at having lost control of his men, he had learned a lesson and would seek redemption in the next battle.

During the fall of 1861, Grant had seen the significance of the location of Fort Henry, Kentucky, on the Tennessee River and adjacent to the Cumberland River. These passages were vital to the flow of arms and men from south to north and vice versa. Furthermore, as long as Fort Henry was held by the Confederacy, the border state of Kentucky was not safe. Grant planned a joint land and water assault, assisted by Flag Officer Andrew Foote and his gunboats.

"To-morrow will come the tug of war," he wrote to Julia the night before the attack. "One side or the other must to-morrow night rest in quiet possession of Fort Henry."

But at Fort Henry, Brigadier General Lloyd Tilghman, knowing of Grant's approach, secretly evacuated most of his men to Fort Donelson, ten miles down the Cumberland River. There was little left to capture at Fort Henry, and Grant continued on, fighting flooded roads and bad weather before making a final approach to Donelson.

At Fort Donelson, Grant would encounter General Simon Bolivar Buckner, his old West Point friend who had served with him in the Mexican war. Once as close as fighting comrades could be, they were now poised in bitter opposition. Buckner had tried valiantly to keep Kentucky out of the war, and he was far from an avid combatant. Now, at Fort Donelson, he was forced to follow a failed military strategy devised by Brigadier General John B. Floyd and Brigadier General Gideon Pillow, both of whom had fled the scene as Grant's forces approached, leaving Buckner to fight alone. He had sixteen thousand men to Grant's twenty-seven thousand. It was a heavy siege, but Buckner finally knew he had to surrender for the sake of his men.

Buckner sent word to Grant asking about terms of surrender. He might have expected his old friend to offer a gentleman's agreement. Instead, Grant showed some of the iron spirit that would distinguish his military career. He felt no pressure to make accommodations out of friendship. This was war, and there would be no negotiation. He sent this message to Buckner:

Sir: Yours of this date proposing Armistice, and appointment of Commissioners, to settle terms of Capitulation is just received. No terms except unconditional and immediate surrender can be accepted. I propose to move immediately upon your works.

From this, Grant gained the nickname "Unconditional Surrender Grant." And Buckner had no choice but to agree. (Future presidents would often cite Grant as the pioneer of the concept; during World War II, Franklin D. Roosevelt took great delight in telling the story of Grant's call for unconditional surrender to justify the decision that he and Winston Churchill made to do the same with the Germans and the Japanese.)

When the two men finally met, Grant asked Buckner, now a

prisoner, "Where is Pillow? Why didn't he stay to surrender his command?" Grant knew Pillow well, having witnessed his poor response as a brigadier general at Belmont; Pillow's own biographer dubbed him a gift to Grant from the tooth fairy. Grant also recalled his laughable performance during the Mexican-American War, when it was said that his command was granted as a favor by his friend President Polk. As Grant scornfully wrote to his sister, "I do not say he [Pillow] would shoot himself. I am not so uncharitable as many who served under him in Mexico. I think, however, he might report himself wounded on the receipt of a very slight scratch."

"He thought you were too anxious to capture him personally," Buckner answered.

Grant grinned. "Why, if I had captured him, I would have turned him loose. I would rather have him in command of your fellows than as a prisoner."

Buckner nodded ruefully. He told Grant that if he'd been in charge, Grant's army would not have found it so easy to move on the fort. Grant acknowledged this possibility, remarking that if Buckner had been in command, he wouldn't have conducted the siege the way he did.

Grant was saddened by the plight of his old comrade, but the price was worth it—Kentucky was saved. Later Grant wrote to Julia: "I am in most perfect health and ready for anything even to chasing Floyd & Pillow. There is but little hope however of ever over-hawling [sic] them. They are as dead as if they were in their graves for any harm they can do."

However, Grant and Buckner's story was not quite finished. Recalling a kindness that Buckner had done him before the war, Grant went aboard the prisoner transport and found him. "Buckner, you may be going among strangers," he said, "and I hope you will allow me to share my purse with you." Buckner was touched by the gesture, but he assured Grant that he had funds of his own.

After Fort Henry and Fort Donelson fell, Grant was promoted to major general of volunteers. His name achieved some acclaim, and he was the subject of intense curiosity. Who was this man who scored such significant victories? What did he look like? His countrymen envisioned him as an imposing man, tall in the saddle—the Union counterpart to the stately general Robert E. Lee. Several newspapers rushed to use the fraudulent image of such a man, who was rumored to be Grant. His sturdy body, erect posture, and lustrous beard perfectly fit the ideal, and the false picture would continue to appear now and then during the course of the war. (The temptation to polish images of Grant survived for a century. In a 1959 biography by Roy Meredith, *Mr. Lincoln's General, U. S. Grant*, a photograph of Grant on horseback in Virginia is actually a composite, employing the body of a taller and more elegant soldier.)

But a strange cloud was falling over Grant just as he was finding fame. Grant's commanding officer, Major General Henry W. Halleck, was not entirely pleased with Grant's leadership. Halleck did not know Grant well, but his early impression of him was unfavorable. Grant lacked the carriage of a great soldier. He lacked the temperament of a hero. Furthermore, it irked Halleck that Grant was getting so much acclaim for the Fort Henry/Donelson victory, when it was Halleck who had given the order to proceed. (In truth, this order was reluctantly issued. When Grant had first approached Halleck with a plan for the attack, he'd been dismissive.) It's an inescapable conclusion that Halleck's attitude about Grant was largely driven by envy.

In his correspondence with Union Army chief George B. Mc-Clellan in Washington, Halleck repeatedly downplayed Grant's leadership in battle, going out of his way to praise other officers at

Grant's expense. He even suggested that Brigadier General C. F. Smith, one of Grant's subordinates, be promoted over Grant for his actions at Donelson.

So, as others were calling out Grant's skill and heroism and the newspapers were lauding him, Halleck was trying to get him sidelined. He found his opportunity when Grant left camp for a few days to travel to Nashville, where he planned to meet with his counterpart Don Carlos Buell, commander of the Army of Ohio, to plan the next campaign. When Halleck could not reach him for a few days, he complained to McClellan that Grant had deserted his men and his army was in disarray.

Then Halleck struck what he hoped would be a final blow to Grant, writing: "A rumor has just reached me that since the taking of Fort Donelson General Grant has resumed his former bad habits. If so, it will account for his neglect of my often-repeated orders. I do not deem it advisable to arrest him at present, but have placed General Smith in command of the expedition up the Tennessee. I think Smith will restore order and discipline."

The missive was full of blatant lies: Grant was on a mission, not drunk. His army was not in disarray. It is doubtful that any such rumor had been received. But Washington was a long way from the front in a time of war, and Halleck no doubt expected his word to be taken as fact. As he ordered Grant to turn over command to Smith, he thought that would be the end of it. But President Lincoln demanded an explanation. How was it that Grant, the heroic commander who had finally scored an important victory for the Union, was being relieved of his command? What was the evidence behind these rumors? Without substance to back him up, and with Grant's very cogent explanation for his absence on hand, Halleck was forced to restore Grant to command. He now led the Army of the Tennessee. The article "the" is important: named for the river, not the state, the Army of the

Tennessee was not to be confused with the Confederate Army of Tennessee. Grant's army would become one of the most significant of the war, distinguishing itself in the great battles.

Restored to command, Grant continued on. But it would hardly be the last time Grant would tangle with Halleck. In fact, it was excessive caution in following Halleck's orders that soon led to calamity.

The Union Army was setting its sights on the rails—in particular, the rail center in Corinth, Mississippi, over the border of southwestern Tennessee. Grant led his forty-two thousand troops south, where he would be joined by twenty thousand more from Buell's army. Among his troops was a newly formed division led by Sherman, who had returned to full battle mode and had pleaded with Halleck to assign him to Grant.

Once Grant's army arrived at Pittsburg Landing, near Corinth, it settled in to wait for Buell, who was delayed by heavy rains and muddy roads. Grant was eager to get to it, but Halleck ordered him to hold off until Buell's reinforcements arrived. Grant stayed put.

Nearby was the masterful Confederate general Albert Sidney Johnston, with over forty thousand troops of his own. Both sides were hampered by a heavy rainfall that turned the camps and trails into bogs. As Grant rode through the torrents to check on his men, his horse slipped and fell, bringing Grant to the ground with his leg under the heavy animal. The soft, waterlogged earth prevented serious injury, but Grant's ankle was damaged and he had to use crutches.

The two sides waited. Buell had still not arrived. Then, in the predawn hours of July 6, 1862, Johnston launched a surprise attack. "Tonight we will water our horses in the Tennessee River," he proclaimed, confident of victory.

Sherman, who had camped next to the church in Shiloh, Tennessee, looked out and "saw the rebel lines of battle in front coming down on us as far as the eye could reach."

Several miles down the river, Grant heard the sound of gunfire and ordered his men to action. He limped to his horse on his crutches and was helped astride. They rode quickly toward Shiloh church and the scene of a mass attack. The cry went out, "The rebels are coming!" Indeed, they were already there.

Sherman was nearly killed early on. As he sat on his horse, surveying the scene through field glasses, one of his men shouted a warning. He threw up his hand as musket shrapnel slashed into it and then went past him to kill his orderly. Sherman quickly wrapped his hand and continued on. Against the onslaught, Sherman's men held the line, but by the time Grant reached him many of his men had fled or been felled. The rest, brave beyond all measure, stood and fought. Grant was impressed by Sherman, writing later that throughout the day, as he'd moved about the field giving directions to division commanders, he'd never felt it necessary to stay long with Sherman. "Although his troops were then under fire for the first time, their commander by his constant presence with them, inspired a confidence in officers and men that enabled them to render services on that bloody battle-field worthy of the best of veterans."

As the day wore on, the Union forces were not faring well. The rebels had captured more than two thousand prisoners, including entire divisions, while their brethren lay in the field. By the time darkness fell and the fighting ceased for the day, it appeared that the Confederate forces were winning.

Long after midnight Grant stood under a tree, near a camp of the wounded, whose screams of agony he found hard to endure. The rain was still pouring down around him. Sherman found him there and was ready to propose a plan of retreat. He didn't believe there was a way that their rapidly decimated forces could prevail. He would later recall that he saw something in Grant's face as he approached that kept him from mentioning retreat. Instead, he said, "Well Grant, we've had the devil's own day of it, haven't we?"

"Yes," said Grant, staring ahead in thought. Eventually he added, "Lick 'em tomorrow, though."

There was no apparent cause for optimism, but Grant had thought it through. The enemy was tired, he reckoned, and it had no reinforcements, while he, finally, had Buell's army approaching just over the horizon. That day the advantage had gone to Johnston because he had attacked. Grant believed that the advantage in battle always went to the attacking party. The next day that party would be his Union Army.

General Johnston had already sent news of a Confederate victory to Jefferson Davis when Buell's Union reinforcements arrived. Grant, who had organized the rest of his forces for an aggressive assault, was ready to attack. The fighting was heavy throughout the day. Johnston confidently rode into battle on his horse Fire-Eater, with the Union gunfire nicking at him as he fought. One bullet struck him in the leg, but he thought little of it and kept on going. He didn't realize that the bullet had hit an artery. Suddenly he began to falter, and those around him noticed his peril and his blood-soaked boot. They helped him off his horse, and he died on the field. General Beauregard replaced him in command, but it was almost too late.

Grant's prediction about the exhausted, hungry Confederates was coming true. As the afternoon wore on, Grant could tell that the Southern forces were weakening. His own men were also exhausted beyond measure, but the reinforcements had given them just the support they needed. As Beauregard was making the calculation that Grant would withdraw until morning so his men could rest, Grant ordered an extra push—roaring at the Confederates with loud cheers and ferocious might. The Southerners retreated, their battle lost.

Sherman felt gratified by the victory, his sins erased. He wrote to Ellen with pride that General Grant had made a special mention of him in his report to headquarters and had shown it to him. But he added soberly, "The scenes on this field would have cured anyone of war. Mangled bodies, dead, dying, in every conceivable shape, without heads, legs; and horses!" He tucked that trauma away, deep inside. He would see many more such sights in the years to come, but he never again lost his resolve.

Grant was struggling with the same reality. Shiloh was won, but at what cost? Surveying the field of battle in its aftermath, Grant reflected on the devastation: "I saw an open field, in our possession on the second day, over which the Confederates had made repeated charges the day before, so covered with dead that it would have been possible to walk across the clearing in any direction, stepping on dead bodies, without a foot touching the ground."

And the terrible truth, beneath it all, was captured in the clash of brother against brother, both figuratively and literally:

The Boston Traveller: **AN INCIDENT OF THE BATTLE OF SHILOH**—The following incident of the battle of Shiloh is related by an eye and ear witness. Two Kentucky regiments met face to face and fought each other with terrible resolution, and it happened that one of the Federal soldiers wounded and captured his brother, and after handing him back began firing at a man near a tree, when the captured brother called to him and said: "Don't shoot there any more—that's father."

At Shiloh there were an estimated thirteen thousand Union casualties—dead, wounded, or captured. The Confederate casualties numbered over ten thousand. The criticism from

Washington was swift and biting. Halleck led the accusations against Grant, while others expressed concern about what seemed an unacceptable loss of life. Rumors started that Grant had been inattentive in letting the enemy attack by surprise. Some wondered if Grant had been drinking.

Halleck, for one, was persuaded by the negative media narrative. He seemed to take delight in once again robbing Grant of his command. He handed Grant's army to a commander under Buell and promoted Grant to an empty position as his second of command—with no authority and no troops.

Completely dispirited, Grant wrote to Julia, "I am seriously thinking of going home."

When Sherman heard, he went looking for Grant and found him at his camp table. Was it true that he was thinking about leaving?

"Yes," Grant said, falling into self-pity. "You know that I am in the way here. I have stood it as long as I can and can endure it no longer."

Sherman asked where he was going. St. Louis, Grant replied. As Sherman recalled, "I then begged him to stay, illustrating his case by my own. Before the battle of Shiloh, I had been cast down by a mere newspaper assertion of 'crazy,' but that single battle had given me new life, and I was now in high feather." He told Grant that because of one reporter's slander, he had been "riding a whirlwind of innuendo." But he was there to prove that it was possible to come out the other side. Perhaps Sherman uniquely understood that once a charge of crazy or drunk was leveled, it was hard to live it down. The only solution was to rise above it and excel.

Sherman now warned Grant that were he to step aside, he would be permanently left out, whereas if he stayed, "some happy accident might restore him to favor and his true place."

Bolstered by Sherman's encouraging words, Grant decided to stay, and soon afterward the "happy accident" occurred. Halleck informed Grant that he was restoring his command of the Army of the Tennessee. And then Lincoln sent for Halleck to come to Washington as general-in-chief, replacing McClellan. The pressure eased slightly.

Long after the war, Grant would render his verdict on Halleck, which was notably fair-minded, given the way Halleck had tormented him. He praised Halleck's "immense knowledge of military science," but said that this knowledge prevented him from being a successful commander in the field. He thought it made Halleck timid. "I do not mean timid personally," Grant said, "because no one ever doubted his courage, but timid in reaching conclusions. He would never take a chance in a battle. A general who will never take a chance in a battle will never fight one."

Grant felt changed by Shiloh. Until then, he had mentally separated the rebel warriors from their countrymen. He'd taken pains to preserve the Southern land—to protect the property of citizens. But now he saw that he could only fight full out, not holding back. So, from then on, while he ordered protection for Southern civilians, he treated their property and goods as fair game for seizure. This approach reduced the resources that could be made available for the Confederate Army, while also supplying Union forces with ready goods at hand and making them less reliant on the long supply trains that followed their march south. All along, Grant was surveying the countryside, analyzing its natural provisions, especially cattle and corn, to determine if seizing property would enable his forces to begin to survive off the land. The process of seizing property was delegated to the quartermaster, who would issue receipts to the owners. Grant did not authorize "promiscuous pillaging," which would be punished, but the immediate effect of the property seizures he did allow was less food for the Confederacy.

At one point, the Confederacy was growing so alarmed by the specter of hunger in the South that members of the cabinet suggested making a deal with the Union—the South would supply cotton to the North in exchange for provisions. Jefferson Davis refused to consider it. Now Grant understood that cutting off the food supply to the enemy was a strategy to weaken them. Basil Gildersleeve, a Confederate officer who became a classics professor at Johns Hopkins University after the war, wrote, "Hunger was the dominant note of life in the Confederacy, civil as well as military."

Lincoln fought a war to save the Union. He did not fight it to free the slaves. He knew that Northerners would not have embarked upon a civil war for that purpose. But as the war progressed the tangled chords of Confederate principles became clearer, and by 1862 Lincoln realized that the war could not be won without also freeing the slaves. It was impossible to imagine reverting to the status quo.

Privately, without informing his cabinet, Lincoln drafted what would become the Emancipation Proclamation. He called the cabinet together in late July and read them the terms he was considering. He made one thing clear: he was not asking their advice. He had decided on this course, and he was now informing them that the proclamation would be made on January 1, 1863. As of that date, all slaves within the Confederacy would be freed.

Abolitionists considered the proclamation a half-measure, since it did not also free slaves in the border states, which had not joined the Confederacy. But Lincoln held to his point. When *New York Tribune* editor Horace Greeley criticized his lackluster policies, Lincoln shot off a letter: "My paramount object in this struggle is to save the Union and is not either to save or to destroy slavery. If I could save the Union without freeing any slave I would do it, and if I could save it by freeing all the slaves I would do it; and if I could save it by freeing some and leaving others alone, I would also do that." As it turned out, freeing the slaves and saving the Union would become a joint effort.

The Emancipation Proclamation ushered in a change on the battlefield. With the creation of the Bureau of Colored Troops in May 1863, freed Blacks began signing up to serve. It wasn't a smooth path for them. There was substantial bias against Blacks within the Union Army, but in time they proved their worth. By the end of the war, 180,000 Black men had served—bravely and proudly. As the former slave and abolitionist Frederick Douglass proclaimed of the moment:

Who would be free themselves
must strike the blow.
Better even to die free than to live slaves.

Grant quickly recognized that not only did Black soldiers perform at exceptionally high levels, but they might well be the secret weapon in the conflict. However, there were issues of deep concern to him. It was well known that the armies of the South treated captured Black Union soldiers quite differently than their white counterparts. Black soldiers were considered to have committed treason, and capture often meant torture or death by lynching. Grant could not abide such treatment of his men, and he announced an end to prisoner exchanges unless Black soldiers were treated properly. Unfortunately, this wouldn't happen until the war was almost over.

Grant appointed John Eaton, an Army chaplain, as the superintendent of freedmen, an effort that was the origin of the Freedmen's Bureau. Grant was interested not only in protecting newly freed Blacks in the South but in putting them to use—for example, picking cotton at abandoned plantations and shipping it north to support the war effort.

In his quiet moments, Grant often contemplated the ultimate outcome of the war. With a Northerner's sensibility and a pragmatist's eye, he perceived it this way: "There was no time during the rebellion when I did not think, and often say, that the South was more to be benefitted by its defeat than the North." Grant wrote in his memoir that "with the outside world at war with this institution [slavery]," there were many reasons why the South would have been unable to form a nation. For instance, "they could not have extended their territory. The labor of the country was not skilled nor allowed to become so. The whites could not toil without becoming degraded." Grant believed that the entire unholy mess of slavery and its future exposed the real truth: no matter the outcome of the war, the South could not return to the way things were, and for the sake of its future, it should hope for a Northern victory to release it from the burden of governing in acrimony a land of freed slaves.

By the autumn of 1862, Grant was setting his sights on Vicksburg, for good reason. From Washington, Lincoln pronounced, "Vicksburg is the key. This war can never be brought to a close until that key is in our pocket." Even Davis described it as "the nail head that holds the South's two halves together." The Mississippi River was the lifeblood of the South, the main shipping and transport channel from the North and the West. Vicksburg was strategically situated on the east bank of the Mississippi, equidistant between Memphis to the north and New Orleans to the south. If the Union took Vicksburg, it would choke off the flow of goods and military supplies to the Confederacy.

At the Confederate capital in Richmond, Virginia, Davis saw Grant's strategy and felt some alarm. He knew that the Union forces were determined to close off the ports, the rail lines, and the flow of goods—to starve his troops into defeat.

The Vicksburg campaign would take five months. During the fall months, Grant stayed in Corinth, focused on consolidating his forces for the great surge. He sent for Julia, who arrived with their four children. They stayed for six weeks in Grant's head-quarter house, which Julia described as "a handsome and very comfortable country house, situated in a magnificent oak grove."

Grant, who had grown quite thin, thrived under Julia's minis-trations. She arranged to have his favorite foods prepared, cleaned and mended his frayed uniform, and lightened his spirits with her love and comfort. In her presence, with his children around him, he could begin to imagine a life beyond war.

In December, Sherman tried and failed to take Vicksburg from the north. Grant's efforts to get a foothold also failed. Survey-ing the scene from a high bluff, hundreds of feet above the river, Grant thought about his options. Vicksburg was very strongly garrisoned—almost impregnable, he thought. Heavy brush and swamps made the approaches difficult. His final strategy, which seemed counterintuitive and few believed would work, was to move *away* from Vicksburg rather than toward it and to come up on the site from the south.

In early March, Grant marched forty thousand men south, along the western shore of the Mississippi to a point thirty miles below Vicksburg. There, with the help of River Admiral David Porter, commander of the Mississippi River Squadron and a sea-soned veteran from the Mexican-American War, they crossed over to the eastern shore and began their move north.

It turned out that much of Grant's presumed floundering during the preceding months had been part of a ruse meant to disguise his true plan to attack from the south. But he kept it quiet, even from Washington. From their distant perch, the wags in the capital—with Halleck at the forefront—were beginning to lose confidence. What was taking so long? Was Grant falling apart? Was he drinking? Finally, Charles A. Dana, the newly appointed assistant secretary of War, was dispatched as a spy to find out what was really going on and to report back. As Dana later described his mission, the president and Secretary of War Edwin Stanton "wanted someone to go to Grant's army . . . to report daily to him the military proceedings, and to give such information as would enable Mr. Lincoln and himself to settle their minds as to Grant, about whom at that time there were many doubts, and against whom there was some complaint." Dana's cover was to arrive as a commissioner of the War Department overseeing the pay service of the western army. Little did the plotters in Washington realize that Dana's true purpose would be plain to everyone in camp, especially Grant, or that Grant would welcome him happily. Dana's daily dispatches relieved Grant of the onerous duty of reporting daily himself. He was glad to have Dana by his side. For his part, Dana grew in the role and relished becoming an indispensable part of the mission of a man he came to admire.

Dana observed, "Grant was an uncommon fellow—the most modest, the most disinterested, and the most honest man I ever knew, with a temper that nothing could disturb, and a judgment that was judicial in its comprehensiveness and wisdom. Not a great man, except morally; not an original or brilliant man, but sincere, thoughtful, deep, and gifted with courage that never faltered; when the time came to risk all, he went in like a simple-hearted, unaffected, unpretending hero, whom no ill omens could deject and no triumph unduly exalt."

Dana recalled the sight as he neared Grant's camp for the first time:

The Mississippi at Millicent's Bend was a mile wide, and the sight as we came down the river by boat was most imposing. Grant's big army was stretched up and down the river bank over the plantations, its white tents affording a new decoration to the natural magnificence of the broad plains. These plains, which stretch far back from the river, were divided into rich and old plantations by blooming hedges of rose and Osage orange, the mansions of the owners being included in roses, myrtles, magnolias, oaks, and every other sort of beautiful and noble trees. The negroes whose work made all this wealth and magnificence were gone, and there was nothing growing in the fields.

As the army moved toward Port Gibson, Dana kept to the rear. There he encountered twelve-year-old Fred Grant, and the two of them followed along. Amazingly, Julia had been in favor of Fred joining his father during the Vicksburg campaign, despite the clear dangers. She would never know the half of it, as Fred was a daring boy who managed to get himself into near-calamitous scrapes when his father's attention was elsewhere. On one occasion when he rode his horse near a Confederate camp, a sharpshooter fired and a musket ball hit him in the leg. A Union soldier who raced to his aid found him not severely injured but in quite a state.

"I am killed!" Fred cried.

The colonel didn't flinch. "Move your toes," he ordered, and when this was accomplished, he declared Fred a survivor.

Grant, who didn't know about Fred's most daring exploits, was proud of his son and glad to have him along. He even arranged for him to have a uniform. "My son accompanied me throughout the campaign and siege, and caused no anxiety either to me or to his mother who was at home," he wrote. "He looked out for himself and was in every battle of the [Vicksburg] campaign. His age, then not quite thirteen, enabled him to take in all he saw, and to retain a recollection of it that would not be possible in mature years."

Fred had a special insight into his father that military men could not match. He watched him with reverence and a sharp eye, memorizing his ways. He shared these recollections many years later, when he was an adult:

> On the battlefield General Grant would ride with his head erect from one point to another on his line where the heaviest fighting was heard, and though quiet in his movements, he seemed to take in account everything—the very smallest and seemingly unimportant details. He gave close attention to all that occurred about him, directing his officers and troops with prompt decision. During the Vicksburg campaign, he was on horseback during the day, and then late into the night he would be writing his orders which were full of the minutest details. He seemed always to be the last to retire and the first to rise in the morning. I know because I slept in the same room or tent with him many a night.

Fred also shared a surprising detail—that his father was sickened by the sight of blood and repulsed by the sight of human suffering. It increased Fred's admiration that he bore up under this weakness.

At Port Gibson, Grant's forces were met with resistance by Confederate major general John S. Bowen. Although his small force was no match for Grant's, they fought fiercely. At last Bowen sent a message to Grant asking for a twenty-four-hour suspension of hostilities to treat the wounded.

Grant refused. "A dispatch now in my possession shows that you are expecting reinforcements and additional munitions of war," he shot back. "I deem therefore the request unreasonable and one you could not expect me to comply with."

In early May, Grant's army neared Vicksburg, and Grant felt hopeful that the goal was finally in sight. He judged the enemy to be exhausted, demoralized, and short on armor, but he also expected a lengthy fight. Too much was at stake for the Southerners to give in easily. On May 7, Grant sent a general order. After thanking his men for the victory at Port Gibson, he wrote, "More difficulties and privations are before us. Let us endure them manfully. Other battles are to be fought. Let us fight them bravely."

General Halleck was openly skeptical that Grant was following the right course. Lincoln wasn't so sure himself, but he was loath to denigrate his favorite general. "I think Grant has hardly a friend left, except myself," he told Halleck. But, he explained, "what I want and what the people want, is generals who will fight battles and win victories. Grant has done this, and I propose to stand by him."

It was a long and unrelenting battle. Confederate general John C. Pemberton had fewer than thirty thousand men to Grant's seventy thousand, and he and his troops were hunkered down near Vicksburg, fighting off Grant through waves of assault. Pemberton and Grant had a history from the Mexican war, where they had served side by side. It was Pemberton who was assigned to bring General Scott's compliments to Grant on his clever use of a church belfry to gain a foothold in Mexico City.

Now they went at each other brutally, and Grant had Pemberton on the run toward Vicksburg. Pemberton burned the Big Black bridge behind him and assembled his troops on the other side. Grant had no choice but to rapidly rebuild the bridge and then follow Pemberton across. By nightfall of June 18, Grant was at Vicksburg.

By then, Pemberton had received impressive reinforcements. General Joe Johnston (not to be confused with Albert Sidney Johnston, who died at Shiloh) was positioned behind Grant's forces with twenty-five thousand men. Johnston would be a constant threat to Grant throughout the siege, although Johnston was flanked by Sherman, who kept careful watch over his movements. Day after day, week after week, the pounding continued.

The genteel surroundings with their many homesteads were demolished in the fight, and the remaining residents were left terrorized. Some of them dug caves into the hillsides to hide from the roar of the cannons and the ferocity of the assault. Sherman wrote poignantly to Ellen of the heartbreaking plight of these civilians, and their undying hatred for the Union soldiers who despoiled their countryside: "Not a man is seen—nothing but women, with houses plundered, fields open to the cattle & horses, pickets lounging on every porch, and desolation broadcast—Servants all gone and women & children bred in luxury, beautiful & accomplished, begging with one breath for the soldiers rations."

Grant kept his eye steadily on the main battlefield, welcoming massive reinforcements when they arrived. The eighty-five thousand men he now had under his command dwarfed the rebel numbers. Reports of hunger and exhaustion from behind enemy lines grew more persistent, but there was no letup in the fighting.

In Richmond, Davis was alarmed by the news from Vicksburg. He summoned General Robert E. Lee, the commander of the Army of Northern Virginia, to plot a strategy for stopping Grant. This had been a rough period for the Confederacy, and Lee was still reeling from the loss five days earlier of his closest military companion and most reliable second, Stonewall Jackson. His army had fought daringly in Chancellorsville, Virginia, against the Union Army of the Potomac, a force twice its size, and Jackson had been grievously wounded by friendly fire. His shattered left arm was amputated, an unimaginable price for such a devoted soldier, and soon pneumonia set in and he died. Lee was grieving his loss and trying to find a way to compensate.

But Lee was above all a soldier, so he buried his grief and set his mind to making a plan. An idea began to take shape: Lee would launch an assault on southern Pennsylvania, which might ultimately reach the capital. Such a threat would require an exceptional response, surely including the need for Grant to leave Vicksburg and bring his army north. The planned battle would come to be known as the Battle of Gettysburg.

Toward the end of June, Lee began to march his army north to Pennsylvania. This caught the attention of the Union Army, whose commanders didn't know what he had in mind. However, General Joseph Hooker, commander of the Army of the Potomac, noted that Lee had left Richmond vulnerable, creating an opportunity to attack there. Lincoln disagreed. He'd lost confidence in Hooker since the defeat at Chancellorsville, and he replaced him with General George Meade. His instructions: find Lee's army and attack.

So, two massive armies were on the march—Lee's going north, composed of 71,699 soldiers, and Meade's going south, composed of 91,921 soldiers. Neither knew the exact intention of the other, but by Lee's design they were headed for Pennsylvania.

On July 1, Lee's army arrived at an innocuous little town in Pennsylvania called Gettysburg, distinguished mainly by its railroad station, built right before the war, and its position as a strategic gateway to Baltimore and Washington beyond. Almost simultaneously Meade's forces arrived. A Union division under the command of General Winfield Scott Hancock set up a position on the high point of a cemetery, called Cemetery Ridge, and a nearby elevation known as Culp's Hill, named for its owner, Henry Culp. This gave Meade's army a dominant position from the outset. It also put them on the defensive for the first two days of the battle. Meade lost twenty thousand men in that period, most of them on the second day. But they continued to fire, endlessly, relentlessly.

In a desperate move, Major General George Pickett, who commanded a hardy and determined division of rebels, marched his men for a mile across an open field. Their screams battered his ears as they were cut down. By the end, he had lost two-thirds of his soldiers. So, while casualties were about even, Meade had the stronger position. Pickett had been unable to shake the Union soldiers loose from their advantageous elevation.

By July 3, there was one last chance for Lee to take Cemetery Ridge, and he was determined to do it whatever the cost. Longstreet, who had replaced Stonewall Jackson in Lee's command, advised him strongly not to attempt it. He favored a strategy that would move in from the left, not a straight-on approach to the ridge. Lee rejected Longstreet's advice. "No, I'm going to whip them [on the ridge] or they are going to whip me."

Lee joined Pickett, who had lined up his remaining fifteen thousand men for the assault. Staring with dread toward the enemy's position, Pickett said to Lee, "Take a drink with me; in an hour you'll be in hell or glory." Lee declined.

Pickett set off, his men in formation, determined to take the ridge. They were butchered by enemy fire, except for a few who managed by some miracle to get past the bullets aimed for their hearts. They planted a flag before they were driven off the ridge. Lee's army was defeated. Reflecting later on the disastrous loss, Longstreet wrote critically, "The Confederate chief at Gettysburg looked something like Napoleon at Waterloo."

Lee's Army of Northern Virginia was so broken that the battle had given Meade a perfect opportunity to end it once and for all. From Washington, Lincoln begged him to deliver the final blow. Instead, Meade allowed Lee and his men to return to Virginia, as both sides tried to comprehend the enormity of their losses—twenty-eight thousand casualties for the Confederates and twenty-three thousand for the Union. Failing to chase Lee's army when it was at its most vulnerable was a mistake that would prolong the war and mar Meade's reputation.

As the Army of the Potomac was claiming victory at Gettysburg, Grant was dominating Pemberton at Vicksburg, and the end was near.

On July 3 at ten in the morning, white flags appeared along the Confederate line. Major General John S. Bowen arrived at Grant's camp with a message from Pemberton offering to discuss a truce. Word spread that the battle was ending, and elation rose from the troops. Grant replied that he would meet Pemberton at 3:00 that afternoon.

They met on a hillside near the rebel lines. Grant noted that "a stunted oak tree, which was made historical by the event," was later taken apart by eager trophy hunters. Also present at this fateful meeting was Grant's son Fred, standing as tall as his child's body allowed.

Grant greeted Pemberton cordially as one would an old acquaintance, recalling their time of service together in the Mexican war. Pemberton asked that his army be allowed to leave with the honors of war, carrying their small arms and field artillery. Grant rejected that plan and told Pemberton that he would send a letter with terms that night.

From a pragmatic standpoint, Grant did not want the burden of holding Pemberton's troops as prisoners. He lacked the wherewithal to guard and care for thousands of enemy soldiers, and he needed his own men for the fight. In fact, the thinning Union forces were an urgent concern, and in that same month Lincoln would call for the establishment of a draft. The draft wasn't popular, and it was considered perfectly acceptable to dodge it by paying a $300 commutation fee or hiring a substitute. The newspapers were full of ads by well-heeled men willing to pay someone else to take their place on the front.

In the surrender accord with General Pemberton, Grant agreed to parole Confederate soldiers in exchange for their vow not to rejoin the war. He allowed them to march out with their side arms and clothing. Field staff and officers could take one horse each, thirty wagons, and as many of their rations as they desired. It was typical for Grant to be ferocious in battle and compassionate in the aftermath. As he explained, "While a battle is raging one can see his enemy mowed down by the thousand, or ten thousand, with great composure; but after the battle these scenes are distressing, and one is naturally disposed to do as much to alleviate the suffering of an enemy as a friend."

Once the surrender was formalized on July 4, a day of great significance, Grant observed his men sharing their rations with the hungry rebels. It was a touching sign of brotherhood.

Elated by the Vicksburg victory, the most significant of the war, Lincoln wrote to Grant on July 13: "I write this now as a grateful acknowledgment for the almost inestimable service you have done the country." Referencing the much-maligned Vicksburg strategy, he added, "I now wish to make the personal acknowledgment that you were right and I was wrong."

It was a generous act on Lincoln's part. Surely, at that point in the war, his heart and mind were filled to overflowing with the suffering on many fronts. He was moved by the tremendous death toll on both sides at Gettysburg. Months later, Lincoln would dedicate a cemetery on the hallowed ground and deliver an address that would be considered the most famous in American history, concluding:

From these honored dead we take increased devotion to that cause for which they gave the last full measure of devotion—that we here highly resolve that these dead shall not have died in vain—that this nation, under God, shall have a new birth of freedom—and that government of the people, by the people, for the people, shall not perish from the earth.

After Vicksburg, Grant was promoted to major general, but he remained the same person to all who knew and served under him. The characteristic that distinguished Grant most as a leader was the clarity of his strategy and his fearlessness. "The art of war is simple enough," Grant told his officers. "Find out where your enemy is. Get at him as soon as you can. Strike at him as hard as you can and keep moving on."

This unexpected hero had an inner steel that wasn't immediately apparent from his quiet demeanor. His men knew he could also be ruthless when the situation warranted. "He is a butcher and is not fit to be at the head of an army," Mary Todd Lincoln complained to her husband. The president merely responded, "But he has been very successful in the field."

"The General never talked war matters with me at all," Julia later told an interviewer. "He wrote very little about the war, even after the taking of Vicksburg. I don't remember that he wrote me any letter of exultation of joy. He was so sorry for the poor fellows who were opposed to him that he never could exult over any victory. He always felt relieved, of course, and glad that it seemed to promise to shorten the war, but he never exulted over them."

After Vicksburg, Grant established headquarters in Nashville and summoned Julia to join him there. Throughout the war, Grant urged Julia to join him whenever she could, and she logged thousands of miles of treacherous travel in the course of the war—often with children in tow. Grant's aide-de-camp, Horace Porter, recalled his boss's high-spirited engagement with the children: "The children often romped with him and he joined in their frolics as if they were all playmates together. The younger ones would hang around his neck while he was writing, make a terrible mess of the papers, and turn everything in his tent into a toy."

Jesse remembered those visits with great delight. "To the small boy it was 'father's army,'" he wrote, "and the soldiers made me very welcome, carving all sorts of toys and regaling me with molasses candy made over the camp fires."

When Julia arrived in Nashville, Grant was away at the front, so she busied herself accompanying the Southern ladies of Nashville to the hospitals, trying to comfort and aid the wounded soldiers. When Grant returned, she told him about her work and shared messages and petitions from the men. He was unhappy. "I hear of these all day long and I sent for you to come that I might have a rest from this sad part," he admonished her. "I do not want you to know about these things. I want you to tell me of the children and yourself. I want and need a little rest and sunshine." He told her that if she continued going to hospitals, he would send her home. Julia obeyed, but she always felt an affinity for the Southern women, knowing that in another circumstance she might have shared their plight. Also, Julia and the Dent family had friends among the Confederates, and her sympathies for them didn't expire because of their different loyalties—it didn't matter who her husband was.

On one occasion, an old friend of Julia's from St. Louis, whose husband had fought and died at Vicksburg on the Confederate side, asked for her help in getting a permit to join her husband's friends in Georgia. Julia asked her to call, and she gave her the permit, wrapped around a roll of Confederate money captured at Vicksburg, worth about $4,000. She enclosed a note: "Dear Mary, I hope the enclosure may be of use to you. They were given me simply as souvenirs." Afterward, Julia worried that her action had abetted the enemy, and she confessed what she had done to Grant. He "only smiled at my fears and said I had done a service to the Union in doing just as I had; that the more of that kind of money there was in circulation, the better it would be for us."

In September, Grant traveled to New Orleans to confer with General Nathaniel Banks about the next western campaign. While there, he was lavishly feted by Banks in a long celebration and given an unbroken horse to ride back to his hotel at the end. As they raced along, the horse lost its footing and slipped, throwing Grant heavily on the ground, where he lay unconscious. His companions feared that he'd been killed. As he wrote of the incident, "I was rendered insensible, and when I regained consciousness I found myself in a hotel near by with several doctors attending me. My leg was swollen from the knee to the thigh, and the swelling almost to the point of bursting, extended along the body up to the arm-pit. The pain was almost beyond endurance." He spent a week in bed before being taken by steamer to Vicksburg, where, despite being barely able to move, he conducted his war planning, with Sherman's help.

As might be expected, Grant's accident raised concerns about his drinking. Banks himself wrote to his wife that Grant had been drunk, although other witnesses did not support his story. Grant biographer McFeely challenged the repeated claims of Grant's drunkenness, citing little actual evidence and noting, "All the rivers of alcohol—imagined or real—flow down from the Fort Humboldt days." It's like he learned from Sherman: Once they call you drunk or crazy, it's hard to shake it off.

While Grant had still been in New Orleans, he'd received a telegram from Halleck, asking him to send all available forces to the aid of General William Rosecrans, who had suffered a defeat near Chattanooga, Tennessee. Chattanooga was a critical intersection and a rail hub—the last stage of the Tennessee strategy. Confederate troops, under the leadership of General Braxton Bragg, had used it as a stronghold but had been driven out of the city by Rosecrans's forces. That was when things turned upside down for Rosecrans. At Chickamauga Creek, twelve miles southwest of Chattanooga, Bragg, fortified by reinforcements led by Grant's old friend General James Longstreet, forced Rosecrans's army into retreat. Only the brave stand of one of his men, Major General George Henry Thomas, allowed Rosecrans's army to safely make it back to Chattanooga. Meanwhile, Bragg's forces held a dominant position, taking over Missionary Ridge, a high abutment overlooking Chattanooga, as well as Lookout Mountain to the west, a position that Rosecrans had abandoned.

In mid-October, Grant and his staff left Vicksburg and headed by rail to Louisville, where he would receive an update on the situation in Chattanooga. To his surprise, he came across Secretary of War Stanton at the station. It was the first time the two men had met. Stanton had Grant's orders for Chattanooga. He would be in command of the Military Division of the Mississippi, with Sherman replacing him as commander of the Army of the Tennessee.

Grant's first act on reaching Chattanooga was to replace Rosecrans with Major General Thomas, the brave soldier who had distinguished himself at Chickamauga Creek. Rosecrans's failures were by then epic. As Dana, who had been on hand to see him in action before the Battle of Chickamauga, wrote scathingly, "General Rosecrans seemed to be insensible to the impending danger; he dawdled with trifles in a manner which scarcely can be imagined. With plenty of zealous and energetic officers ready to do whatever needed to be done, precious time was lost because our dazed and mazy commander could not perceive the catastrophe that was close upon us, nor fix his mind upon the means of preventing it."

Now that Rosecrans had failed in the first battle, only adding to the favorable position of the enemy, things grew increasingly dire. Grant found the troops bedraggled, hungry, and poorly fortified for the fight ahead, although quite willing and eager to follow Grant's lead. He was dismayed to see that they were living on half rations of dried bread and beef from starved animals that was so poor it was barely edible. At the time of Grant's arrival, Rosecrans's forces had come to believe that they faced either starvation or capture. Grant realized that before he did anything else, he had to get them food. He immediately opened a line of transport to Bridgeport to bring in food and supplies. Within a week the men were on full rations. "It is hard for any one not an eye-witness to realize the relief this brought," Grant wrote. "Neither officers nor men looked upon themselves any longer as doomed." The same could not be said for Confederate General Bragg's troops, who were now cut off from supplies.

On November 24, Grant's attack on Lookout Mountain began, led by General Joseph Hooker. Hooker's men—twelve thousand in number—barreled up the side of the fog-shrouded mountain. The fog provided some cover for their advance, and they ascended easily. By the time they reached the twelve hundred men stationed at the top, it was too late for the defenders to offer much resistance. They were outmanned and outmaneuvered. By afternoon, they had abandoned their post on the mountain.

The next day Sherman's army was joined by Hooker's troops for an assault on the valley and above it Missionary Ridge. Having sent Longstreet and his forces to Knoxville (a critical tactical error), Bragg was in a weakened position. By contrast, the exuberance of Grant's army was a remarkable sight. Amid the whooping, cheering, and pounding at the enemy of the Union troops, a reporter described the scene: "With bands playing, flags flying, soldiers cheering and yelling, our men three lines deep in perfect alignment, poured out through the young cottonwood timber, swept the rebel skirmishers out of the underbrush into the open cotton field, and pursued them on the run under a severe musketry fire." Then they raced to the mountain and began scurrying up the ridge before the order was even given. Thomas was worried that they would be shot down in so reckless an approach, but Grant stopped him from intervening. "The boys seem pretty good. Let them alone awhile."

Soon word came back that they had taken the lower trenches, and the order came: "Take the ridge!" Within hours, the top of the ridge was a sea of blue. Bragg's army had been driven off and was on the run. It was a sublime victory, especially satisfying given Rosecrans's earlier defeat.

Lincoln was elated by the victory at Chattanooga. In its honor, he announced a national thanksgiving celebration for November 26 and declared that the holiday of Thanksgiving would continue to be celebrated every year on the fourth Thursday in November.

The acclaim grew for Grant, and it was not uncommon for people to ask whether he'd consider running for president in 1864. Grant found the idea laughable, and he had a stock reply: "I never aspired but to one office in my life. I should like to be mayor of Galena—to build a new sidewalk from my house to the depot."

Through it all, despite the acclaim, Grant was humble, lacking any of the imperious remove that leaders often adopt. His aide Porter's recollection of meeting Grant for the first time perfectly captured the experience of countless others: "In an arm-chair facing the fireplace was seated a general officer, slight in figure and of medium stature, whose face bore an expression of weariness. He was carelessly dressed, and his uniform coat was unbuttoned and thrown back from his chest. He held a lighted cigar in his mouth, and sat in a stooping posture, with his head bent slightly forward. His clothes were wet, and his trousers and top-boots were spattered with mud." He was a common man's hero.

Victories were welcome, but Lincoln was deeply troubled by the larger course of the war. Three years in, despite some important successes, it was no closer to being won. There were many brave men and strong leaders, but no grand central strategy. The president had often controlled military strategy himself, including giving orders to generals in the field. It was not a sustainable arrangement. He needed a military leader worthy of the cause. "The first three years of the war might almost be termed the period of search for a general," Franklin Spencer Edmonds wrote in 1915. That was the question that kept Lincoln awake at night: Who would that man be?

CHAPTER 5

LINCOLN'S GENERAL

When it came time to decide on a military leader, Lincoln realized he had always known that the man he needed was Ulysses Grant. But when he began to share his thinking with confidants, he was warned about Grant's drinking. According to one version of the story, he didn't care. "Do you know what brand of whiskey Grant drinks?" he was said to have asked. "I would like to get barrels of it and send it to my other generals." This story has been frequently disputed, including by the president himself, who nevertheless acknowledged, "That would have been very good if I had said it." For years, he'd been listening to the piles of criticism heaped upon Grant by men who couldn't find their way in or out of a battlefield. He was tired of the rumors because the facts were so compelling. And he loved Grant's spirit. Grant, he told his secretary, was "the quietest little fellow you ever saw. The only evidence that he is in any place is that he *makes things go*—wherever he is, they *move*."

That's not to say that Lincoln's motivations were entirely pure. It was an election year, and he had political considerations in mind as well. He knew he was in danger of losing reelection if he didn't appear to have the war in hand. And he wondered if he had reason to fear a challenge from his popular general. At one point, he privately asked the lawyer J. Russel Jones, an Illinois friend, who was also close to Grant, to come to Washington. Once he was there, Lincoln got straight to the point: "I have sent for you, Mr. Jones, to know if this man Grant wants to be President."

Jones didn't hesitate. "No, Mr. President."

"Are you sure?"

"Yes," Jones replied. "Perfectly sure. I have seen General Grant frequently and talked fully and freely with him about that and every other question, and I know he has no political aspirations whatever, and certainly none for the Presidency."

"Ah, Mr. Jones," Lincoln said with relief, "you have lifted a great weight off my mind, and done me an immense amount of good, for I tell you, my friend, no man knows how deeply that presidential grub gnaws till he has had it himself."

Relieved of any political concerns about Grant, Lincoln asked Congress to approve the general for a rank not held by any other man—that of lieutenant general. On March 2, the Senate confirmed Grant for the rank. By then, it was no longer a secret. The news was out that Grant would be in command.

Lincoln summoned Grant to Washington for his appointment, and he arrived on March 7, accompanied by Rawlins and Fred, who was now fourteen. While Rawlins reported in at the War Department, Grant and Fred walked over to the Willard Hotel to check in. The Willard Hotel was an elegant place, favored by a high-ranking and prosperous clientele. The clerk looked at Grant skeptically. He appeared down on his luck, shrunken by weight loss, and shabby in an old uniform. Not knowing who he was, the clerk said that all rooms were booked except for a tiny space on the top floor. Indifferent to prestige and comfort, Grant said that was fine, and he signed the register.

The clerk glanced down and read, "U. S. Grant and son, Galena, Illinois." Then his head jerked back up and his eyes widened. He stumbled away from the desk, calling for a manager. Within moments, Grant and Fred were ushered into the bridal suite, one of the most lavish accommodations. They dropped their bags and headed for the Willard's large dining room, which was packed. When someone recognized Grant, the word spread, and suddenly the large roomful of diners rose to its feet as one, cheering and waving napkins. "Really, it was very embarrassing," Grant told Julia. "I heartily wished myself back in camp."

Later, he went to the White House to meet Lincoln, only to find him hosting a reception in the Blue Room. Grant still looked scruffy in his worn uniform. His shoulders were characteristically stooped, but his face calm. When Grant entered, his eyes went to the tall frame of Lincoln, and Lincoln's eyes went to the short frame of his general. They were meeting physically for the first time, but they might have recognized something in each other. Lincoln was an uncommon commoner, just like Grant. He shared the quality of extreme reserve when it came to personal matters, rarely sharing true emotions or feelings of self-doubt. A close friend of Lincoln's might have been describing Grant when he said, "Mr. Lincoln never had a confidant, and therefore never unbosomed himself to others. He never spoke of his trials to me, or, so far as I know, to any of his friends." These two interior men, protective of their inner lives yet calmly certain of their purpose, now met.

"I'm glad to see you, General," Lincoln said, holding out a welcoming hand. Grant shook it before greeting Mrs. Lincoln, who was eager to introduce him around the room. Everyone wanted to meet the star general.

A torch was being passed, and it was now Grant's war. The downtrodden leather store clerk with a savant-like gift for military strategy and a devastating fearlessness was to be in command of the Union Army. Of his partner, the president, he had kind thoughts. The qualities he admired most in Lincoln were those he sought to emulate: "What marked him [Lincoln] especially was his sincerity, his kindness, his clear insight into affairs. . . . It was that gentle firmness in carrying out his own will, without apparent force or friction, that formed the basis of his character."

In a quiet moment, Lincoln took Grant aside to describe the ceremony planned for the following day when he would be named lieutenant general. Lincoln mentioned that he knew Grant was inexperienced in public speaking, so he shared some thoughts on what he might say when it was time for his remarks. Grant expressed appreciation, although notably he didn't use any of Lincoln's suggestions. It was late in the evening before Grant made his escape and returned to the Willard.

The next day, with Fred at his side, Grant received his promotion and the order of the president in a White House ceremony. Lincoln read:

General Grant, the nation's appreciation of what you have done and its reliance upon you for what remains to be done in the existing great struggle, are now presented with this commission, constituting you Lieutenant General in the Army of the United States. With this high honor devolves upon you also a corresponding responsibility. As the country herein trusts you, so, under God, it will sustain you. I scarcely need to add, that with what I here speak for the nation goes my own hearty personal concurrence.

Grant responded humbly, reading a statement he'd prepared the previous night in his hotel room. He concluded, "I feel the full weight of the responsibilities now devolving on me; and I know that if they are met, it will be due to those armies; and, above all, to the favor of that Providence which leads both nations and men."

Later, Lincoln and Grant met privately. Lincoln explained, somewhat defensively, that he was not a military man and had little understanding of how to conduct a campaign. The only reason he'd been involved up until then was that there had been so much procrastination from the generals and so much pressure from the people. All he'd ever wanted, he assured Grant, was a commander who would take responsibility and *act*—and to that man he would give his full support.

Grant promised to do the best he could and said he'd avoid as much as possible annoying Lincoln and the War Department.

As to where Grant would have his headquarters, Sherman had passionately weighed in on that in a letter to Grant: "For God's sake and for your country's sake, come out of Washington. I foretold to General Halleck before he left Corinth the inevitable result to him, and now I exhort you to come out West. Here is the seat of the coming empire, and from the West, when our task is done, we will make short work of Charleston and Richmond and the impoverished coast of the Atlantic." His point was gladly taken by Grant, who had no intention of bunking in the capital, the place of bureaucratic quicksand.

However, now that he was in a position to fully evaluate the army's needs, Grant saw the necessity of headquartering with the Army of the Potomac in Virginia, which was under Meade's command. It wasn't the same as being in Washington, he hastened to tell Sherman.

Grant paid a visit to Meade the day after the ceremony, taking the train for the sixty-mile trip to Brandy Station, Virginia, where he was encamped. The Army of the Potomac had a history of struggles, evidenced by how frequently Lincoln had changed its command. After the demoralizing defeat at Bull Run near Manassas Junction, Virginia, at the beginning of the war, Lincoln had assigned General George McClellan as commander. McClellan seemed up to the task, driving his army south of the Confederate capital at Richmond, in preparation for taking on General Lee. But McClellan could never quite bring himself to *charge*. The more aggressive Lee became, the more McClellan retreated. Inexplicably, he blamed Lincoln for his clear failings as a leader, writing, "They (the President and others) determined to ruin me in any event and by any means." This accusation seemed absurd, given how desperately Lincoln wanted McClellan to succeed.

In a fateful battle, after Lee had launched an invasion into the Union state of Maryland, McClellan's response was so lackluster that Lincoln finally had to replace him, on November 7, 1862, with General Ambrose Burnside. Burnside went down to defeat at the Battle of Fredericksburg and was replaced on January 26, 1863, by General Joseph Hooker. Hooker was a good soldier, but he too suffered a major defeat at Chancellorsville and was replaced by Meade shortly before the Battle of Gettysburg.

Meade, a West Point man a few years older than Grant, had also fought in the Mexican war, but Grant did not really know him. What he *did* know was that their command relationship would be very delicate and potentially contentious. Civil War historian Shelby Foote notes that Meade had leadership problems, such as his "hair trigger temper," but his real problem was that "he lacked the quality which Grant not only personified himself but also prized highest in a subordinate: the killer instinct."

In particular, Meade had drawn down after his victory at Gettysburg the previous year, instead of pressing his advantage against Robert E. Lee's army. Many officers believed that he had missed the opportunity to decisively defeat Lee. Now Grant told him, "Lee's army will be my objective point. Wherever Lee goes, there you will go also." He was careful not to step directly on Meade's toes, but it was certainly clear that with the lieutenant general in the camp, only one man would really be in charge.

Grant returned briefly to Washington, but his mind was elsewhere. On March 11, as he was preparing for a journey west to consult with Sherman, Lincoln informed him that Mrs. Lincoln had organized a military dinner at the White House in his honor that evening. Twelve other generals would be in attendance.

Grant replied that he hoped Mrs. Lincoln would excuse him, as he was needed back in Nashville.

"I don't see how we can excuse you," Lincoln said. "It would be *Hamlet* with the Prince left out."

"I appreciate the honor Mrs. Lincoln would do me," Grant said sincerely, "but time is very important now—and really, Mr. Lincoln, I have had enough of the *show* business."

The next day he set off for Nashville to close his headquarters and strategize with Sherman about how they would execute the finale of the war. They met for two days, Sherman peppering the conversation with ideas presented in his rapid-gunfire style; Grant was calmer—steady and analytical. Cigar smoke hung heavy in the air between them. Any observer would have seen how these two men came to be such effective partners. Grant and Sherman complemented each other perfectly. They devised what amounted to a two-pronged strategy. Grant would pursue General Lee in the Potomac, and Sherman would pursue General Joe Johnston, who had replaced Bragg after Chattanooga as the head of the Army of Tennessee, now headquartered at Atlanta. They parted, each with his marching orders.

Lee the aristocrat and Grant the plebe represented different sides of the same coin of American life. Their roots were unalike, but as leaders they had many qualities in common. Both were un-flappable, relentless, unsentimental, and clever. Many thought the older, more experienced Lee had the edge. Grant's own men heard this from their Eastern counterparts—"Well, Grant has never met Bobby Lee yet." Grant shrugged off the rumors of Lee's might, believing that they had been grossly exaggerated by the entire Southern press and some of the Northern press as well. The media's attention to the Southern general, Grant felt, "was calculated to give him the entire confidence of his troops and to make him feared by his antagonists."

Grant was well aware of the hero worship the South heaped on Lee. The men under his command believed him invincible. "The natural disposition of most people is to clothe a commander of a large army whom they do not know, with almost superhuman abilities," Grant wrote in his *Memoirs*. "A large part of the National army, for instance, and most of the press of the country, clothed General Lee with just such qualities, but I had known him personally, and knew that he was mortal; and it was just as well that I felt this."

For his first move on Lee, Grant chose a daring approach—getting to Lee through the Wilderness, a twenty-mile stretch of brush and bramble, interspersed with marshland and lacking any real roads. But he didn't anticipate Lee's clever ruse. Instead of waiting until Grant's army emerged from the forest, Lee attacked him there in the thicket, where sight lines were poor and mobility was halting. Shallow graves, upended by heavy rains, left an eerie trail of skulls to greet the armies. A fierce day of fighting produced a great number of casualties on both sides. By nightfall, the underbrush was a sea of dead and dying men, the rivers of blood from both sides mingling. The howling of the wounded was an eerie chorus in the thicket.

An officer (by some accounts Meade) approached Grant, deeply worried that Lee was plotting some spectacular feint that would do them in.

"Oh, I am heartily tired of hearing about what Lee is going to do," an exasperated Grant replied. "Some of you always seem to think he is suddenly going to turn a double somersault and land in our rear and on both of our flanks at the same time. Go back to your command and try to think what we are going to do ourselves, instead of what Lee is going to do."

Grant did have information that Longstreet was expected to arrive the next day with reinforcements of twelve thousand men. He decided that they'd better get up and at them before then. He ordered the fight to commence at 5:00 A.M.

It was a fierce battle the following day, and Grant's army had driven the Confederates into retreat by the time Longstreet arrived. Fortified, they decided to reengage, but Longstreet was wounded in the neck by friendly fire and would not be fit for battle for many weeks. At the end of the day, Grant claimed a victory, but the losses were heavy.

Grant called it "as desperate fighting as the world has ever witnessed . . . the armies now confronting each other had already been in deadly conflict for a period of three years, with immense losses in killed, by death from sickness, captured and wounded; and neither had made any real progress accomplishing the final end." It was a nightmare experience, trying to slog through the tangled brush, stumbling over bodies, as the sun poked through the trees with a cruel spotlight.

In the coming days, heavy casualties piled up on both sides, and Grant recognized that it was something of a standoff. He believed that the only way to break it was to fight more aggressively than ever, to be bolder and more brutal in achieving the ultimate result. Mrs. Lincoln's hand-wringing aside, the only way to save the Union and save countless other lives was to strike hard. And it worked. Lee's army was pushed back toward Richmond, having gained no ground.

Henry Wing, a reporter with the *New York Tribune* who was with Grant during the battles, announced that he was returning to Washington. Grant pulled him aside to give him a private message for the president. When he arrived in the capital, Wing was welcomed to the White House, and after a lively discussion on the state of the war in the field, he said, "Mr. President, I have a personal word for you." Everyone left the room until they were alone.

Lincoln moved in close and stooped down until his face was level with Wing's and whispered, "What is it?"

Moved by Lincoln's intensity, Wing struggled not to stammer. "General Grant told me to tell you, from him, that, whatever happens, there is to be no turning back."

Then, as Wing described it, "the vision that opened through these wonderful eyes from a great soul glowing with a newly kindled hope is the likeness of Mr. Lincoln that I still hold in my memory, and ever shall. . . . Mr. Lincoln put his great, strong arms about me and, carried away in the exuberance of his gladness, imprinted a kiss upon my forehead."

Lincoln, who was used to running things on his own, with the advice of those whose guidance he didn't always trust, felt relieved to have a confident general commanding the troops. He was very sensitive about not appearing to meddle in the business of generals, so while Grant always welcomed his company, Lincoln hesitated to overstep. When Secretary of War Stanton protested one of Grant's decisions, Lincoln told him, "Now, Mr. Secretary, you know we have been trying to manage this army for nearly three years, and you know we haven't done much with it. We sent over the mountains and brought Mr. Grant, as Mrs. Grant calls him, to manage it for us, and now, I guess, we had better let Mr. Grant have his own way."

However, Grant was respectful of the president and did his best to keep him in the loop. After the Wilderness campaign, he fully outlined his forward strategy. In essence, he would continue to focus on Lee, holding him to a narrow territory around Richmond, where he could ultimately be defeated. Sherman would take on the Confederacy's remaining western strongholds.

"Oh, yes! I see that," Lincoln replied. "As we say out West, if a man can't skin he must hold a leg while somebody else does."

Grant believed that the path to victory ran through Petersburg, which was a major rail hub twenty-four miles south of Richmond. Working around Lee's Army of Northern Virginia, Grant brought his forces south to the James River. There the engineers constructed a pontoon bridge more than two thousand feet long to enable them to cross the river and come up to Petersburg. Swaying under the heavy weight of thousands of boots, the bridge fulfilled its purpose.

Grant's army numbered almost one hundred thousand men to Lee's sixty-five thousand, but Lee had the advantage of being in place. He held Grant off during the first battle on May 15 and continued to do so in repeated encounters that ended in standoffs. By July, the two sides were still in opposition. Grant noted that Lee was on the defensive, but "in a country in which every stream, every road, every obstacle to the movement of troops and every natural defence [sic] was familiar to him and his army. The citizens were all friendly to him and his cause, and could and did furnish him with accurate reports of our every move."

By that point, Grant had reached the conclusion that holding Lee's army stuck in place had its own advantages. So he settled in for trench warfare, a nine-month stationary battle of endurance and attrition. He established his headquarters at City Point, a small town at the intersection of the James and Appomattox Rivers. From there, he aimed to exhaust, starve, and deplete the enemy.

"That camp life at City Point can never be forgotten by those who shared it," his aide Adam Badeau recalled, "living in summer in a group of tents, in winter in rude huts, of which the commander-in-chief's was larger but in no other respect better than that of the humblest captain on the staff." According to Badeau, Grant would join his aides at the table and then sit with the men around the campfire, where he would engage in the conversation, smoking a cigar and whittling a piece of wood.

Grant ate very little during the long sieges and normally drank only water or coffee with his simple meals of hard bread and perhaps a slice of cucumber or fruit. But he was rarely seen without a cigar, and observers noted that he smoked most in times of greatest stress. According to his aide Porter, he smoked twenty-four strong cigars on the second day of the battle of the Wilderness. His son Fred recounted how the habit grew after the battle at Fort Donelson, when he was seen carrying a cigar stump, long since unlit, during battle. The news spread that he'd been smoking a cigar during the fight, and suddenly cigars began to arrive at camp from all over the nation; at one point he had eleven thousand cigars.

He was everywhere in the sight of his men during those months. If they saw him astride his horse, it was a signal that movement was coming. When they were in battle, Grant always appeared in the distance or close up, checking out the strategy and terrain and directing his commanders.

"General Grant's courage was supreme," an officer on his staff later told a reporter, requesting anonymity:

At one time I saw the general escape death by a very slight margin. We were breaking camp at Spottsylvania Court House, and under the fire of a Confederate battery. All of the headquarters equippage had been removed except a camp stool, and on this the general was sitting, while the shells of the enemy's guns shrieked over our heads. A shell passed just over the general, not missing him, apparently, more than a few inches, and struck the ground about thirty feet away. Without showing the slightest nervousness, he called to me, "Get the shell," saying: "Let's see what kind of ammunition the battery is using." I went and picked up the shell, which was a six-pound spherical case, and the general examined it as coolly as if there was not an enemy's gun within a hundred miles of him.

Those who grew frustrated as the months passed could not see Grant's strategy for an end game, which only became clear in retrospect. Lee's entrenched army was functionally in its final throes, but Lee didn't seem to recognize it. In staking out his narrow territory while the rest of the war was being lost, Lee tunneled his vision with devastating consequences. Sherman later reflected that Lee "never rose to the grand problem which involved a continent and future generations. His Virginia was to him the world. He stood like a stone wall to defend Virginia, stood at the front porch battling with the flames whilst the kitchen and house were burning."

It's hardly surprising that many people were wondering whether a presidential election could legitimately happen in 1864. How would a nation at war with itself organize a fair vote? But Lincoln was adamant that the election should not be postponed. "We cannot have free government without elections," he said. "If the rebellion could force us to forgo or postpone a national election it might fairly claim to have already conquered or ruined us."

At the same time, Lincoln had every reason to believe that he might lose the election. Although Grant's appointment had raised Northern spirits, the war seemed to be trapped in a circular battle that was never completed. The cost in lives and money was unsustainable. And, Lincoln knew, it was all happening on his watch. The situation was so dire that Lincoln was contemplating a second draft call of five hundred thousand men, even though the first draft had been unpopular. This time Congress had closed the loophole that allowed people to pay their way out of service for a $300 fee.

Once again, Lincoln grew paranoid about Grant's popularity. Disturbed by rumors that a nonpartisan group was plotting to run Grant in the election, he sent an envoy to surreptitiously feel Grant out about his presidential aspirations. When Grant heard that people were promoting his candidacy, he erupted. "They can't do it! They can't compel me to do it!" he shouted.

Lincoln was relieved to hear of Grant's disinterest in politics. But he still had sleepless nights fearing he would be defeated. On those nights the cloud of failure fell over him. Not only the failure of his army to defeat the rebels and restore the nation, but the failure of the country as a whole to embrace what Lincoln viewed as the great moral imperative of the time—the fulfillment of the constitutional promise that "all men are created equal."

John Hay, Lincoln's personal secretary, wrote in his diary, "I do not know whether the nation is worthy of him for another term. I know the people want him. There is no mistaking the fact. But politicians are strong yet, and he is not their 'kind of cat.'"

Many Republicans were worried that, with emancipation made a condition for peace, the war would drag on and end with the South in ruins. All along Lincoln had insisted that two conditions were necessary for a peace agreement: the sovereignty of the Union and the freedom of slaves. However, many Republicans thought that getting Jefferson Davis to agree to abide by the Constitution was enough. They argued that matters like slavery could be hammered out later. Lincoln refused to consider it.

Separating the constitutional restoration from abolition was the position widely held by many Democrats who had adopted the slogan "The Constitution as it is and the Union as it was"—to which Lincoln scornfully responded, "The Union as it was, barring the already broken eggs."

But the Democrats had bigger problems: they were hopelessly divided between the War Democrats, who were pro-Union, and the Peace Democrats, who wanted peace at any price, even if the price was to let the South go. Republicans called the Peace Democrats "Copperheads," comparing them to deadly poisonous snakes.

Republicans and War Democrats decided to unite in a rare—but they felt necessary—coalition to prevent the Copperheads from taking the presidency. They formed the National Union Party, with Lincoln as their candidate.

Once the party shift had happened, Lincoln knew he had to have a vice presidential running mate who reflected the coalition. He replaced his Yankee vice president, Hannibal Hamlin, with a Southern Democrat named Andrew Johnson. As the US senator from Tennessee, Johnson had refused to support secession, making him a hero to some and the devil to others. He'd made it clear that as a slaveholder he wasn't opposed to slavery, but he was against breaking up the Union. When Tennessee was restored to federal control in 1862, Lincoln appointed him military governor of the state. Although Johnson was initially against the Emancipation Proclamation, he had come around to it by the time Lincoln began considering him for vice president.

The Peace Democrats nominated a familiar face—former general George McClellan, whose failures were legendary, as was his contempt for Lincoln. The nomination wasn't without controversy. After all, McClellan had been general-in-chief of the Union Army early in the war. But he no longer felt any loyalty to

Lincoln or his cause. In spite of the heated rhetoric of a noisy convention, McClellan won the nomination easily, and after he was confirmed, the band played "Hail to the Chief."

There was one startling difference in this election, never repeated. It was effectively nonpartisan. There was only one issue: the future of the Union. Established less than one hundred years earlier, the relatively new United States was still fragile when compared to the old monarchies and regimes across the ocean.

Yet, as the cruel summer waned, Lincoln's reelection was becoming even less certain. John Hay was beside himself, writing to a colleague, "If the dumb cattle are not worthy of another term of Lincoln then let the will of God be done & the murrain [plague] of McClellan fall on them."

Deep in the heart of the Confederacy, General Sherman had set out from Chattanooga in May to confront General Joe Johnston at Atlanta. Johnston was settled in there, and to the surprise of many, including Sherman, he made no move to attack as Sherman's forces approached. Day after day, he kept delaying, as if to draw the battle out as long as he could. Was his hesitation due to Sherman's much larger army? It was unclear. Delay certainly could not put off the inevitable and only showed weakness. Disgusted by Johnston's inaction, Jefferson Davis pulled him from the field. (He would be restored to command in early 1865, as the war neared its conclusion.)

Johnston's replacement, General John Bell Hood, a notoriously fearless soldier, rode confidently into the battle, despite missing his right leg, courtesy of the Battle of Chickamauga, and having a crippled left arm, courtesy of Gettysburg.

Hood immediately proved himself with an aggressive attack on Sherman's forces on July 20. Sherman held the line but lost nearly two thousand men in the first encounter. Still southeast of the city, Hood launched a second attack two days later.

Sherman had sent a young major general named James McPherson to the east of the city to destroy the Georgia Railroad and cut off the supply chain. McPherson, who had been with Grant at Shiloh and then with Sherman, was dearly beloved by both men. They thought of him as a little brother, and Sherman often mentioned him in his letters to Grant. In battle, Sherman trusted McPherson implicitly. He was brave, smart, and reliable. But on July 23, as McPherson rode through the woods east of Atlanta, he came upon a group of Confederate soldiers. They fired on McPherson, killing him.

Sherman wept when he heard the news, and so did Grant. It was a terrible personal loss. Sherman was further gutted by the fact that months earlier McPherson had requested a short leave to marry his sweetheart but was denied the leave. Tearfully, Sherman told an aide, "I expected something to happen to Grant and me, either the Rebels or the newspapers would kill us both, and I looked to McPherson as the man to follow us and finish the war."

McPherson's eighty-seven-year-old grandmother wrote to Grant: "When it was announced at his funeral, from the public prints, that when General Grant heard of his death he went into his tent and wept like a child, my heart went out in thanks to you for the interest you manifested in him while he was with you." She humbly requested that Grant spare a few words for McPherson's grieving family and friends.

Grant complied, though he struggled to find the right thing to say. He wrote of his love for McPherson, but also paid tribute to the place he'd had in the hearts of his comrades: "It may be of some consolation to you, his aged grandmother, to know that every officer and every soldier who served under your grandson felt the highest reverence for his patriotism, his zeal, his great, almost unequaled ability, his amiability, and all the manly virtues that can adorn a commander. Your bereavement is great, but cannot exceed mine."

Although he did not live to see it, McPherson's mission to cut Atlanta off from the railroad to the east succeeded. However, as Atlanta was a major rail hub, there were still railroads in the west, and the city remained well fortified. Sherman set to work breaking up the railroads to the west, while bombarding the city with constant shelling. Three weeks in, on August 7, he sent a telegram to Halleck: "We keep hammering away all the time, and there is no peace, inside or outside of Atlanta. . . . One thing is certain, whether we get inside of Atlanta or not, it will be a used-up community when we are done with it."

During the coming month, Hood launched battle after battle, losing them all to Sherman's superior forces. Sherman never let up on the direct assault, while he was crippling the supply chain to the west. By September 1, with the loss of his last railroad and half his men, Hood knew he could not prevail. He abandoned Atlanta on September 2.

After the mayor of Atlanta officially handed the city to Sherman's army, Sherman made a proclamation that would shake its citizens to the core: "I have deemed it to the interest of the United States that the citizens now residing in Atlanta should remove, those who prefer to go South, and the rest North. . . . Atlanta is no place for families or noncombatants."

Sherman had decided that he would crush the city so that it could not in any way become a source of commerce or support for the rest of the war. After the citizens were driven from the city, cursing Sherman's name, he began destroying the military assets, eventually setting much of the city on fire. The people of Atlanta, who had suffered long years of deprivation and heartache, now found themselves cast from their homes and robbed of the last vestige of their dignity. Writing to Halleck, Sherman refused to apologize. "If the people raise a howl against my barbarity & cruelty, I will answer that War is War & not popularity seeking," he wrote. "If they want Peace, they & their relations must stop War."

Sherman's victory at Atlanta was met with great joy and relief in Washington. For a time, there was so much enthusiasm for Sherman as the hero du jour that there was even a campaign to elevate him to Grant's rank. The impression was strong that Sherman was more effective than Grant because, as Badeau pointed out, Grant "had accomplished nothing in front of Richmond," although he had been sitting there quietly for months. This was false. It did not account for Grant's constant oversight of hundreds of thousands of troops and constant troop movements within a thousand-mile arena. Nor did it factor in Grant's master strategy, which, while mysterious to the broader population, was clear to him.

Sherman was appalled at the talk of his elevation and wrote to assure Grant that he had no such designs on the top position. Grant, characteristically, was unbothered. "No one would be more pleased at your advancement than I," he wrote Sherman, "and if you should be placed in my position and I put subordinate, it would not change our relations in the least. I would make the same exertions to support you that you have done to support me, and I would do all in my power to make our cause win."

More than anyone else, Sherman recognized that special character of Grant's military leadership that no other commander, regardless of skill and dedication, could match. "I am a damned sight smarter man than Grant," Sherman once confessed to his chief of cavalry James Harrison Wilson. "I see things more quickly than he does. I know more about law, and history, and war, and nearly everything else than he does; but I'll tell you where he beats me and where he beats the world. He doesn't care a damn for what he can't see the enemy doing, and it scares me like hell." In other words, Grant studied the enemy's position and sought as much information as he could about its tactics and capabilities, and then he crafted his own plan. He didn't worry himself silly about whether he was right; he didn't change his mind on the fly; and he was always cool in action. His temperament made him the steadying influence on men of passion, warriors with personal agendas, and those whose discipline might slip in the heat of battle.

Lincoln was well aware that his presidency might have been saved by highly publicized and important victories like Sherman's. But that did not stop him from worrying. On election day, it was quiet at the White House and Lincoln was in a pensive mood. "It is a little singular," he told his secretary, "that I, who am not a vindictive man, should have always been before the people for election in canvasses marked for their bitterness."

Standing at the window with his young son Tad, Lincoln could see the line of soldiers quartered on the White House grounds preparing to cast their votes. When he saw Tad's pet turkey wandering among them, he asked teasingly, "What business has the turkey stalking about the polls in that way? Does he vote?"

"No," Tad replied. "He's not of age."

Lincoln laughed—not a common sight in those days.

That night he went to the telegraph office to receive news of the results. Early numbers from Philadelphia, Boston, and Baltimore were promising. It was a long wait for more precise numbers, but by midnight it seemed clear that Lincoln had won. By the time all the votes were counted—in a matter of days, not hours—Lincoln had secured 212 electoral votes to McClellan's 21. McClellan carried only Delaware, Kentucky, and New Jersey.

Long after midnight on election night, Lincoln returned to the

Executive Mansion, where supporters were waiting for him to make a statement. "I am thankful to God for this approval of the people," he said. "But while deeply grateful for this mark of their confidence in me, if I know my heart, my gratitude is free from any taint of personal triumph. I do not impugn the motives of anyone opposed to me. It is no pleasure to me to triumph over anyone; but I give thanks to the Almighty for this evidence of the people's resolution to stand by free government and the rights of humanity."

As soon as the election was over, the cities of the North began bustling with activity, gathering provisions to provide the soldiers of the Union Army with a full Thanksgiving dinner on the second year of the holiday's celebration. The largest effort was launched by the Union League, which raised enough money to provide 250,000 pounds of turkeys and other fowl (not including Tad Lincoln's pet, who had received a presidential pardon), plus all the trimmings. Other volunteer efforts from cities across the North made sure that the men at war had a lavish turkey dinner. This celebratory meal was in contrast to the starvation rations received by the Confederate soldiers. There would be no feast for them.

Gradually, in hunger and despair, the entrenched line of Lee's army was being drained in size as soldiers deserted—seventy-two thousand of them east of the Mississippi—easing back to their nearby homes and farmlands. In their hearts the war was over, and now their attention turned to the survival of their families.

In Georgia, Sherman's army was ensuring that it would be a harsh, cold Christmas for the civilian population, as well as for the Confederate Army. With Grant's approval, he planned to take sixty-two thousand of his men on a "March to the Sea"—some 250 miles from Atlanta to Savannah. His purpose was not so much the capture of Savannah as sowing fear and horror throughout the state. He aimed to send a message to Georgians as his troops pounded through their towns and across their farmlands, stealing food and livestock, harassing the citizens, and burning the homes and barns of anyone who resisted. His strategy was callous and cruel and also psychologically strategic, as if to say to Southerners: *This is what you face.*

"We cannot change the hearts of the people of the South," Sherman wrote to Grant, "but we can make war so terrible that they will realize the fact that however brave and gallant and devoted to their country, still they are mortal and should exhaust all peaceful remedies before they fly to war."

The March to the Sea lasted from November 15 to December 21 and culminated in the capture of Savannah. Sherman telegraphed Lincoln: "I beg to present you as a Christmas gift the City of Savanna with 150 heavy guns & plenty of ammunition & also about 25,000 bales of cotton."

Lincoln replied with thanks and praise, adding, "But what next? I suppose it will be safe if I leave it to you & General Grant to decide."

CHAPTER 6

SURRENDER

More than fifty thousand people gathered under overcast skies to witness Lincoln's second inauguration on March 4. Andrew Johnson took his oath first, and it immediately became apparent that he was very drunk. If Lincoln was chagrined as he watched his vice president slur his way through his oath and remarks, he might have been comforted by the thought that Johnson had served his electoral purpose and need not have much of a role going forward.

As Lincoln took the oath and began to deliver his inaugural address, the sun broke through—or so it was reported. (It's truly remarkable how often this magic has occurred in records of presidential inaugurations.) What is most remembered from that speech were his healing words of union:

> With malice toward none; with charity for all; with firmness in the right, as God gives us to see the right, let us strive on to finish the work we are in; to bind up the nation's wounds; to care for him who shall have borne the battle, and for his widow, and

his orphan—to do all which may achieve and cherish a just and lasting peace, among ourselves and with all nations.

After the inauguration, knowing this moment was upon them, Grant sent a message to Lincoln: "Can you not visit City Point for a day or two? I would very much like to see you, and I think the rest will do you good."

The enervated president brightened at the idea of getting away from the prison of the White House and breathing the honest air of the field. He responded quickly with an acceptance, mentioning that Mrs. Lincoln and Tad would be accompanying him as well. Sherman, who had continued his "march" through the Carolinas, was planning a visit at the same time.

Lincoln arrived and settled in on his steamship, the *River Queen*, which was docked at the City Point dock, while Grant awaited Sherman's arrival on a blockade runner that had been captured from the Confederates. Sherman jumped ashore, and the two men ran toward each other, crying, "How d'you do, Sherman?" "How are you, Grant!" They stood together, grasping hands and smiling. "Their encounter was more like that of two school-boys coming together after a vacation than the meeting of two actors in a great war tragedy," Porter observed.

They soon went aboard the president's vessel, where Grant assured Lincoln that the decisive moment of the war was now at hand. Lincoln asked if they might bring the war to an end without the massive suffering and bloodshed that was sure to occur. Grant would dearly have loved to comply, but he told Lincoln that he had no control over that. It was up to the enemy to choose whether to fight or to lay down its arms.

The following day there was an informal council aboard Lincoln's vessel. Only Lincoln, Grant, Sherman, and Rear Admiral David Dixon Porter, commander of the Navy, were present.

Lincoln had deliberately come without members of his cabinet or other advisers, wanting to hear the unfiltered truths from Grant, Sherman, and Porter. It was, noted the aide Horace Porter, "an informal interchange of views between the four men who, more than any others, held the destiny of the nation in their hands." A famous 1868 painting captured the scene. *The Peacemakers* by George P. A. Healy portrays the four men: Lincoln is at the center, chin resting on his hand, flanked by Grant and Porter, as Sherman gestures and speaks. A rainbow is visible through the window as they talk strategy.

Grant and Sherman had already worked out the endgame between them. Grant believed that Johnston and Lee would try to find a way to join forces to launch an overwhelming attack, and he aimed to prevent it. His entire attention was focused like a laser on Lee. If Lee fled Richmond to join up with Johnston, Virginia would be lost to the Confederacy, and that might be a fatal blow.

It also seemed unlikely that Johnston could move north to meet up with Lee. Sherman had Johnston pinned down in North Carolina, with eighty thousand Union troops ready to pounce. Lee was similarly trapped in Virginia. It was doubtful that either could shake off Union forces long enough to join up with the other, although Johnston was only 150 miles from Richmond.

Lincoln was deeply concerned that Johnston would get away. He was nervous about Sherman being at City Point rather than back in North Carolina making sure his prey was trapped.

"Mr. President," Sherman insisted, "there is no possible way of General Johnston's escaping; he is my property as he is now situated, and I can demand his unconditional surrender; he can't escape."

"What is to prevent him from escaping with his army by the Southern railroads?" Lincoln asked.

"Because there *are* no Southern railroads to speak of," Sherman replied brashly. "My bummers have broken up the roads in sections all behind us—and they did it well." (Sherman's "bummers" were those who destroyed the countryside and foraged for food and provisions from its residents on the March to the Sea.)

Despite his worries, Lincoln felt assured enough of victory to launch into a long discussion about the end of the war and what should become of the rebel forces. "Let them all surrender and reach their homes; they won't take up arms again," he said. "Let them all go, officers and all. I want submission and no more bloodshed." This declaration, which was not formally recorded, would later become a bone of contention when Sherman chose to do exactly as Lincoln proposed.

At the end of the day, Sherman took his leave and hurried off to return to his men. After Sherman had left, Lincoln and Grant talked alone. "I merely told him what I had done, not what I meant to do," Grant recalled. "I was then making the movement by the left which ended in the surrender of Lee. When I returned to Washington [after succeeding], Lincoln said, 'General, I half suspected that movement of yours would end the business, and wanted to ask you, but did not like to.' Of course I could not have told him, if he had asked me, because the one thing a general in command of an army does not know, is what the result of a battle is until it is fought."

Grant's hidden strategy was the final movement he planned against Lee. Prior to Lincoln's visit, Grant had met with Philip Sheridan, his brilliant but brutal general. He knew he could count on Sheridan to rain destruction down on Lee's army. He instructed the general to separate himself from the Army of the Potomac and organize a separate force of infantry and cavalry. Publicly, this move would be characterized as preparation for joining Sherman against Johnston. In reality, it would be a secret mission to destroy

Lee's southern flank. Grant instructed Sheridan to await his order, which would come directly after Lincoln's visit.

Grant prepared to bid farewell to the president, who would travel by train back to Washington. "As the train was about to depart, we all raised our hats respectfully," Horace Porter recounted. "The salute was returned by the President, and he said in a voice broken by emotion he could ill conceal: 'Good-by, gentlemen. God bless you all! Remember, your success is my success.' The signal was given to start; the train moved off; Grant's last campaign had begun."

Grant felt strengthened by Lincoln's visit and reassured by the president's temperament. "He was a great man, a very great man," he later said, reflecting back on the moment. "The more I saw of him, the more this impressed me. . . . What marked him especially was his sincerity, his kindness, his clear insight into affairs. Under all this he had a firm will, and a clear policy."

Lincoln's kindness was a compelling aspect of his character in a time of war, when most men's hearts were hardened. His bodyguard William H. Crook recalled observing the president view prisoners of war with great compassion. "He is the only man I ever knew the foundation of whose spirit was love," he wrote. "That love made him suffer. I saw him look at the ragged hungry prisoners at City Point. . . . I remember his face." Yet this man so suffused with love and compassion still waged war. "I never saw evidence of faltering," Crook added. "I do not believe anyone ever did. From the moment he, who was all pity, pledged himself to war, he kept straight on."

Five Forks was a small Virginia crossroads at Petersburg that would have a big role to play in the end of the war. On April 1, with barely more than ten thousand men behind him, Sheridan attacked General Pickett's right flank while the general was two miles away with other officers enjoying a shad bake. His weak army struggled to resist the assault.

Grant had sent his aide-de-camp to be his eyes and ears in the battle, and what Porter saw was a show of brute force and ferocity, with bodies being thrown everywhere in explosive motion. Sheridan was unstoppable. At one point, Porter saw one of Sheridan's men hit in the neck. As blood spurted out of what appeared to be a cut jugular, he fell to the ground crying, "I'm killed!" Sheridan called to him, "You're not hurt a bit! Pick up your gun, man, and move right on to the front." The soldier grabbed his gun, rose to his feet, and rushed forward a few steps before collapsing and dying. Such was the force of Sheridan's uncompromising command that he inspired dead men to rise and fight!

As Sheridan was decimating Pickett's men on the right, Major General Gouverneur K. Warren attacked on the left, and the flailing Army of Northern Virginia caved in on itself as a third assault was launched at the center. By day's end, Five Forks was in the hands of the Union, with thousands of prisoners captured. Porter rode as fast as he could to Grant's headquarters to deliver the news. Now nothing stood between them and Richmond.

After holding the line for over nine months, Lee's army was being forced back and away. The broken line would allow a stream of blue straight toward Richmond. The exhausted and depleted rebel forces, having been subjected to Grant's long, forced entrapment, fought bravely, but they were little match for the Union forces. Many of their officers had been killed or were too injured to fight. Sleep was beyond them—they were forced to stay in their saddles night and day, catching brief naps when they could. Most telling of their fate was the extreme disparity in strength. Grant's forces numbered 125,000, Lee's a mere 35,000.

On April 2, Lee recognized that Richmond was on the verge of being lost. A telegram from Lee was delivered to Jefferson Davis as he attended Sunday service at St. Paul's Church:

I THINK IT IS ABSOLUTELY NECESSARY THAT WE SHOULD ABANDON OUR POSITION TONIGHT. I HAVE GIVEN ALL THE NECESSARY ORDERS ON THE SUBJECT TO THE TROOPS, AND THE OPERATION, THOUGH DIFFICULT, I HOPE WILL BE PERFORMED SUCCESSFULLY. I HAVE DIRECTED GENERAL STEVENS [SIC] TO SEND AN OFFICER TO YOUR EXCELLENCY TO EXPLAIN THE ROUTES TO YOU BY WHICH THE TROOPS WILL BE MOVED TO AMELIA COURTHOUSE, AND FURNISH YOU WITH A GUIDE AND ANY ASSISTANCE THAT YOU MAY REQUIRE FOR YOURSELF.

By 11:00 that evening, Davis was at the train station, preparing to leave, while the city erupted in anarchy and panic in advance of the Union forces.

The next morning the Union troops arrived to stake their claim as the shell-shocked civilians beheld in horror their city and their dreams in ashes. That day Lincoln paid a visit to Petersburg, and his tour of Richmond on April 4 was a sober acknowledgment that the end was near.

But through it all, Lee failed to acknowledge defeat. On April 7, Grant decided it was time to communicate directly with Lee:

HEADQUARTERS ARMIES OF THE U.S., 5 P.M., APRIL 7, 1865.
GENERAL R.E. LEE COMMANDING C.S.A.

The result of the last week must convince you of the hopelessness of further resistance on the part of the Army of North Virginia in this struggle. I feel that it is so, and regard it as my

duty to shift from myself the responsibility of any further effu-
sion of blood, by asking of you the surrender of that portion of
the Confederate States army known as the Army of Northern
Virginia.

Longstreet was with Lee when he received the message. Lee
read it and passed it to him. Longstreet studied the message and
looked calmly at his commander. "Not yet," he said, and Lee
nodded. He responded that evening:

GENERAL: I have received your note of this day. Though not
entertaining the opinion you express on the hopelessness of
further resistance on the part of the Army of North Virginia, I
reciprocate your desire to avoid useless effusion of blood, and
therefore before considering your proposition, ask the terms
you will offer on condition of its surrender.

R.E. LEE, GENERAL

Grant did not consider Lee's response satisfactory, and the following day he wrote a straightforward response about what it
would take for Lee's surrender to be accepted:

Your note of last evening in reply to mine of same date, asking
the condition on which I will accept the surrender of the Army
of Northern Virginia is just received. In reply I would say
that, peace being my great desire, there is but one condition I
would insist upon, namely: that the men and officers surren-
dered shall be disqualified for taking up arms again against the
Government of the United States until properly exchanged. I
will meet you, or will designate officers to meet you, or will
designate officers to meet any officers you may name for the

*same purpose, at any point agreeable to you, for the purpose
of arranging definitely the terms upon which the surrender of
the Army of Northern Virginia will be received.*

Lee fired back:

*In mine of yesterday I did not intend to propose the surren-
der of the Army of Northern Virginia, but to ask the terms of
your proposition. To be frank, I do not think the emergency
has arisen to call for the surrender of this army, but as the
restoration of peace should be the sole object of all, I desired
to know whether your proposals would lead to that end. I cannot, therefore, meet you with a view to surrender the Army of
Northern Virginia.*

Lee then proposed that they meet at 10:00 the following morning
on the old stage road to Richmond, between the picket lines of
the two armies. When Grant received the message, he refused the
meeting, saying that it would do no good to meet unless it was for
surrender.

Longstreet was not privy to these further communications between the two leaders, but as he and his army set out that day, he
could see the collapse all around him—"The troops of our broken
columns were troubled and faint of heart," he wrote in his memoir. Along the way, many bedraggled soldiers drifted out of the
woods to join them, hoping for food. As they marched, Grant's
army pursued them.

Among the men of Lee's army, there were two schools of
thought on the subject of surrender. The first was that they had
no choice. They were starving and depleted in ranks, and they
were no match for the sheer numbers of the enemy. The other,
however, was that no opponent could equal in spirit and drive the

will of Confederate soldiers to fight to their last breath. An order to stand down would surely be met by great recrimination.

The next morning a desultory scene greeted Lee as he rode among the men, who were busy organizing their next attack. He summoned Longstreet to his side. Longstreet was struck by Lee's appearance: "He was dressed in a suit of new uniform, sword and sash, a handsomely embroidered belt, boots, and a pair of gold spurs." Lee's face bore a weight of profound depression as he described their circumstances: a formidable force lay ahead of them, impossible to break through, and Meade and his men were at the rear. What were their options?

It was the final moment of truth. Even Longstreet, Lee's most gallant and determined commander, who had vowed to never surrender, could not hold off the advance of Grant's endless army, which reached back as far as sight allowed and then some, replenishing itself constantly, so that even as soldiers fell it was never diminished. "I asked if the bloody sacrifice of his army could in any way help the cause in other quarters. He thought not. Then, I said, your situation speaks for itself."

"There is nothing left to do but to go and see General Grant, and I would rather die a thousand deaths," Lee replied. He mounted his horse and, leaving Longstreet in charge, set off to find Grant.

Grant woke the morning of April 9 with a bad headache. On the field, the two armies were already engaged, but suddenly there was a light flash along Lee's line—a white flag. Lee sent messengers to Meade and Sheridan to inform them of his desire to reach Grant for the purpose of surrender. Grant, who was on his way to Appomattox Court House, was out of immediate communication, but when the message reached him, he agreed to the meeting, which was hastily arranged at a private home. Grant, who had not anticipated such a high-level meeting when he'd left camp that morning, was dressed in the uniform of a private, which bore only the shoulder straps of his rank. His boots and portions of his clothing were spattered with mud, and a felt hat was pulled low on his forehead.

Porter, who was accompanying Grant and knew he'd felt ill earlier, asked him how he was feeling. Grant told him, "The pain in my head seemed to leave me the moment I got Lee's letter."

When they arrived, they found Sheridan and some of the troops milling around.

"How are you, Sheridan?" Grant asked.

"First-rate, thank you; how are you?" Sheridan replied, his voice full of joy.

Grant gestured up the road. "Is Lee over there?"

"Yes. He is in that brick house, waiting to surrender to you."

"Well then," Grant said placidly, "we'll go over."

As they rode up to the house, Grant saw Lee's large gray horse, Traveller, standing in the yard. Lee had purchased Traveller in early 1862, and the impressive steed had become his favorite, owing to his stamina and calm under pressure. Now he was waiting to carry his master out of the war.

As Grant entered the house, General Lee, immaculate in his formal dress, stood erect to greet him.

Confederate colonel Charles Marshall, who accompanied Lee, described the men: "Grant, restrained in victory . . . Lee dignified in defeat."

Grant greeted Lee cordially. The two men reminisced for a while about the Mexican war. Lee said he remembered Grant quite well, a pleasantry Grant seriously doubted, as he had been much younger and of a much lower rank than Lee. He, however, did in fact remember Lee from that period.

Their conversation was so friendly that it was tempting to

carry on in that vein. Finally, Lee began to discuss the subject at hand—the reason he had called for this meeting. What terms would Grant offer? Lee might have been steeling himself for a sword to his throat. Instead, Grant offered him his dignity. There would be no talk of the spoils of war. In victory, Grant was generous to the Confederate soldiers, telling Lee he would allow the Confederate officers to keep their sidearms, private horses, and baggage. Lee was genuinely moved. "This will have a very happy effect upon my army," he said.

However, Lee had an additional request. "There is one thing I should like to mention. The cavalrymen and artillerists own their own horses in our army. . . . I should like to understand whether these men will be permitted to retain their horses."

Grant frowned. That had not been part of the plan. It hadn't even occurred to him, since Union soldiers did not own their animals. But he quickly thought it over and responded, "I think we have fought the last battle of the war—I sincerely hope so—and that the surrender of this army will be followed soon by that of all the others. . . . I take it that most of the men in the ranks are small farmers, and as the country has been so raided by the two armies, it is doubtful whether they will be able to put in a crop to carry themselves and their families through the next winter without the aid of the horses they are now riding, and I will arrange it in this way."

Lee was relieved. "This will have the best possible effect upon the men. It will be very gratifying and will do much toward conciliating our people."

Grant summoned his aide, Ely Parker, who brought three sheets of blank paper, a pen, and an ink bottle, so that Grant could write the terms of surrender. Parker had been born on a Seneca reservation in western New York and had spent his life trying to maintain a balance between two worlds. He and Grant had become friends before the war when Grant was working at his father's leather goods store and Parker was an engineer for the US Treasury Department in Galena. Now Parker was one of Grant's most loyal aides. Grant worked over the terms, erasing and rewriting several times before the final document was handed to Lee. Lee put on his glasses and read the document, approving it verbally. Then Grant handed it to Parker to transcribe onto official paper, with a copy for Lee.

Grant signed the articles of surrender in front of Lee, and then Lee wrote a letter accepting the terms and gave it to Grant. The deed was done.

A story later made the rounds that Lee had surrendered his fine sword to Grant and Grant had then handed it back. The story seemed credible, as it reflected exactly how the two men might act given their temperaments. But Grant noted in his *Memoirs* that no such incident had occurred. Porter recalled Grant telling him that he had briefly considered asking Lee to surrender his sword, but that he'd felt it would be an unnecessary humiliation. Some years later, Grant told a reporter with a smile, "I did not want his sword. It would only have gone to the Patent Office to be worshiped by the Washington rebels."

Finally, Grant asked Lee if there was anything he could do for Lee's men. Lee said that his army was in a very bad condition because of lack of food—they'd been living for some days on only dried corn. Could Grant spare rations for his men?

"Certainly," Grant replied, and asked how many.

"About twenty-five thousand."

Grant said that Lee could send his quartermaster to Appomattox Station, where he could get provisions from the trains stopped there.

This moment of surrender would not fully end the war. There were still other armies on the march. In February, Davis had restored General Johnston to his command of the Army of Tennessee and other scattered forces, which were still active. But as a practical matter, the war was over.

As news of Lee's surrender reached the Union lines, the men began firing a hundred-gun salute. Grant sent word for them to cease so as not to denigrate their opponents. He said, "The rebels are our countrymen again." Even in those first moments he was thinking about unification. He did not savor a victory that had caused such massive death and destruction.

It had been borne out time and again how close the ordinary soldiers of the two armies were—brother had been fighting against brother, and cousin against cousin. The morning after Lee's surrender, Grant received a note that a captured rebel, claiming to be his West Virginia cousin, wanted to see him. Grant summoned him.

"Are you one of Aunt Rachel's sons?" Grant asked kindly. Rachel was his father's younger sister, who lived with her pro-Confederacy husband in West Virginia.

"Yes," he said. "Charley."

"What are you doing here?"

"I have been fighting in Lee's army."

"Bad business, Charley. What do you want to do now?"

"I want to go home."

Grant laughed. "Have you got a horse?"

"No, mine was killed under me, day before yesterday."

"Have you got any money?"

"No."

Grant arranged for Charley to receive a horse, $50, and a parole. It was a kindness. As soon as it could be arranged, all the prisoners of Lee's army would be paroled to return to their homes.

Before leaving for Washington, Grant wanted to see Lee once more. He set off for Lee's headquarters, with a bugler and an officer holding a white flag ahead of him. When Lee saw him coming, he mounted his horse and rode to greet him. They sat side by side for half an hour or so, quietly talking about the next phase in their journey. Lee remarked that the South was big; it might take some time and effort to end the fighting in every corner of the Confederacy. He was pleading for Grant's forbearance, hoping his army would not cause further bloodshed as they wrapped up the war. Grant felt that result was largely up to Lee and his forces, and he suggested that if Lee now openly called for the surrender of all the armies, they would surely oblige. Lee said that he had to consult President Davis first—it was his call.

Grant did not press further, but Lee's nod to Davis felt gratuitous. Davis was no longer "president" in any true sense of the word. He wasn't even attempting to lead. As they spoke, Davis was in hiding—although that day he would be found in Georgia and captured.

Not that Grant faulted Davis's leadership for the collapse of the Confederacy. As far as Grant was concerned, Davis was a good enough leader, one who could be credited with "gallantry and persistence." Grant would always believe that Davis and the Confederacy did not lose the war, but that it was lost from the outset because "there was no victory possible for any government resting upon the platform of the Southern Confederacy."

Before leaving the area, Grant shared a personal moment with Longstreet, lingering on a memory of their former friendship. "Pete," he said, using Longstreet's nickname, "let's have another game of brag to recall the old days." Longstreet agreed and gratefully accepted a cigar before Grant rode off. Longstreet was left with the melancholy question, "Why do men fight who were born to be brothers?"

On April 11, a weary Grant made his way back to the headquarters steamboat, where Julia was waiting for him. She had prepared the best meal she could for the celebratory occasion, but he did not arrive until early morning and missed dinner. Julia arranged a sumptuous breakfast for Grant and many of the officers at the headquarters. As they ate, conversation turned to conquest. Julia excitedly asked Grant if they could visit Richmond, the jewel in the crown of their victory.

"Hush, Julia," he said. "Do not say another word on this subject. I would not distress these people. They are feeling their defeat bitterly, and you would not add to it by witnessing their despair, could you?" Julia felt chastened by his words. He was correct, and she would say no more.

Grant did not linger to savor his victory. His mind had already turned to postwar matters, and he felt the urgency of his responsibility. For one thing, he had to organize his army for the job, which would include oversight of the seceded states, while substantially reducing the army's cost and numbers. Within months, he would have to reduce the army by two-thirds.

In Washington, he busied himself mustering out the Army and attending cabinet meetings. Before a meeting on April 15, the president asked him if he and Julia would accompany the Lincolns to the theater that evening. Grant sent word to Julia and was inclined to accept the honor. But Julia had other ideas. That day she had received a visit from Mrs. Stanton and learned that the Stantons had also been invited to the theater. Mrs. Stanton, whose relationship with Mary Todd Lincoln was poor, told Julia, "Unless you accept the invitation, I shall refuse. I will not sit in the box with Mrs. Lincoln."

Julia wasn't inclined to go either. Her dealings with Mrs. Lincoln had also been most unpleasant. Besides, she had already pleaded with Grant that morning to visit their children, who were in school in Burlington, New Jersey. She quickly sent a message to

Grant reminding him of this plan and asking him to give the president and Mrs. Lincoln their regrets. Conceding to Julia's wishes, Grant boarded a train with her at Union Station later that day. It would take them to Philadelphia and then on to Burlington.

In Washington, Lincoln confided to his bodyguard that he didn't really want to go to the theater. Earlier he had told him, "Crook, do you know, I believe there are men who want to take my life? And I have no doubt they will do it." Now Crook thought his reluctance to attend a public performance was related to his premonition that his life was in danger.

The Grants left Washington, and as they arrived at the Broad Street Station in Philadelphia, Grant was handed a telegram from the War Department. He read it and turned deathly white. It was the worst possible news.

THE PRESIDENT WAS ASSASSINATED AT FORDS [SIC] THEATRE AT 10:30 TONIGHT & CANNOT LIVE. THE WOUND IS A PISTOL SHOT THROUGH THE HEAD. SECRETARY SEWARD AND HIS SON FREDERICK WERE ALSO ASSASSINATED AT THEIR RESIDENCE & ARE IN A DANGEROUS CONDITION. THE SECRETARY OF WAR DESIRES THAT YOU RETURN TO WASHINGTON IMMEDIATELY.

"Is there anything the matter?" Julia asked. "You look startled."

"Yes, something very serious has happened," he replied quietly. "Do not exclaim. Be quiet and I will tell you. The President has been assassinated at the theater, and I must go back at once." He arranged to accompany Julia to Burlington, briefly see the children, and then return to Washington before dawn.

As they rode, Grant was overcome by melancholy for the opportunity lost. "The President was inclined to be kind and magnanimous," he told Julia, "and his death at this time is an irreparable loss to the South, which now needs so much both his tenderness and his magnanimity." Grant understood that it wasn't so much Lincoln's plan for Reconstruction or his philosophy of the South that made him a valuable guardian of the fragile nation, but his temperament: "His goodness of heart, his generosity, his yielding disposition, his desire to have everybody happy." Grant recalled a meeting he'd had with Lincoln, shortly before the end of the war, when the president's tone had shifted from fighting to healing. Even as his men remained on the battlefield, he was looking ahead, knowing that the end of the war would not automatically heal the nation. But now Lincoln was gone, and his steady stewardship had ended.

In the coming days Grant would be confronted by a chilling reality—that he too had been targeted for assassination and had escaped by mere chance. He and Julia recalled an aggressive horseman who had pursued the Grants to the train station that night. As Julia later described it, the "man rode past us at a sweeping gallop on a dark horse—black, I think. He rode twenty yards ahead of us, wheeled and returned, and as he passed us both going and returning, he thrust his face quite near the General's and glared in a disagreeable manner." When one of the coach's occupants said, "General, everyone wants to see you," he replied, "Yes, but I do not care for such glances." They now knew that man was John Wilkes Booth, the assassin. Had the Grants accompanied the Lincolns to the theater, it seemed likely that Grant would have fallen as well. Later, Grant received an anonymous letter from a man claiming to have been hired to kill him on the train. He'd been unsuccessful because Grant had kept his carriage locked.

But Grant had little interest in the threat to his own life. Instead, according to biographer Geoffrey Perret, he was beset with feelings of guilt that he had not been at the theater to save Lincoln. "Grant always regretted leaving," Perret wrote. "He blamed himself for not going to Ford's Theater that night. Grant was certain he would have heard Booth open the door to Lincoln's box and been able to get his body between Booth's derringer and the seated President."

Grant found some comfort in the solemn and moving tributes to their fallen leader, including a beautiful ceremony in the East Room of the White House, with the honor guard of an African American regiment standing over Lincoln's black-draped casket. During the ceremony, Grant stood silent at the head of the catafalque, tears falling from his eyes.

In life, Lincoln had suffered his share of controversy. He wasn't universally popular. But death transformed him into a towering figure, a saint, the savior of the Union. For many, it felt unthinkable that the nation could be stitched back together without the steady hand of their leader—in the words of poet Walt Whitman, their "Captain." Whitman's elegy, "O Captain! My Captain!" captured the shock and despair of a country that, having reached the shore after a treacherous voyage, awoke to find its captain dead.

> O Captain! my Captain! our fearful trip is done,
> The ship has weather'd every rack, the prize we sought is won,
> The port is near, the bells I hear, the people all exulting,
> While follow eyes the steady keel, the vessel grim and daring;
>   But O heart! heart! heart!
>   O the bleeding drops of red,
>   Where on the deck my Captain lies,
>   Fallen cold and dead.

Heartbroken at Lincoln's murder, his visions of the postwar collaboration shattered, Grant steeled himself to cooperate with—and devote his loyalty to—Andrew Johnson, a man he didn't really know, except that temperamentally he was very different from Lincoln.

Born of humble roots in Raleigh, North Carolina, Johnson was raised with few aspirations except to adopt a trade. As a young man, he apprenticed as a tailor, but after moving to Tennessee he became interested in politics. From his tailor's bench, he ran for and won a place in the state legislature and used it to launch an impressive political career. Before the Civil War, Johnson served in Congress, for two terms as governor of Tennessee, and in the US Senate. When the Southern states began to secede, Johnson took a bold position: "Show me the man who fires on our flag and I will show you a traitor."

Johnson's courageous stance at the start of the war as the only Southern Democrat to support the Union, and his faithfulness throughout the long years of battle, had endeared him to Lincoln, who also recognized a political opportunity in embracing a Southern Democrat. The question now was what kind of president Johnson, a son of the South, would be. Johnson, known to be hot-tempered and rigid, was not well-liked in Washington. Particularly problematic was his inability to collaborate and make necessary concessions. He adopted a view and hung on to it for dear life.

The cabinet was in disarray. Suspicion ran high that Confederate leaders—perhaps Jefferson Davis himself—were behind Lincoln's assassination. Investigations were under way, citing other potential targets—chief among them Grant—who might still be in jeopardy.

Meanwhile, the war needed to be fully won. To that end, Sherman was in North Carolina, engaged in crafting a surrender agreement with General Johnston for his Confederate Army of the South. Grant had cautioned Sherman to keep it simple and avoid adding extraneous political and social conditions to the surrender. He felt that the terms should be modeled on Appomattox. But Sherman still had Lincoln's words from City Point burned in his mind, and he took that as his template, offering generous concessions. When the terms reached Washington, there was an uproar. A particularly egregious concession, according to many, was his decision to allow all of the Confederate soldiers to keep their muskets and for cannons to be stockpiled in the state capitals. Some viewed this as tantamount to arming the next revolution.

Stanton in particular was outraged and declared Sherman's action treason. Grant calmed him down, assuring him and the president that Sherman was misguided but well-meaning and reminding them of his heroism over the course of the war. He promised to remedy the situation, but this was no easy matter, as Stanton had ordered the Army to "resume hostilities at the earliest moment" once Sherman's treaty was discarded.

Fearing that the hard-won peace would be undone, Grant headed south to confer with Sherman. He wrote to Julia: "I find my duties, anxieties, and the necessity for having all my wits about me, increasing rather than diminishing. I have a Herculean task to perform and shall endeavor to do it, not to please any one, but for the interest of our great country."

Stanton, still furious with Sherman, was back in Washington, spiking the punch with some dangerous mischief. Even as Grant was trying to salvage the peace, Stanton described in detail for *New York Times* and *Chicago Tribune* reporters the private meetings of the cabinet and berated Sherman for his actions, which Stanton melodramatically suggested had set the Union up to be overthrown.

It is fortunate that Sherman knew nothing of this public scorching before he met with Grant at his headquarters. Calm as always, Grant privately told Sherman that his terms had been rejected and asked him to inform Johnston that he must accept new terms similar to those agreed upon at Appomattox or the fighting would resume within forty-eight hours. Sherman complied without argument and sent a message to Johnston.

It was a credit to Grant's even temper and Sherman's loyalty that the effort succeeded. Johnston signed the new agreement, · and soon Grant was headed back to Washington, having avoided a return to war. But once the matter was settled, Grant had time to look at the newspapers and was shocked by the vitriol against Sherman, instigated by Stanton. The papers were in a fever of speculation: Was Sherman a traitor? Had he been involved in Lincoln's assassination? Should he be tried for treason?

In Raleigh, Sherman had finally read the papers too, and predictably, he flew into a rage. He was deeply wounded by the unfair accusations and would not soon forgive Stanton. Only the love and loyalty of his armed forces and the steady friendship of Grant kept him on the rails.

"Tell the world that I only loved America," Jefferson Davis would say on his deathbed twenty-four years later. The stripped, barren land of the South might have testified to something darker—a hopeless, self-inflicted stab to the heart. The Civil War nearly destroyed this object of love. An estimated 620,000 to 750,000 people (depending on the source) lost their lives in the war, its toll extending beyond the battlefield to claim lives from disease and starvation. The bereavement of loved ones could not be soothed by military honors and stately grave markers; many of the corpses dissolved into the ground, unclaimed and anonymous.

As if the blood and misery were not enough, the long war had been unimaginably costly for that era—around $5 billion. What a high price for the nation's people to pay in order to fight and kill one another and destroy their own countryside!

Were it not for Ulysses Grant, the agony might have dragged on until the Union itself was destroyed. The humble warrior, such a failure in ordinary life, had found his purpose on the battlefield. Every day he held the lives of his countrymen in his hands. He alone chose the ending of the war, crafting its finale with razor-fine precision. Others might have followed a different strategy or dragged the misery out much longer. That's certainly where the war was headed when President Lincoln stepped in and put Grant in command. War is often conducted by an unwieldy bureaucracy—even more so than peacetime bureaucracy—and that was certainly true of the Civil War, with its surfeit of generals. Grant cut through it, bypassing channels—and Lincoln let him.

Grant had believed from the start that the Confederacy was a lost cause, and every man's death weighed on him as having been preventable. As soon as he took command, he had one mission—to end the war by cutting off the Confederate leaders, to go for the source. Although Sherman, his brother-in-arms, was temperamentally hotter than Grant, he shared his vision and was in on the plan. And so these two men performed their synchronized assault and brought the Confederacy down.

Great joy in the North was tempered by the suffering in the South. Imagine those soldiers returning home to their plundered world. Already spent and half-starved, they had to put themselves to the task of rebuilding.

So too was any rejoicing of the liberated slaves short-lived. A declaration of freedom did not tell them how to bargain for their daily rights. It did not feed their children. It did not force their countrymen to treat them with respect.

Lincoln had achieved his "house united" before his death, but it was a shaky structure requiring a gut renovation. The engineers of war would now have to be the architects of the peace.

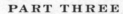

PART THREE

THE POLITICAL
JOURNEY

CHAPTER 7

CHAOS

Ulysses Grant's slight figure was front and center on the viewing stand across from the White House, and the eyes of a massive throng of spectators sought him out—his stature no impediment to his commanding presence. On his lap, held close, was seven-year-old Jesse, whose eyes were alight in anticipation of the parade. Julia sat near them, alongside General Sherman's wife, Ellen, with President Johnson close by. Members of the cabinet and civilian and military dignitaries filled out the viewing stand.

On May 23 and 24, the dark funereal mood in Washington was lifted as a tribute to the Union's great victory excited the population. On those two days, the eagerly awaited "Grand Review of the Union Armies" took place, with the victorious soldiers marching up Pennsylvania Avenue before the president. The flag over the Capitol Building, which had been lowered to half-mast after Lincoln's assassination, was finally raised.

Elated at having something to celebrate, crowds of people,

numbering an estimated two hundred thousand, poured into Washington, clogging the streets with jubilation and pride. A banner hung outside the Treasury building:

**The only national debt we can never
pay is the debt we owe to the
victorious Union soldiers**

More than 150,000 soldiers from two armies would march over two days. On the first day, 90,000 from Meade's Army of the Potomac, buffed and groomed, looking the way a victorious army ought to look, put on a mighty show. On the second day, 60,000 from Sherman's Army of the West dominated, having marched to Washington straight from the final battle.

Sherman recognized that his army would not have the polish of Meade's. With only threadbare uniforms, dusty and torn, and worn shoes or none at all, his men were rough-looking. On the first day, as the two generals watched Meade's fine troops marching, Sherman told Meade, "I'm afraid my poor tatterdemalion corps will make a poor appearance tomorrow when contrasted with yours." Meade magnanimously assured him that the crowds would forgive their shabbiness, and Sherman hid a smile. He knew his men would put on a superior marching show that would capture the hearts of the crowds in a way that the slick Potomac troops never could. In fact, he felt that his men's rugged authenticity was an advantage. Let the nation see them as they were! When the Army sent fresh uniforms to his encampment the night before the march, he refused them.

On the second day, the crowds turning out to see Sherman's troops were bigger than ever. Banners across the avenue heralded the marchers:

Hail to the heroes of the West

**Hail champions of Belmont, Donelson, Shiloh,
Vicksburg, Chattanooga, Atlanta, Savannah,
Bentonville—pride of the nation**

The crowds roared as Sherman appeared on his steed, leading his sixty thousand men down Pennsylvania Avenue. Marching bands played "The Battle Hymn of the Republic," "When Johnny Comes Marching Home," and "Marching Through Georgia." Adoring women and girls wrapped garlands around the men's necks and tossed so many bouquets of flowers that the soldiers sometimes had to wade through them.

Watching the scene, Grant felt proud and somewhat sentimental:

> They gave the appearance of men who had been thoroughly drilled to endure hardships, either by long and continuous marches or through exposure to any climate, without the ordinary shelter of a camp. They exhibited also some of the order of march through Georgia where the "sweet potatoes sprung up from the ground" as Sherman's army went marching through. In the rear of a company there would be a captured horse or mule loaded with small cooking utensils, captured chickens and other food picked up for the use of the men. Negro families who had followed the army would sometimes come along in the rear of a company, with three or four children packed upon a single mule, and the mother leading it.

Neatly dressed in a fresh uniform, and handsome with his red hair gleaming, Sherman led his men. He had never felt such pride. As he neared the viewing stand, he could not resist taking a look behind him and was struck with awe by the smooth discipline of thousands of men who in spite of their shabby dress had perfected a natural synchrony. "I believe it was the happiest and most satisfactory moment of my life," he would later say.

At the viewing stand, Sherman dismounted and saluted the president, greeted Grant with an enthusiastic embrace, and went around and shook everyone's hand. As he approached, War Secretary Stanton began to put his hand out. Sherman ignored the secretary, brushing past him as if Stanton were not even there. The public snub was well noted and became a subject of eager gossip. Julia, with a close-up view, reported, "What a defiant and angry glance he [Sherman] shot at Stanton." She seemed to approve.

Grant pulled his friend down onto a seat so that the two generals flanked the president. They watched Sherman's men march by, delighting in them, though Grant seemed embarrassed by the accolades the soldiers shouted at him. Young Jesse, observing it all, later wrote, "I recall the enthusiasm of the marching soldiers and the shouts of, 'Grant! Grant! Good-by, old man!' I wondered why father did not respond or join them. Always before father had participated in the reviews I had witnessed. It was much later in life before I understood father's embarrassment at the continuous ovation to him and the very patent neglect of the President sitting beside him, who was, in fact, the commander-in-chief of that army."

With Lincoln in the grave, postwar hero worship fell on Grant. When the Grants toured the North that spring, the general was surrounded by large crowds wherever he went. The adulation took a material form as well. The Grants were in a much better position financially than they had ever been before, thanks to the largesse of a grateful nation. In Galena, residents built a new home for them, and recalling Grant's long-ago comment that he might run for mayor so he could build a sidewalk in front of his house, they hung a banner: GENERAL, THE SIDEWALK IS BUILT.

In addition, a beautiful house on Chestnut Street in Philadelphia had been gifted to the Grants. Obviously, this was a different time, when such gifts were considered by many to be a natural and appropriate gesture of thanks. Others disapproved; later, at the first hint of scandal in the Grant administration, critics cited suspicious links to this donor generosity. Originally, the Grants thought the family could live in the Philadelphia house and he could commute to Washington. This suited Grant well, because he did not want to live in the capital. But the plan soon became untenable. In the fall of 1865, the Grants rented out the Philadelphia house and purchased a four-story Federal-style house on I Street NW in Washington.

Grant was not used to the public displays, and he was a bit uncertain about how to fashion himself. Eager politicos were still trying to adapt to Grant's lack of political interest. His presidential ambitions were a great topic of conversation, for although he had never said a word about aspiring to be president, much of the population wanted it, and Republicans imagined him as a dream candidate in 1868. But that day seemed a lifetime away.

As general of the Army, Grant's role in peacetime would be essential. It was under his direction that the fragile reunion would be conducted, for although the war was over, the seceded states remained in limbo as officials in Washington debated the best way to restore them. It was a tortured transition that had incongruously elevated Johnson, a Southerner who had been vice president for only one month, and who had not won the allegiance of a united nation. Grant wondered if Johnson, a Tennessean, could be trusted with the delicate task of Reconstruction.

It's not that he lacked a blueprint. Lincoln had mapped out a plan for the South that recommended forgiveness in exchange for loyalty to the Union and the agreement to accept the equal status of former slaves. Johnson was certainly in favor of the leniency part of the plan, but he was less committed to the conditions.

The Republican Party in Congress was split between the Radical Republicans and the more moderate wing. The Radicals, who were unflinching in their belief that African American suffrage was the cornerstone of Southern revival, were Johnson's chief nemesis. They were determined to ensure that African Americans, now free, would be able to exercise their full rights. Johnson favored a more nuanced approach that would ultimately result in less African American suffrage, not more. As a Southerner, he felt better equipped to understand the Black population and to evaluate its potential. He did not think it was prudent to press for freed Blacks to get the vote, because he simply did not believe that Blacks were capable, intellectually or socially, of fully participating in the political and economic life of the states. Johnson trafficked in the worst stereotypes about Blacks, and he covered his dismissal of their rights with a demeaning paternalism that would undermine their independence and their status.

Johnson didn't care much about improving the lives of Black citizens. John Eaton, who had supervised the freedmen during the war, recalled a meeting with Johnson when he was the military governor of Tennessee. Eaton spoke to Johnson of his work and his hopes for the revival of the South and of the Black population. He recounted, "Johnson, it will be remembered, was fond of referring to himself as the 'Tribune of the people,' but when I spoke of the opportunity of establishing schools and organizing new industries for farmers and mechanics, he was quite obviously bored, and all that might have been said on the subject had no more inclination to stay by him than has water to stay on a duck's back."

Johnson's belief system was drastically different than his predecessor's. In particular, he maintained that African Americans, while "free" in the literal sense, were lesser members of society. For Johnson, their freedom was less a matter of rights and more of white beneficence. David Priess, presidential author and former CIA officer, described Johnson in *How to Get Rid of a President*:

> The president of the United States was both a racist and a very difficult man to get along with. He routinely called blacks inferior. He bluntly stated that no matter how much progress they made, they must remain so. He openly called critics disloyal, even treasonous. He liberally threw insults like candy during public speeches. He rudely ignored answers he didn't like. He regularly put other people into positions they didn't want to be in, then blamed them when things went sour.

Johnson's pretense of supporting Lincoln's plan gave him little cover with Radical Republicans in Congress, who also thought Lincoln's method showed a fatal weakness. They believed that unless there was military oversight and stricter terms to regain admission, the Southern states would not protect the rights of Blacks.

Where did Grant stand in this debate? In spite of his father being a passionate abolitionist, Grant's view of slavery had initially been purely pragmatic. Whatever else people might say about it, whether the suffering of slaves or the offense to human rights, his practical approach was simple: slavery was unsupportable in a democracy. But by the end of the war, Grant had warmed to the abolitionist argument as the only answer to a divided nation, stating, "A state half slave and half free cannot exist."

He wrote, "Slavery was an institution that required unusual guarantees for its security wherever it existed; and in a country like ours where the larger portion of it was free territory inhabited by an intelligent and well-to-do population, the people would naturally have but little sympathy with demands upon them for its protection."

However, he accepted an uncomfortable truth about the prewar North. That is, many whites had no real problem with slavery, as long as it didn't affect their lives. It had been a common sentiment in the North from the start that what the South chose to do was its own business. The starkest evidence of this attitude was prewar Abraham Lincoln, who repeatedly stated his intention not to interfere with the states that practiced slavery. Only when this blind-eye was tested by fugitive slave laws requiring Northerners to hand over fugitives did Northerners begin to wake up. "Prior to the time of these encroachments the great majority of the people of the North had no particular quarrel with slavery, so long as they were not forced to have it themselves," Grant wrote with honesty. "But they were not willing to play the role of police for the South in the protection of this particular institution."

President Johnson was determined to have his way on reconciliation with the South, even if it meant going it alone. With Congress out of session, he went ahead and declared his plan to eliminate the barriers to reunion with broad offers of immunity. While the Radical Republicans in Congress were adamant that the seceded states needed to earn their way back into the Union, Johnson believed that the seceding states did not lose their status as states when they withdrew and that they were still states now. All that was required was their adherence to the Constitution.

In one school of thought, no actual secession had occurred; instead, the South had merely staged an insurrection, because the states didn't have the constitutional authority to secede. This idea had been favored by none other than Lincoln, whose appointment of military governors in several Southern states during the war (including Andrew Johnson in Tennessee) had marginally kept them in the Union.

Radical Republicans in Congress disagreed. Secession was an abdication. Senator Charles Sumner was one of the most impassioned and controversial of the Radicals. Before the war, he had given an antislavery speech so fiery that he was assaulted on the Senate floor and had to step down from office for three years to recover from his injuries. Once back in the Senate, Sumner kept the drumbeat going, and now it was directed squarely at President Johnson.

It's interesting that Johnson's principles of reconciliation did not extend to the Confederate leadership. Viewing them as elites, the aggrieved former poor boy wanted to shame and punish them. After Robert E. Lee wrote to Grant with an application for a pardon, Grant took it to Johnson. The president pushed it aside. "When can these men be tried?" he asked, meaning Lee and his cohorts.

Grant was horrified. "Never," he replied, "unless they violate their parole."

Johnson glared at him. "I would like to know by what right a military commander interferes to protect an arch-traitor from the laws," he demanded.

Grant, usually so calm in the face of conflict, erupted in anger. Such arrests and trials, he told Johnson, would violate the understanding at Appomattox. Surely, Lee would not have surrendered had he known that he and his officers might be subject to arrest, trial, and even execution. Grant stared down his belligerent commander-in-chief and issued a threat: if he was ordered to arrest Lee, he would resign his command rather than obey.

Johnson continued to glower at Grant, but he knew he'd met his match. "Upon the rock of his inflexible resolution the rage of the President broke without effect," wrote the author Hamlin Garland of the moment. "He had met a man he could neither wheedle nor intimidate." Johnson never mentioned the matter again.

When Badeau, who had remained with Grant after the war, wrote about the incident, he concluded that Johnson "found a will more stubborn, or at least more potent with the people, than his own." The moment was a precursor of future encounters with Grant's iron will—battles Johnson lost every time.

In November 1865, Johnson asked Grant to make a fact-finding tour of the South, and Grant reluctantly agreed. He distrusted Johnson's motivations, fearing the president wanted to use him for political cover. The president, he knew, was eager to have the whole Southern question wrapped up.

But Grant found things far from settled. On the matter of security, Blacks were fearful of white retaliation, and whites were fearful of Black uprisings. And while there seemed to be a general consensus that the South wanted to rejoin the Union and begin to rebuild, there remained large pockets of antagonism that, Grant felt, required the continued presence of the Army. He also found many well-meaning Southerners who longed for reconciliation. In Jonesborough, Tennessee, Grant was surrounded by locals who wanted to shake his hand. An older man, a former Confederate soldier, announced to the crowd, "I fought that man pretty hard, but I would like to see him." Grant turned to him. "That does not keep you from being a good citizen," he said. "I had as soon see you as anybody."

Grant had a great store of compassion for the Southern soldier that he would never lose. Once, meeting a former Confederate soldier who had fought Grant's troops at Fort Donelson and Champion Hill, Grant said to him, "I honor all Confederate soldiers, as I do all brave, conscientious men. You were not at fault; your leaders were. They knew that a Southern confederacy was impossible and ought not to be. I was fighting not against the South, but for it. In every battle I felt a sympathy for you, and I felt that I was fighting for North and South—for the whole nation."

Back in Washington, Grant delivered a mixed verdict to Johnson. "The mass of thinking men of the South accept the present situation in good faith," he reported—that was the good news. However, he added, there was much work to do, and the Army was still needed to ensure order—both among the whites and among the Blacks. Johnson was extremely unhappy with this recommendation, and he chose to ignore it, announcing that Reconstruction had been successful. He quickly moved to grant amnesty and allowed the states to elect their own leaders, without much concern for whether those leaders would fairly represent national principles, especially in their treatment of freed slaves. The Southern states, Johnson announced, could retake their places in Congress. These members counted among them some of the leaders of the Confederacy, including its former vice president, Alexander Stephens.

Outraged, the Radical Republicans refused to seat the former Confederates. Johnson continued to battle Congress, but the real progress was realized only with constitutional gains. At the end of the year, the Thirteenth Amendment was ratified by the states, giving more power to the antislavery forces. It declared:

> **Neither slavery nor involuntary servitude, except as a punishment for crime whereof the party shall have been duly convicted, shall exist within the United States, or any place subject to their jurisdiction.**

It was a first step. But clearly, constitutional advances had to be supported by a change in public thinking or they would be ineffective. And that thinking started with the president. In early 1866, Johnson's agreement to a White House meeting with a delegation of five African Americans, led by Frederick Douglass, might have briefly given some hope that the president was becoming more open-minded. Douglass couldn't help but recall the remarkable occasion in 1863, when President Lincoln sat down with him in the White House and conversed with him about the state of the nation, treating him as an equal. Perhaps Johnson would become an ally after all.

Douglass and his committee went to great pains to be highly respectful of Johnson, even calling him "your Excellency." But when they politely asked him to consider their case for enfranchisement and the right to vote, Johnson's mood turned sour. The request set him off on an insulting diatribe about his supposed kindnesses toward the Blacks he had held as slaves. He told them that he had been so good to them that he'd essentially been "their slave instead of their being mine." He then gave a lengthy treatise on the threat that freed slaves posed to poor white workers, arguing that Black equality meant poor whites might become slaves themselves.

Johnson left the meeting annoyed with Douglass and his committee. He thought they were trying to trick him into agreeing to something against his principles. Soon after, he vetoed a congressional measure to extend protections through the Freedmen's Bureau, the agency established under Lincoln to protect the interests and well-being of freed Blacks. And when Congress overwhelmingly passed the Civil Rights Act of 1866, which declared that citizenship rights should be given to all "without distinction of race or color, or previous condition of slavery or involuntary servitude," he vetoed that too. Congress had the numbers on its side, and Johnson's veto was overridden.

How did Johnson, who was Lincoln's choice as vice president, find himself so completely on the wrong side of history? John Russell Young, a prominent journalist with the *New York Herald*, had a theory at the time: "Andrew Johnson, one of the ablest of the poor white class, tried to assert some independence; but as soon as the slave-holders put their thumb upon him, even in the Presidency, he became their slave."

Another explanation was that expediting legitimacy for the South would enable Southerners to go about the business of building prosperity. In retrospect, it was the height of naivete to expect a new understanding to simply appear as if by magic. A change in law does not automatically transform the hearts and minds of the people, and many Southerners simply could not grasp that their former slaves were now their equals. As a Southerner, Johnson preferred to simply forget the whole sorry mess of secession, hoping that a peaceful coexistence would eventually work itself out. But certain realities were impossible to ignore.

Unsettled in their new circumstances, the Southern states were erupting in violence and codifying efforts to keep Blacks under white control. With the South flooded by waves of emancipated Blacks, and in the absence of an orderly national system for putting the economy back together, individual states began establishing their own "Black Codes," which were based on racist notions about Black incompetence and laziness. For as long as slavery had existed, it was believed that Blacks were not self-motivated—that the threat of the whip was the only way to get them to work. This belief, which ignored the obvious enervating factor of forced labor, was so essential to slavery that it informed every common bias about Black people. Just because Blacks were now free didn't mean that those prejudices would simply disappear. Southern states, beginning with South Carolina and Mississippi, began to tighten their rules. Black Codes required Blacks to contract for work and to be able to show proof of those contracts or else be subject to forced labor or arrest. In South Carolina, Blacks were prohibited from any profession except farmer or servant, unless they paid a heavy tax for the privilege. In some areas, the codes placed restrictions on property ownership and denied Blacks the right to vote or serve on juries. If the essence of freedom is self-determination, the Black Codes robbed the freed slaves of this basic right as they became ubiquitous throughout the South. The codes were created in what Douglass would later call "the spirit of caste." In every endeavor, whether in work, in society, or in political influence, Blacks were considered less-than. President Johnson had no argument with the Black Codes. He believed that white men should determine the way of life in the South, and that all others should abide by it.

The fate of "forty acres and a mule" is an example of this thinking. Near the end of the war, General Sherman, with the support of War Secretary Stanton and in consultation with African American leaders, determined that the newly emancipated Blacks could prosper only by owning their own land. Sherman gave the directive known as Special Field Order No. 15, which distributed coastal land in Georgia and South Carolina to Black families. Each family received forty acres, and later a mule. This was a remarkably progressive program that went to the heart of what it really means to be free and to have opportunity. Unfortunately, in late 1865, less than a year into the program, Johnson reversed the order, and most of the land was returned to its previous owners. If freed Blacks were experiencing a sense of whiplash, it was understandable—as soon as Blacks were given more rights and opportunities, they were taken away.

"This was the condition of the Colored people at the close of the war. They were set free without a dollar, without a foot of land and without the wherewithal to get the next meal even," wrote former slave Henry Clay Bruce, after the "forty acres" debacle.

"It does seem to me that a Christian Nation, which had received such wealth from the labor of a subjugated people, upon setting them free would, at least, have given them a square meal. Justice seems to demand one year's support, forty acres of land and a mule each." The failure of the government to construct some form of economic way forward for the four million former slaves showed a shameful indifference to human rights, which surely must include basic sustenance. Unfortunately, the narrative took hold early on that freedmen were looking for a handout they had not earned.

Even though Congress had overridden Johnson's veto of its extension of the Freedmen's Bureau Bill and the Civil Rights Act, it was clear to everyone that these bills lacked the teeth and permanence of constitutional mandates. The Fourteenth Amendment, recently ratified, established without nuance the principle of equal protection:

> All persons born or naturalized in the United States, and subject to the jurisdiction thereof, are citizens of the United States and of the state wherein they reside. No state shall make or enforce any law which shall abridge the privileges or immunities of citizens of the United States; nor shall any state deprive any person of life, liberty, or property, without due process of law; nor deny to any person within its jurisdiction the equal protection of the laws.

This was progress, but the reality was plain to see. Throughout the South, as well as in the White House, there was resistance to the very notion of equality, regardless of what the Constitution stated. Seeing this dissonance within the administration he served, Grant did everything he could to voice his support for the Fourteenth Amendment.

His relationship with President Johnson was worsening. In the early period of the administration, following Lincoln's assassination, Grant had been supportive of Johnson, believing he was following Lincoln's blueprint. But this had ceased to be the case. Grant found himself often disagreeing with the president. Stanton, too, was growing increasingly outspoken about Johnson's abject failure to manage Reconstruction and protect the rights of Southern Blacks.

Especially troubling was Johnson's failure to address the growing violence against Blacks in the South. On May 1, 1866, a fight took place between several policemen and a group of Black Union veterans in Memphis, attesting to the rising tensions in the community. The fight was broken up by soldiers from Fort Pickering, but it wasn't the end of the matter. That night a large white mob raided the Black community, creating havoc throughout the night. By morning, when the riot was quelled, forty-six Blacks had been murdered and more than seventy-five injured. Three Black churches and five schoolhouses were burned. The Memphis riot, along with a summer riot in New Orleans, only strengthened the determination of Radical Republicans in Congress to push for legislation to protect the rights of freed Blacks—an effort that elicited no sympathy from Johnson.

In spite of Grant's resistance, Johnson pulled him into his political orbit, enlisting him to join a campaign trip. Grant didn't want to go, and his friends urged him to refuse. Johnson was only using him because of his popularity, they said. Grant would have liked to decline, but he didn't think he could. "I am a soldier," he told his friends. "He is my superior officer. So long as I retain my present position, it is my duty to obey."

Grant was miserable throughout most of the trip. By the end, he could barely stand to look at the president. He certainly couldn't speak his mind. Johnson was intolerant of anyone who challenged him and probably would have fired Grant if he thought he could get away with it. One thing had been evident on their tour: Grant was vastly more popular than Johnson. Even in Johnson's presence, citizens didn't hesitate to call out to the general, shouting their desire to see him in the White House.

Annoyed at having the thorn of Grant pricking his side, Johnson came up with the idea of sending him off on a diplomatic mission to Mexico and bringing Sherman in to take his place. He thought he had devised a clever way to get rid of Grant. But Grant refused to go.

When Johnson presented him with the order in front of the Cabinet, Grant declined. This, of course, infuriated Johnson. He turned to the attorney general. "Mr. Attorney General," he said, "is there any reason why General Grant should not obey my orders?"

Before the AG could reply, Grant jumped to his feet. "I can answer that question, Mr. President, without referring it to the attorney general. I am an American citizen, and eligible to any office to which any American is eligible. I am an officer of the army and bound to obey your military orders. But this is a civil office, a purely diplomatic duty, and I cannot be compelled to undertake it. Any legal military order you give me I will obey, but this is civil, and not military, and I decline the duty. No power on earth can compel me to it."

There was a shocked silence in the room. No one had ever heard someone confront the president so boldly. Especially not Grant, whose modus operandi was conciliation.

Johnson had already summoned Sherman, and he was sure he'd get his way in the end. However, when Sherman arrived, he shocked the president by telling him that he was wrong to force a diplomatic mission on Grant. He further admonished Johnson that it would be a big mistake for him to get into a public argument with Grant.

He added, if anyone could be spared to go to Mexico it should be Sherman himself. And that's what happened. As Sherman left to conduct diplomacy in Mexico, he observed that his real diplomatic purpose had already been served in preventing a "serious quarrel" between the president and Grant.

The Washington standoff continued, and Johnson received disappointing results in the midterms. The Republicans maintained their dominant position in Congress, with a veto-proof majority. In February 1867, Congress passed a major Reconstruction bill. In what was becoming a familiar dance, Johnson vetoed the bill, a move Grant decried as "ridiculous." The president's veto was overridden. Three more Reconstruction bills were passed, vetoed, and overridden in the course of the year. Technically, Congress was winning, but in reality it was impossible for legislation so vigorously opposed by the president to gain a foothold. Even so, Johnson's opponents were gathering strength and visibility.

With reports pouring in of violence against Blacks in the South, Stanton felt more firmly than ever that a strong Army presence was needed in the states to provide protection. Every day he was forced to stand up to Johnson, who was determined to remove federal troops from the South.

Grant was feeling the stress. Increasingly, he was required to stay close to the home base, because tensions were so great between Johnson and Stanton that he worried about an eruption. Apologizing for missing a family trip that Julia had looked forward to, Grant told her, "Well, Stanton was hectoring the President, and I could not leave, as he feared some trouble." Julia noticed how burdened her husband looked.

The next morning, as they were preparing to leave for church, a messenger from the White House came to the door and said that Grant's presence was requested. Leaving Julia to attend church without him, Grant headed in to see the president. He was gone for several hours, and when he finally returned to I Street, his face was grim. He described the scene to Julia. The president, who had "worked himself up to a white heat of indignation" over Stanton, had finally decided to fire him and replace him as secretary of War with Grant. "And I consented to do so," Grant told his wife, "as I think it most important that someone should be there who cannot be used." It was notable that Johnson took this action in August, with Congress out of session until December.

But there was more. Johnson informed Grant that he planned to remove General Sheridan and to begin putting an end to military control in the South. This alarmed Grant. He feared that a military withdrawal from Sheridan's territory of Louisiana and Texas would be viewed as tantamount to the end of Reconstruction. When Johnson countered that Sheridan was a tyrant and the Southerners hated him, Grant had no defense. Sheridan's roughness was well known; as biographer Joseph Wheelan put it, "He believed ends justified practically any means, no matter how harsh." That being said, Grant relied on Sheridan to maintain order in the most volatile areas of the South.

Johnson got his way with Sheridan, sending him west to deal with Native American conflicts. Predictably, Southerners were elated to see what they hoped was the last of Sheridan. Finally, their president, a son of the South, was standing up for them.

Uneasy about the changes Johnson was instituting, Grant took Stanton's place and waited for Congress to return and deliver its verdict on Stanton's ouster. In December, it did, declaring that Johnson's removal of Stanton was a violation of the Tenure of Office Act, a law passed in 1867 that prevented a president from removing appointed officials, such as cabinet members, without the approval of Congress. Congress now ordered Stanton reinstated.

This was fine with Grant, who didn't want the job. He immediately stepped down and handed the keys back to Stanton. This set off a fresh wave of fury from Johnson. He couldn't believe that Grant was caving so readily. Grant just wanted to be as far away from the conflict as possible. He thought remaining in Stanton's office would be improper. But, according to Grant's bodyguard William Crook, Johnson thought Grant's action "was that of a traitor."

Stanton's return lasted less than two months. On February 21, Johnson informed Congress that he was firing Stanton again, replacing him with Lorenzo Thomas, adjunct general of the Army. This time Stanton refused to leave. Day after day, as Thomas arrived to take possession of the office, he found Stanton stubbornly there. Finally, Congress declared the firing illegal. The remedy it proposed was impeachment. On February 24, 1868, the House of Representatives voted 126 to 47 to impeach Johnson for "high crimes and misdemeanors."

There's no question that the Tenure of Office Act, a highly suspect law, was a thin basis for impeachment. Many believed that the law was unconstitutional, and that a president should have the right to choose his cabinet. (Grant certainly believed it. As soon as he was elected president he would try to get rid of the Tenure of Office Act, but it would linger for twenty years before being ended.)

But if the impeachment proceedings were technically about Johnson breaking an obscure law, they were *actually* about a much greater rift between the White House and Congress. Behind the scenes of the impeachment hearings was the question of which men and which philosophies would advance. On one side was Johnson. On the opposite side was Stanton and, by extension, Grant. In an ordinary time, the impeachment story would have ended with Johnson's conviction or his exoneration. But in an election year a different calculation had to be made. Would a president wounded by the impeachment but not removed be more easily defeated in the election than a strong new candidate?

The Senate trial lasted three weeks, and Johnson never appeared to testify. He remained in the White House, trying to conduct business as normal. A two-thirds majority was required for removal, and when the vote was cast in the Senate, the count fell one vote short of that number. The final turn toward acquittal was in the hands of Senator Edmund G. Ross from Kansas. His vote to acquit earned him a place in John F. Kennedy's Pulitzer Prize–winning book *Profiles in Courage*:

> Unable to conceal the suspense and emotion in his voice, the Chief Justice put the question to him: "Mr. Senator Ross, how say you? Is the respondent Andrew Johnson guilty or not guilty of a high misdemeanor as charged in this Article?"
>
> . . . As Ross himself later described it, "I almost literally looked down into my open grave. Friendships, position, fortune, everything that makes life desirable to an ambitious man were about to be swept away by the breath of my mouth, perhaps forever."

Hearing the news of his acquittal, Johnson poured whiskey and raised a toast at the White House. Less happy was Ross's office. His Republican colleagues voiced outrage, and his constituents in Kansas turned their backs on him. But in truth, even some of Johnson's enemies were not really disappointed in the vote. Now the election could be fully engaged without worrying too much about Johnson. He was diminished—in every sense a lame duck. Even though he was acquitted, nearly two-thirds of the nation's senators had voted against him, signaling a lack of confidence across the country. According to Hamlin Garland, Johnson had dreamed of "being the Presidential Candidate of a new Democratic party, made up of a union between the reconstructed South and the Democratic party of the North." But when the Democrats met to choose their presidential candidate, Johnson barely registered in the vote count. He was finished.

After Johnson's acquittal, Stanton stepped down from the War Department and was replaced by John Schofield, a well-regarded military leader who had served as military governor of Virginia. He would essentially be a placeholder until the next president made his selection.

Grant had been supportive of Stanton, but privately he could sympathize with Johnson's frustration. "I should not have liked to have been in Johnson's place," he said later. "Stanton required a man like Lincoln to manage him." In his love for the Union, Grant observed, Stanton was "volcanic in his fierceness," and that made life difficult. Yet Grant found him a man of superior qualities, "one of the great men of the Republic." They would later become close friends.

Stung by the ugliness of the early Reconstruction process, the nation was in the mood for change. The era of radical Republicanism was fading, while the idea of moderate Republicanism was taking hold. Grant was viewed as a principled moderate. He fit the national mood.

The movement to back Grant for president had been growing in 1868, although Grant did nothing to advance his own cause. He was so inscrutable that a reporter from the *New York Tribune* likened his face to masonry: "The square straight brow knows the meaning of the wary unchanging eyes, and will not tell it. The eyes watch the heavy unquivering nostrils; the nostrils command the locked mouth: when the mouth opens the strong chin keeps the secret of patient brain and tyrannous will." No political operative, reporter, or friend was successful at cracking the granite. Grant knew he was favored for the nomination, but he would not seek it.

While others speculated about his future, Grant, a solitary, deep-thinking man, did his job and kept silent. As Geoffrey Perret observed, "There was something about him which made Grant seem always to be alone, no matter how large the crowd, as if he lived within some personal force field that kept other people and their concerns on the periphery while the real Grant was somewhere else."

What was Grant really thinking? To his intimates, Grant's views were clear, but he refused to speak publicly. He wrote to Sherman, "No matter how close I keep my tongue each tries to interpret from the little I let drop that I am with them."

Those closest to Grant understood just how indispensable he was to the political orchestration. Behind the scenes, members of Congress, lacking an ally in the White House, chose to consult with Grant instead. His son Jesse, whose concerns were those of a typical child's, nonetheless noticed that their house on I Street was a busy place. "Always father seemed in consultation with some one [*sic*], Senators and Congressmen more in evidence than army men," he wrote in his memoir. "When he was at home the stream of callers was unbroken, often until late at night. It was long after before I understood that father had been consulted by Congress upon practically all the legislation of the period, and particularly upon every reconstruction measure."

In the privacy of their home, Julia gently pressed her husband. "Ulys, do you wish to be President?"

He told her, "No, but I do not see that I have anything to say about it. The convention is about to assemble, and from all I hear, they will nominate me; and I suppose if I am nominated, I will be elected."

Julia was troubled. She'd seen what had happened to Johnson and wondered if it was even possible to bring together the disparate factions. "To satisfy one section you must hurt another," she complained to Grant.

Now Grant quietly admitted to his wife what he would never acknowledge in public, telling her, "I feel, too, that if I am elected I can give to the widely separated interests and sections of the country more satisfaction than any other man." He was particularly confident of his influence in the South, where he believed the goodwill he'd earned at the end of the war would help him govern.

Grant was not being boastful. He was in every way the man for the moment, perhaps the only one who could unite the country. He had won the admiration and trust of Northerners and was still respected by many former Confederate soldiers. He had a reputation for fairness and goodwill to all, presenting a striking contrast to President Johnson. He had shown himself in war to be a master strategist; could that same skill be applied to the problems of postwar civilian life? Increasingly, Grant believed that it could—and others agreed.

Days after the final impeachment vote, the Republican convention was held at Crosby's Opera House in Chicago, and Grant was unanimously nominated. Schuyler Colfax, the Speaker of the House and a Radical Republican, was nominated as his vice presidential running mate.

Back in Washington, Grant was busy at his desk at Army headquarters when he heard the news. Stanton, who had yet to resign and was monitoring the convention news via telegraph at the War Department, saw the report and hurried across the street to Grant's office. Bursting in, he declared, "I have come to tell you that you have been nominated by the Republican Party for President of the United States."

Grant accepted the news without emotion. Badeau, who was present, recalled, "There was no shade of exultation or agitation on his face, not a flush on his cheek, nor a flash in his eye." By day's end, though, he was swept up in a parade, accompanied by a Marine band, as his supporters in Washington gathered to celebrate. Afterward, Grant delivered his first ever political address—typically self-deprecating and noble:

> Gentlemen, being entirely unaccustomed to public speaking and without the desire to cultivate the power, it is impossible for me to find appropriate language to thank you for this demonstration. All that I can say is, that in whatever position I may be called by your will, I shall endeavor to discharge its duties with fidelity and honesty of purpose.

Later, he sat down and wrote a letter of acceptance. Pausing at the end before adding his signature, he wrote, "Let us have peace." It became his campaign slogan.

Sherman warned Julia that she must be prepared to have her husband's character "thoroughly sifted." She balked. "General Grant is my Admiral Crichton. He does all things well. He is brave; he is kind; he is just; he is true."

Sherman smiled at her enthusiasm and replied, "Oh, my dear lady, it is not what he has done, but what they will *say* he has done, and they will prove too that Grant is a very bad man indeed. The fact is, you will be astonished to find what a bad man you have for a husband."

Julia knew he was teasing her, but there was truth in his words, and indeed, Grant was slammed in the press as a coward, a drunk, a cheat, and more. She got used to it, as political spouses learn to do.

The Democratic candidate was New York governor Horatio Seymour, who was nominated at a rousing convention at the newly built Tammany Hall in New York City. Despite the Northern location, according to Garland the convention was as completely dominated by the South as the Republican convention had been dominated by the North. Seymour had insisted before his nomination that he didn't want to run. But when forced to it, he ran a campaign of states' rights—an end to Reconstruction that might shift the nation back to a war footing. As if to underscore this possibility, the slogan of the Democratic convention was "This is a White Man's Country; Let White Men Rule." Although Democrats tried to align Grant with the Radicals, most Americans still trusted Grant to be the arbiter who would stand in the middle and calm the opposing forces.

As a June 3 *New York Times* editorial proposed: "Peace—a settled, just and permanent peace—not merely the end of war, but the end of the discord, resentment and hatred which survive the war—is what the American people, without distinction of section, of party, or of race, most of all, at this moment, most fervently desire." Could Grant's election bring about that coveted result?

Grant did no real campaigning himself, and he had little stomach for it. However, his son Jesse recalled a telling incident during the campaign when he accompanied his father to Utica, New York, where they happened to meet Seymour. Jesse watched in stunned horror as the two men greeted each other in a friendly way. "My impressions of [Seymour] had been formed by the cartoons of a fiercely partisan press," he noted. "I believed him to be a terrible man." Yet here was his father greeting the governor nicely. And here was Seymour, setting aside all conflicts and seeming a bit starstruck. "I fear you will have slight cause to remember me as your political opponent, General, but I am very glad to have this opportunity to meet you."

That's not to say that the Democrats weren't ferocious in their attacks on Grant. Henry Whitney Cleveland, a former Confederate officer, recalled that "it became a sort of Democratic fashion to belittle General Grant," especially his skill on the battlefield.

Cleveland thought the strategy self-defeating. "It is not too much to the credit of the South if we were defeated by a weak and incompetent man," he said, reminding friends of the proverb, "Great let me call him, for he conquered me."

Grant returned to Galena to vote. On November 3, he went to the polls, accompanied by a group of neighbors. He voted for Congressman Elihu Washburne and other Republicans on the ticket. But he left the ballot for president blank. He thought it unseemly to vote for himself.

On election night, Julia waited at home while Grant settled in with Badeau and Washburne at the congressman's house. A telegraph hookup had been arranged so that they could receive the results, and soon they were joined by other men from Galena. The results were closer than expected, given Grant's hero status—he was up only 300,000 in the popular vote. However, his electoral college victory was decisive—214 to 80.

It was after 2:00 A.M. when Grant trudged home. Julia met him at the door. "I am afraid I am elected," he told her apologetically.

Julia and others who knew him well recognized his typical humble pose but also understood that the victory meant the world to him. He was so sensitive to the way he was perceived that a defeat would have been a crushing verdict on his life's achievements.

A crowd had gathered outside his home, and he turned to face them, speaking in the language of battle. "The responsibilities of the position I feel," he told them, "but accept them without fear."

CHAPTER 8

THE OUTLIER PRESIDENT

Shortly after 11:00 A.M. on March 4, 1869, Ulysses S. Grant stepped out of the family home on I Street, wearing a well-cut dark suit, and boarded his carriage beside Rawlins for a short ride to the Capitol. Julia had already gone separately with the family. As they drove past buildings whose windows were festively draped with flags, they felt the bite of the cold air and the mist of a steady drizzle. The day was gloomy, but by the time Grant took his oath a tentative sun would have broken through.

Grant's ride to the Capitol was absent the usual ceremony. Normally the outgoing president joined the president-elect in his carriage. However, Grant had refused to ride with Johnson (or Johnson had refused to ride with Grant—it was never entirely clear), and as a result Johnson and his staff were boycotting the inauguration. While his successor took the oath of office, Johnson and his small cadre of loyalists sat in the White House, in a disappointing show of pettiness. Shortly before noon, Johnson said his goodbyes to the remaining staff and left the premises. He made a point of gathering up all his office records to take with him, saying, "I found nothing here when I came, and I am going to leave nothing here when I go."

In modern times we have usually experienced a comfortable tradition of transition conversations between outgoing and incoming presidents. But these rituals are voluntary, not prescribed. In the four-month period between Grant's election and the inauguration, no such courtesy had been extended. In his final months, Johnson was busy absolving the Confederacy. On Christmas Day, he issued clemency to all remaining Confederates under threat of conviction, including Jefferson Davis. And then he waited. As Crook described it, "During the last two months Mr. Johnson sat at the White House waiting for the man whom he hated to take his place."

As a footnote to Johnson's life of public service, he was elected to the Senate from Tennessee in 1874, during Grant's second term. As soon as he took his seat on March 4, 1875, Johnson sent for Crook and told him, "I have come back to the senate with two purposes. One is to do what I can to punish the Southern brigadiers. They led the South into secession, and they have never had their deserts. The other is to make a speech against Grant." He did make the speech two weeks later. "He was the best hater I ever knew," Crook concluded.

During the transition period before Grant's inauguration, there had only been silence from the incoming president. Not even his closest intimates had any idea what he planned. Badeau speculated that this was a leftover habit from his military days, when he had been used to "appointing commanders without consulting their wishes and to ordering movements without informing his inferiors, and he kept up the practice in civilian life." This habit would be a stumbling block in his presidency.

A huge crowd surrounded the east portico of the Capitol to see their war hero sworn in as president by Chief Justice Salmon

P. Chase. On the platform, the Grants were present in full force, with the notable exception of Grant's mother, Hannah, for whom this was just an ordinary day back in Ohio. She'd concluded that the hoopla surrounding her son's inauguration was unseemly, later telling a reporter, "We are not a demonstrative family. None of us care a penny for all the demonstrations in the world."

Grant took the oath of office and leaned in to kiss the Bible. He then turned to face the crowd, which extended as far back as the eye could see.

Grant was never an orator or a gifted speechwriter; prior to the *Memoirs* he wrote late in life, his public writing was confined to directives and strategic planning. His first inaugural address, which he wrote himself, with only the smallest consultation with Badeau, had something of that flavor. Badeau, with an ear for the poetic phrase, urged him to use the line that had so moved him on election night: "The responsibilities of the position I feel, but accept them without fear." Grant complied, and it was included as the fourth line of the speech.

The speech itself was dry but to the point, with straightforward language and repeated assertions that he would be faithful and forthright as president. He delivered it in a conversational voice, so quiet that many in the huge crowd could not hear a word.

> On all leading questions agitating the public mind I will always express my views to Congress and urge them according to my judgment, and when I think it advisable will exercise the constitutional privilege of interposing a veto to defeat measures which I oppose; but all laws will be faithfully executed, whether they meet my approval or not.

He paid substantial attention to the national debt, expressing strong support for the gold standard:

> To protect the national honor, every dollar of Government in-
> debtedness should be paid in gold, unless otherwise expressly
> stipulated in the contract. Let it be understood that no repudi-
> ator of one farthing of our public debt will be trusted in pub-
> lic place, and it will go far toward strengthening a credit which
> ought to be the best in the world, and will ultimately enable us
> to replace the debt with bonds bearing less interest than we
> now pay. To this should be added a faithful collection of the
> revenue, a strict accountability to the Treasury for every dollar
> collected, and the greatest practicable retrenchment in expen-
> diture in every department of Government.

On Reconstruction he was at last in a position to exert leadership,
and he made a bold pronouncement:

> The question of suffrage is one which is likely to agitate the
> public so long as a portion of the citizens of the nation are ex-
> cluded from its privileges in any State. It seems to me very de-
> sirable that this question should be settled now, and I entertain
> the hope and express the desire that it may be by the ratifica-
> tion of the fifteenth article of amendment to the Constitution.

As Grant spoke, thirteen-year-old Nellie suddenly broke away
from her mother and ran over to stand beside her father. She
grasped his hand, and he held it as he spoke, until a chair was
brought for her. He did not object to her presence. People were
moved by the sight of their new president, his daughter at his side,
speaking to a troubled nation.

His final words were calm and hopeful as he asked for "patient forbearance one toward another throughout the land, and a
determined effort on the part of every citizen to do his share toward cementing a happy union; and I ask the prayers of the nation

to Almighty God in behalf of this consummation." As the huge crowd, which included many African Americans, roared its approval, Grant walked over and handed Julia the text of his speech, leaning in to kiss her on the cheek. She beamed with pride.

The nation wanted to love Grant, to prove themselves right for backing him, and the press complied. He received good reviews for his speech, even though it was mostly workmanlike. The *New York Times* review was typical: "General Grant had something to say, and he has said it strongly and well." (It didn't refer to him as President Grant, however; to some, he would always be General Grant.)

Afterward the Grants returned to their I Street house, where they would continue to live for a few weeks before moving into the White House. That evening there was an inaugural ball at the Treasury Department building, which was still under construction. Six thousand revelers crowded the hall, paying $10 each for the privilege, in spite of the construction dust that hung in the air. The journalist Mary Clemmer Ames gave a colorful description: "The air throughout the entire building was perforated with a fine dust ground till you felt that you were taking in with every breath a myriad homoeopathic doses of desiccated grindstone. The agonies of that ball can never be written." Yet there was a high mood of celebration, and a good time was had by all.

Long years of service to Grant had made Badeau an adept student of his ways, and on inauguration day he recognized something familiar in Grant's posture. Recalling Grant in the days after he was promoted to lead all of the Union armies and face his opposition in the Wilderness, he noted an unusual sternness in his manner and a formality in his dress that was in keeping with the seriousness of the moment. Now, in the newness of his presidency, "he bore himself with a distant and almost frigid demeanor" among his associates. "That day there was no geniality, no familiar jest, hardly a smile; but the man who became the chief of a nation of fifty million and stepped into the ranks of earth's mightiest potentates might well be grave."

When Grant took the oath of office, he was only forty-six years old—the youngest man ever to assume the presidency. He was the first president with no political or governing experience. Even George Washington had been a member of the Continental Congress. The great problem of Grant's presidency was his inexperience and his lack of respect for the political class. He was too emotional, too swayed by personal loyalties. He had learned to rely on a circle of indispensable comrades during war, and he tended to choose only those who were most skilled. He relied on them still. But how to gauge skill in the political arena? That was a calculation he had no idea how to make. He might have benefited from consulting with those who had experience in Washington, but he made a point of separating himself from most politicians. This supposedly noble posture was actually foolish.

The anti-politician is a well-known character in American ideology. Dwight Eisenhower, a general whose political trajectory mirrored Grant's nearly a century later, felt the same about the political establishment. Also like Grant, Eisenhower had an unparalleled experience of leadership and felt confident that those qualities would serve him well in the White House.

But once elected, Eisenhower quickly came to understand that the political class had a role to play, and he sought to bring both parties into partnership. His selection of political veterans to serve in the cabinet and Justice Department stabilized his presidency and helped him face controversies around McCarthyism, civil rights, and the Cold War. His close collaboration with the wily elders of the House and Senate, Speaker Sam Rayburn and Majority Leader Lyndon Johnson, helped forge concessions that would have been unthinkable in a more typical partisan standoff.

The citizen president is a romantic notion, yet to openly dismiss politics and politicians is to ignore the value they bring to the table: civic passion, historical knowledge and perspective, relationships and constituencies, and ultimately the flexibility to compromise when it suits their needs. But of Grant, historian Henry Adams, a descendent of presidents himself, observed, "A great soldier might also be a baby politician."

On Grant's first full day in office, he finally came out of the shadows to show his intentions when he sent a list of his cabinet nominees to Congress for confirmation. In advising him, Rawlins had had a key piece of advice: avoid appointing adversaries who would spend their time trying to thwart his plans. In other words, he cautioned Grant to avoid anything like Lincoln's famous team of rivals. Grant took the advice to heart, perhaps going overboard in the other direction by choosing people for whom he felt personal loyalty.

The new president didn't really know how else to judge the members of his team. In the army, he'd found it essential that his senior officers be extremely close and loyal to the death. Had he been willing to listen to people experienced in the political arena, he would have been told of the folly of this approach. They would have suggested that the ideal cabinet should be composed of the best men for the jobs—men who shared his vision but had their own stores of knowledge and insight. These men would not be motivated by the hope of personal wealth or glory, but by the highest ideals of public service. Grant himself was so motivated. But when he sent his cabinet list to Congress, it was met with dismay and confusion. It was a hodgepodge of candidates, some unknown and others ill regarded. While overall it was arguably not such a bad list, it seemed thrown together without any consultation with party leaders.

Grant immediately ran up against a conflict in his selection of

Alexander T. Stewart, a department store magnate, for secretary of the Treasury. Not entirely coincidentally, the wealthy Stewart was a generous benefactor to Grant's campaign and had contributed to the purchase of his house as well. Stewart was generally considered to be a good man, but it turned out that he was ineligible for the treasury post because of a provision that importers could not hold the position. Stewart withdrew his nomination, and Grant named Massachusetts congressman George S. Boutwell, who would serve for Grant's first term. A Radical Republican, Boutwell had been a leading proponent of Black civil rights and was a manager of Johnson's impeachment. During his tenure at Treasury, he would focus on reorganization, but would have his share of crises.

Congressman Elihu Washburne was a valued Galena friend who had heartily recommended Grant to Lincoln at a time when his skill was barely acknowledged by others. Arguably, without Washburne's intervention, Grant might not have so easily come to the attention of those who mattered.

When Grant nominated Washburne for secretary of State, there was loud discussion about his fitness, even after the Senate quickly confirmed him. But Washburne served only five days in the post before stepping down, at which point Grant nominated him as minister to France.

What happened? There are several theories, including Washburne's own admission that he wasn't up to the job. The most persuasive theory is that Grant had nominated him as a personal courtesy, knowing that his tenure would be brief. Washburne would gain his desired ministry to France and serve with the added gravitas of having been secretary of State. It was the kind of personal gesture Grant was known for. He managed to send his friend off to his French mission with the gift of a coveted title.

Once Washburne stepped down, Grant made a strong choice.

Hamilton Fish, who took office after a week, would hold the distinction of being the only cabinet officer to remain for the entire eight years of Grant's presidency.

Fish was extremely experienced and temperamentally suited to the job. He had achieved the trifecta of offices, having been a congressman, governor of New York, and a US senator. Fish understood the importance of Grant's stature in the nation. He described the election this way: "The plain man had not elected Grant; he had elected an indestructible legend, a folk-hero."

Rawlins had made no secret of his desire to be secretary of War, and he anxiously waited for Grant to nominate him. He spent the final days of the transition secluded in Connecticut, growing increasingly anxious over the lack of communication. As the inauguration approached, Rawlins became convinced that he would not receive the appointment, and he decided not to attend. When Grant heard of Rawlins's plan to stay away, he was surprised. Only then did he reach out to Rawlins to tell him that he wanted to keep John Schofield for a brief transition period, but then would appoint Rawlins. Rawlins came out of seclusion and joined Grant for the inauguration. Grant kept his word about appointing Rawlins, but his term was brief. He was suffering from tuberculosis and was unable to fulfill his duties. General Sherman stepped in as acting secretary until Rawlins's death in late 1869. It was believed that Grant's appointment of a dying man was another typical gesture of personal respect.

After Rawlins died, Grant accepted Sherman's recommendation for a replacement. William Belknap, a brigadier general during the war, had served at both Shiloh and Vicksburg. He would remain secretary of War for most of Grant's presidency, before resigning in the midst of a scandal that put a stain on Grant's second term.

For attorney general, Justice Ebenezer Rockwood Hoar was

praised as a good pick. Hoar had served on the Massachusetts Supreme Court for a decade. But he'd only be the first of five attorneys general during Grant's eight years in office, serving a little more than a year and a half. Hoar accomplished much in his brief term, his greatest contribution being the establishment of the Department of Justice.

Grant wasn't always entirely happy with Hoar, and at one point he tried to move him out of office by nominating him to the Supreme Court. When the Senate failed to confirm Hoar, Grant asked for his resignation. He told the shocked Hoar that his advisers were urging him to appoint a Southerner to oversee Reconstruction. He then appointed Amos T. Akerman, the US attorney from Georgia, who was in full support of Grant's Reconstruction efforts.

Grant's Philadelphia friend Adolph E. Borie was appointed secretary of the Navy. A wealthy retired businessman, Borie was virtually unknown, and his only qualification seemed to be that he'd raised money for the Grants' Philadelphia home. It was so clearly a patronage appointment that Borie was an embarrassment to Grant. He lasted only three and a half months but managed to make a mark by stirring up a loud controversy about renaming American ships—some with non-American names. However, he also desegregated the Washington Navy Yard.

Other appointments were less controversial, including former Ohio governor and soldier Jacob D. Cox for secretary of the Interior and John A. Creswell, a former Democrat who had become a Radical Republican, for postmaster general.

Grant was determined that Sherman would succeed him as general-in-chief of the Army, but there was some pushback from Grant's congressional supporters. They argued that the position had been created solely for Grant himself, and that perhaps he would reclaim it after his presidency. But he said, "No, Sherman must succeed me. I shall send his name in at once, and I hope he will be confirmed without fail." He was. The Grants also sold the Shermans their house on I Street.

Grant took the opportunity to take care of several old military friends, including Sheridan, who was restored to his command at New Orleans and promoted to lieutenant general. Grant also went out of his way to help his old friend Longstreet, who had endorsed him for the presidency and attended his inauguration. He nominated Longstreet as surveyor of the port of New Orleans.

In Washington, Grant clearly felt comfortable surrounded by military men; in addition to Badeau, he chose three others to serve on his staff as secretaries—his brother-in-law, General Frederick T. Dent, who had been an aide-de-camp to Grant in the last year of the war; General Horace Porter, who had also served as Grant's aide-de-camp; and General Orville E. Babcock, who had served in the Corps of Engineers before becoming one of Grant's closest aides during the war. As Crook noted,

> There was something about the President's office at this time which, to my way of thinking, suggested a military council. It was not that there were any of the trappings of war, for, of course, all three of the office secretaries wore civilian dress; nor was it in any special ceremoniousness of manner, for they were men of simplicity and geniality. It was rather in the fine, soldierly presence of the men, as well as in a sort of military exactness which pervaded the routine business.

However, Grant's leadership style might have suffered in office by his reliance on his military ways. As his former brigadier general James Harrison Wilson wrote, "He unconsciously treated his Cabinet rather as staff officers than as his constitutional advisers; rather as clerks than as counsellors, and unfortunately for him and for the country, this view of their relations was too frequently accepted without question by his new associates."

Badeau's insight about Grant's inner thinking seems to get to the heart of the matter. "Grant was in reality one of the most sensitive of men. He regarded the feelings of others carefully, and it was always painful to him to inflict pain. Although few supposed so, he felt acutely all the censures and attacks and even the slights of which he was the object. He said nothing, perhaps, when he received them, but there was abundant evidence, which those who were with him closely could detect, that Grant was a thin-skinned man."

It appears that even those who knew him best and were dedicated to serving his interests did not understand him. Hamilton Fish's biographer Allan Nevins underscored this, noting that one of Fish's "first and most imperative tasks was to try to penetrate that great national enigma, the President. Even today Grant is partly an enigma; then he was wholly so. Men waited—and hoped." It might also be noted that, although Grant was beloved as a general, in the presidency Lincoln was a very hard act to follow.

As Julia made an inventory of her new home, she found it unbearably dark and shabby. It was no secret why this was so. First Lady Eliza Johnson had been virtually bedridden with tuberculosis during her husband's time in office and had made only two public appearances. Although the Johnsons' eldest married daughter, Martha, filled in for her mother as best she could, it wasn't the same as having an active first lady. Before that, the Lincoln White House had been a sober place, understaffed and struggling to control the overcrowded receptions. Not only did Mary Todd Lincoln suffer her own share of physical and emotional problems,

including a deep grief over the death of their eleven-year-old son
Willie, but the White House in wartime was devoid of many nice-
ties. There had been no question of decorating.

In the early months of the administration, Julia took on the
job of restoring order, refinishing furniture, and replacing aged
carpets and wallpaper. In particular, she was disgusted by the
disarray of the front reception area, which had become a catch-
all resting place for various messengers and workmen, who also
smoked their pipes and heated up their lunches there. It created
a stinking, messy first impression to anyone who entered. Julia
ordered an immediate change. No longer would eating or smoking be allowed there, and ushers were to wear suits and white
gloves.

It took a while for the White House staff to settle in and get
used to a Grant administration. Crook, who would stay on as
Grant's bodyguard, recalled that everyone was very nervous at
first. There was such acrimony between Johnson and Grant that
the staff wondered if they'd all be fired. The public seemed to
favor the idea of a clean sweep and inundated the White House
with brooms inscribed with the message, "Make a clean sweep."
But the Grants kept the staff on.

The staff especially loved the way Julia took charge. "Her
interest in her domestic household was not a perfunctory one,"
Crook recalled. "She had a motherly sort of feeling of responsibility in the welfare of her dependents. Any morning her stout,
comfortable figure might have been seen making the rounds of
kitchens and pantries, and stopping to hold little colloquies with
maids or men."

The woman who a few years earlier had been so pampered and
incapable of running her own household that she mourned the
emancipation of her slaves now was masterful in running the nation's house. Her warmth filled the place, and her husband's did

too. The staff was witnessing a very different mood—a happiness and a calm. None recalled ever seeing the president lose his temper. "It warmed us all like a glowing fire," Crook wrote.

Much of this more serene atmosphere was undoubtedly due to the pure devotion of the Grants, which was as strong as it had been the day they were married. They always reserved time in the day to be attentive to one another, and it was a rare occasion when they didn't eat meals together. Every morning Grant would wait for his wife, and they would descend the stairs together, smiling and chatting.

Two of their four children came with them to the White House. Fred was at West Point and Buck at Phillips Exeter Academy in New Hampshire. The two youngest, Nellie, thirteen, and Jesse, eleven, lived in the White House. For Jesse, young enough to fully enjoy the sprawling grounds, the experience was magical. The property was wide open for exploration, and he suddenly had a great group of friends who shared the fun. "The White House lot was our playground in good weather, and the big, airy basement, or ground floor, was reserved for rain or storm," he wrote. He added that he didn't think his new position had anything to do with his burgeoning popularity.

The Grants adored their children and suffered greatly when they were absent. Near or far, the little family was a cohesive unit, bound tightly by love, shared experience, and a sense of us-against-the-world that had always been with them. Nellie and Jesse, the acknowledged favorites, were allowed to do much as they pleased. When Nellie begged to come home after two days at boarding school, her parents complied, as they later did with Jesse. Nothing mattered so much as being together. As Mary Clemmer Ames wrote of her impressions then, "the house is brightened by ever-blooming flowers, and the presence of happy children." They regularly took the evening meal together as a family, and Grant playfully rolled bits of bread into little balls and tossed them at the children, to their great delight.

The older generation was represented in the White House as well. Julia's father, who had lived with them off and on since her mother died, moved in with them when Grant became president. Colonel Dent's presence was sometimes awkward, given his pro-Confederacy leanings, though Grant chose to forget his father-in-law's murderous fury when he'd signed up with the Union Army. At that time Colonel Dent had sworn that if Grant ever stepped foot on his land, he would shoot him. Since the war, the old man had softened his attitude toward his son-in-law, but he had not abandoned his fiercely held principles, including his support for the secessionist South. Garland called him "old, gray, irascible, and unreconstructed." At dinner he would sometimes make comments that raised eyebrows, but the family chose to treat him as a doddering relic from another era and paid little attention to his ramblings. He was actually quite happy living in the White House during his final years, although there were occasional fireworks when his true opinions slipped out.

The most comical episodes occurred when Grant's father paid a visit. The two fathers were drastically different in their philosophies, but that was beside the point of their true conflict—determining which of them was more fit. Young Jesse would often hear Grandfather Dent tell his mother, "You should take better care of that old gentleman, Julia"—meaning Grant's father. "He is feeble and deaf as a post, and yet you permit him to wander all over Washington. It is not safe."

Grandfather Grant would overhear this remark, in spite of his alleged deafness, and say to his grandson, "Did you hear him, Jesse? I hope I shall not live to become as old and infirm as your Grandfather Dent."

After a long social drought, Washington was beginning to

sparkle under the bright supervision of a first lady who relished the role. The Grants loved to entertain and to throw open the doors of the people's house. And while the taste of glamour was welcome, the public also appreciated having what seemed like a normal happy family living there. There were no airs or pretenses about the Grants, and no drama—just a family who mirrored the behaviors of ordinary citizens. Growing portly in civilian life, Grant was still physically active, taking daily walks around the area. The neighbors grew accustomed to seeing the president strolling briskly down the road after breakfast or in the evening, puffing on his cigar.

Sometimes in the afternoons he would mount his horse and go for a long ride. Three of his favorite warhorses, Cincinnati, Jeff Davis, and Egypt, lived in the White House stables. A stable hand reported that Jeff Davis was a particularly unruly horse who kicked and bit. All the stable hands were afraid of him. Only Grant could soothe him, stroking him and calming his restlessness.

The White House was surprisingly open given the ever-present dangers of the time. "A correspondent from the Old World was surprised to find the Capitol grounds unguarded, the gates unlocked, and the ruler of the nation dwelling in an open palace, as if the United States were peopled with none but honest men and friends," Garland wrote. Supplicants of all stripes could arrive on reception days and be ushered in to see the president or be greeted by Julia or one of the senators' wives she'd enlisted to help her.

Mary Clemmer Ames painted a vivid picture of Julia's receptions that elevates the president by association:

> Mrs. Grant's morning receptions are very popular, and deservedly so. This is not because the lady is in any sense a conversationalist, or has a fine tact in receiving, but rather, I think,

because she is thoroughly good-natured, and for the time, at least, makes other people feel the same . . . one of the pleasantest facts of these morning receptions [is] the informal coming down of the President to receive with Mrs. Grant. I have never been accused of over enthusiasm for him, but find myself ready to forgive in him the traits which I cannot like, when I see him, with his daughter, beside Mrs. Grant. *Then*, it is so perfectly evident that, whatever the President may or may not be, "Mr. Grant" has a very true and likeable side, with which nobody is so well acquainted as Mrs. Grant.

Grant had been president for two months when he welcomed a surprising and consequential visitor to the White House. Robert E. Lee arrived to pay what he said was a courtesy call, and the media sprang into action with speculation and questionable accounts of the meeting, supposedly from those in the know. But it truly *was* a courtesy call, lasting no more than fifteen minutes. Stiffly polite, Lee said little, and when Grant attempted a joke—in a conversation about railroads, he observed, "You and I, General, have had more to do with destroying railroads than building them"—Lee did not respond with even the barest hint of a smile. No doubt Grant was relieved when the strange meeting came to an end.

It didn't take long for Grant's anti-political persuasion to get him into trouble. Most records of Grant's presidency focus on the corruption of those associated with him—never Grant himself, but others who, because of his ignorance and negligence, were allowed to fester within his government. While these corruptions are not the focus of this book, they are instructive of the folly of Grant's indifference to the political life.

The instigating event of the first scandal involved his brother-in-law Abel Corbin, who had recently married Grant's sister Virginia, known as Jennie.

Two speculators, Jay Gould and James Fisk, hatched a plot to corner the gold market and profit from rising gold prices. Corbin, who was involved with the men, bragged that his association with the president through his wife could benefit them. In particular, Corbin boasted that he could convince the president to stay out of the gold market, which would leave the path clear for them to bid a higher price for gold.

At first, the effort was successful. Introduced to Grant by Corbin, Gould and Fisk convinced him that the sale of gold would be harmful to the economy, and particularly to Western farmers. Grant asked Secretary Boutwell to suspend gold sales. But just in time, Grant figured out the scheme and ordered the Treasury to release $4 million in gold. This wiped out Gould and Fisk, but also created panic on Wall Street—the first Black Friday.

Grant always claimed that his intentions were misunderstood in the whole episode. He told Julia that when he responded "all right" to the delivery of a letter from Corbin by a messenger, his intention was to dismiss the messenger, not approve the content of the letter. Yet his "all right" was taken as an acceptance of the plan. He also instructed Julia, who had a regular correspondence with his sister, to write to her as he dictated: "The General says, if you have any influence with your husband, tell him to have nothing to do with [Gould and Fisk]. If he does, he will be ruined, for come what may, he (your brother) will do his duty to the country, and the trusts in his keeping." She signed the letter "Sis."

This was Grant's first scandal. Others would follow. The incident betrayed a certain naivete on his part, and a penchant for choosing unreliable advisers. The inexperienced politician, Garland noted, was too trusting and subject to betrayal. He found himself "pitted against the keen, shrewd, practiced manipulators of public affairs.

"It was a time of speculation, of cupidity, and of corruption," Garland added. "The war being over, the people had turned their attention to making money, and the corruption that was in private life had . . . rotted official life. The administration shared the characteristics of the times."

Garland had an additional sharp observation about Grant's culpability: "In his desire to avoid politicians, he seemed likely to fall among thieves."

Two sentences in Grant's inaugural address slipped by almost without notice: "The proper treatment of the original occupants of this land—the Indians—is one deserving of careful study. I will favor any course toward them which tends to their civilization and ultimate citizenship."

The final two years of the Johnson administration had seen an escalating tribal war in the West that pitted the Sioux, Cheyenne, and Arapaho against the US Army. The trigger for the violence was a new gold rush in Montana and Wyoming, which had drawn floods of prospectors and miners to the area. They recklessly trampled across lands that had been set aside by treaty as hunting grounds for the tribes. In particular, outsiders trespassed on the Bozeman Trail, which was the most expedient route from Montana through Wyoming to the Oregon Trail. Rather than enforce the existing treaty, the Army built forts along the Bozeman Trail and then called upon the tribes to agree to a new treaty allowing gold miners and prospectors open passage.

Negotiating for the tribes at Fort Laramie in Wyoming (the site of the original treaty, which was now being broken), the dynamic leader Chief Red Cloud of the Oglala Sioux rejected the idea of a new treaty and demanded that the Army remove its forts from the Bozeman Trail. When the army refused, Red Cloud, who would become an icon of the tribes in war and peace, led them in a fight of nearly two years that was known as Red Cloud's War.

The first major battle of the war came in December 1866. It began with a series of minor attacks on protective forces at Fort Phil Kearney in northeastern Wyoming. These small ambushes were a setup for a devastating action on December 21, when Indians tricked Lieutenant Colonel William Fetterman and eighty soldiers into an ambush away from the fort.

The Indians attacked the soldiers with bows and arrows and then, drawing closer, clubbed them or drove them through with spears. Fetterman and his eighty men were killed, and in a final indignity, the Indians stripped and mutilated the bodies, as a warning to others of the horror that awaited them.

For the next year and into the spring of 1868, the Indians kept the Army on its heels, including another brutal attack on Fort Phil Kearney. Finally, the US government had had enough. In the spring of 1868, the government and Indians signed a second Fort Laramie Treaty, agreeing to end all passage on the Bozeman Trail and remove the forts in exchange for an end to the raids. It also handed over the Black Hills to the Sioux for peaceful settlement on what was considered sacred land. (Later, the United States would illegally take back much of the land in the Black Hills when gold was discovered there. The Sioux Nation is still fighting that battle today.)

As Grant came into office, elements of the new treaty were already beginning to break down. Red Cloud and others argued that some of the language in the treaty was deceptive and seemed more designed to corral and subdue the tribes than to ensure their rights. More than any other president, Grant was actually sympathetic to the Indians' plight and was willing to consider their perspective.

His encounter with Native Americans during his Army sojourn at Fort Vancouver in the 1850s had made a tremendous impression on him. There he witnessed the peacefulness of the tribes and their loving attention to family. When Julia wrote to him of her fear that he'd be assaulted, he'd responded, "Those about here are the most harmless people you ever saw . . . the whole race would be harmless and peaceable if they were not put upon by the whites."

Now he was in a position to do something about it. Grant turned to Ely Parker, the Seneca Indian who had been with him at Appomattox, serving as his military secretary, and asked him to serve as commissioner of the Bureau of Indian Affairs.

Parker's appointment was incredibly meaningful to his people. As his great-nephew Arthur Casswell Parker wrote in a biography of his ancestor, "For the first time there was an Indian Commissioner of Indian Affairs, and needless to say *that* Commissioner loved his people, and they trusted him and looked to him with hope. It was the first faint hope of permanent self-government, freedom, and a new day of life."

Grant and Parker organized a coalition of Christians, led by Quakers whose commitment to peace made them effective intermediaries. Representatives of the major Protestant churches nominated board members. Grant also made inroads with the Jewish community when he appointed Dr. Herman Bendell, a Jewish war surgeon, as superintendent of Indian affairs for the Arizona Territory.

Grant knew he had set in motion a project of a grand scale. More than three hundred thousand Indians lived in the nation, and past treaties had failed to bring them into peaceful coexistence with white settlers and travelers. Grant believed strongly that the United States owed the native members of the nation a fair and peaceful settlement, but his view was derided by the propagandists who talked of Indians scalping innocent white women and children. Grant had problems with his own military leaders, who thought that the solution to the "Indian problem" was either the complete subservience of the tribes or their slaughter.

Grant steadfastly maintained that many of the complaints of Indians were justified and that the violence was usually triggered by indignities from the white population. Addressing Congress in 1869, Grant warned that "a system which looks to the extinction of a race is too horrible for a nation to adopt without entailing upon itself the wrath of all Christendom."

Grant's advocacy, with Parker by his side, undoubtedly eased the tensions with Chief Red Cloud, who accepted an invitation to dine at the White House in June 1870. But Red Cloud wasn't there just to hobnob with the elites. During his visit he confronted Secretary of the Interior Jacob Cox, telling him that the treaty signed in 1868 was "all lies. . . . We have been driven far enough; we want what we ask for."

After leaving Washington, Red Cloud traveled to New York, where he addressed a packed crowd at the Cooper Union on June 16. He electrified the audience with his heartfelt words:

> I am poor and naked, but I am the Chief of a Nation. We do not want riches, but we do want to train our children right. Riches would do us no good. We could not take them with us to the other world. We do not want riches. We want peace and love.

Red Cloud challenged the system of treaties made and then broken without a second thought. He told the audience that the treaties were misleading and poorly understood. The Indians needed help getting what was rightfully theirs.

Grant tried to be an honest broker, and he continued to meet with Red Cloud throughout his presidency. But he failed to understand that what he regarded as kindhearted—an opportunity for Indians to forgo their nomadic hunting lifestyle and settle on reservations where they could farm and be protected by the federal government—the Indians viewed as a desecration of their culture and their very identity. Two years in, Grant's Peace Policy collapsed as tribes such as the Sioux were vowing to fight efforts to force them onto reservations.

Grant encountered blowback from Congress as well, but his own Board of Indian Commissioners, a patronage-heavy committee of fat cats who challenged every plan and had little use for Parker, was his ultimate downfall. They were like foxes in the henhouse, and they insisted that a firmer hand was needed with the Indian tribes. They thought that only by stamping out tribal identities and customs could a peaceful coexistence be established.

The commission's chairman, William Welsh, was particularly hostile, challenging Parker's credibility and calling him "one who is but a remove from barbarism." Welsh was also horrified that Parker had married a white woman, and that Grant himself had given the bride away.

Welsh orchestrated a plot against Parker, accusing him of defrauding his own people by stealing funds meant for them. A trial was held, and although Parker was exonerated, he was forced to resign. "In the end General Parker was found without a stain, but his heart was broken," his great-nephew wrote.

In addition to the loss of his mission, Parker's relationship with Grant never recovered. Without Parker by his side, Grant was left with a toothless policy that lacked the inspiring, hopeful spirit he and Parker had ushered in. Although Grant was defended in some circles for the humane considerations that motivated his Indian policy, a fair review shows that under his policy peace was attained almost entirely at the expense of the Indians—their culture, their way of life, their property, and their chosen work. The message came through loud and clear: *We'll accept you only if you become like us.*

These were big, defining issues that demonstrated an American identity still fragile and unformed. For good or ill, Ulysses Grant was the president placed by fate at the heart of these trials. And the biggest one would always be Reconstruction. No matter what issues and controversies vied for attention during Grant's presidency, Reconstruction was at the center. It was the unfinished business of the general's life—the reason he became president. Deep down Grant understood that winning the war would have meaning only if the peace was won as well.

CHAPTER 9

THE BATTLEGROUND OF
RECONSTRUCTION

Since the end of the war, Grant had focused on a dual mission, neither of which aims would happen automatically: bringing the people of the South back into happy union with the rest of the nation and ensuring that the once-enslaved Blacks had an equal part in that society. The bloodshed was too recent for goodwill, and the mixed messages delivered from the North did not give Southerners much confidence. Grant later explained, "The people who had been in rebellion must necessarily come back into the Union and be incorporated as an integral part of the nation. Naturally the nearer they were placed to an equality with the people who had not rebelled, the more reconciled they would feel with their old antagonisms, and the better citizens they would be from the beginning. They surely would not make good citizens if they felt they had a yoke around their necks."

Yet here was the dilemma. Without the yoke, millions of Blacks might be open targets for abuse. The laws protecting them were being ignored in many Southern communities, and it was far too early to fully believe in the new world they'd imagined. As Grant took office four years into an uneasy peace, some hard truths were emerging. "Appomattox signified much but settled little," William Gillette concluded in his seminal analysis of Reconstruction. "The war had reduced the South to rubble and ashes, had destroyed the old regime and discredited its ways, but the martial triumph had succeeded only in preventing disunion. . . . The war had decided vital matters with negative decisions: secession and slavery were closed questions but victory was posing new ones." Gillette pointed out that the way the North would execute the peace and how people from both sides would deal with each other and with the recently freed slaves was left unsettled. In the vacuum, many in the South wrote their own rules. Johnson's disinterest in acknowledging the truths about the Confederacy had wasted any momentum that might have existed after the war.

Sometimes Grant found himself wondering whether Black emancipation was even possible in the Southern United States. Centuries of slavery had hardened the roles and confirmed the biases, so that not even the protective new laws and constitutional amendments could penetrate them. When Grant now contemplated the surrender of the South at the end of the war, he recognized what he had not fully appreciated then—that the Confederacy had been beaten but it had not been bowed. In surrender, General Lee would admit only that Grant's army had superior numbers and firepower. There was no mention of regrets, no acknowledgment of wrongdoing in making war on the United States. In the years since, there had been no self-examination or recrimination in the South—only disappointment, a brewing resentment, and an impatience to return to "normal."

Entering the White House after four years of civil rights backsliding under Johnson, Grant had looked for ways to advance the cause of equality. He felt an urgency to get things moving, and this was in part responsible for his ill-fated idea to annex a Caribbean island and make it a new home for African Americans. Grant set his sights on the island of Santo Domingo (today's Dominican Republic) and began investigating whether it might be advantageous to annex it. He strongly believed that the island could produce many economic benefits for the United States, and as a bonus the Black nation might be a welcoming place for disenfranchised Southern Blacks. Santo Domingo, he said, would be a home where Blacks could express their American citizenry among their own people and thus avoid the brutalities of the South.

To sell the idea to Congress, he had started with Charles Sumner, the chairman of the Senate Committee on Foreign Affairs. The prickly senator had seemed to build his career on conflicts with presidents, and he had a particularly skeptical view of Grant, whom he discounted as unprepared and unsuited for high office. For his part, Grant found Sumner almost unbearably pompous. Told that Sumner didn't believe in the Bible, Grant quipped, "I suppose not. He didn't write it." Grant considered Sumner something of a hypocrite, noting that his high-minded posturing didn't preclude his seeking patronage appointments for his friends. Nevertheless, Grant understood the power Sumner had, and he knew he'd have to convince him if there was any chance of the Santo Domingo plan working.

Eager to share his idea, Grant walked across Lafayette Square to Sumner's home on the evening of New Year's Day 1870. He was not expected. Sumner, who was dining with the journalist Benjamin Perley Poore and the secretary of the Senate, John Forney, invited Grant in. The president sat down and began expounding on his plan. He pleaded for Sumner's support.

After hearing Grant out, Sumner gave a noncommittal reply, just positive enough to convince Grant that he'd favor the treaty. Grant was encouraged by Sumner's parting words that evening:

"Mr. President, I am an administration man, and whatever you do will always find in me the most careful and candid consideration." This is Grant's version of what he said. Sumner's exact wording is subject to some dispute. Whatever Sumner actually said, Grant heard a stamp of approval that Sumner never intended to give. Confident in Sumner's support, Grant sent the treaty to the Senate.

Secretary of State Fish, who was managing the matter from the State Department, saw the handwriting on the wall well before Grant realized that his plan was doomed. Fish did not credit Congress with having legitimate questions about the plan's validity. Rather, he complained that Congress had gotten into the habit under President Johnson of being antagonistic to the executive branch, and Grant was suffering from yet another legislative power play. That defensive posture ignored real questions about the plan's viability.

Throwing himself into a lobbying effort, Grant stalked the halls of Congress, buttonholing senators. It was to no avail. Sumner spewed his customary fire in the Senate. He was appalled at what he deemed an attempt by a powerful white nation to take control of an island nation of Blacks. "We are called to consider commercial, financial, material advantages, and not one word is lisped of justice or humanity," he raved. "What are these, if right and humanity are sacrificed?" Although Frederick Douglass supported Grant's plan, Sumner managed to turn people against it.

The more the public heard about the proposed annexation, the less they liked it. The United States was a big country, full of undeveloped land and presumably great opportunity. The idea of sending disaffected Blacks to a turbulent island nation—even if that nation were annexed—seemed ludicrous. What better example of America's failure to solve its race problems? When the Senate vote was cast in June 1870, only twenty-eight senators voted yes. The final count was twenty votes short of the number needed.

It was a sad episode. The toil of war and the struggle to rebuild were centered on the proposition that America should fulfill its foundational standard that all men are created equal. To say that vision was impossible in the South, that the country was so inhospitable to Blacks it was necessary to create an offshore alternative, was a blow to the constitutional promise.

Failures aside, Grant kept his promise to push through the Fifteenth Amendment and cheered when it was ratified on February 3, 1870. In a major step toward Black equality, this constitutional mandate boldly pronounced their suffrage in the plainest possible terms:

> The right of citizens of the United States to vote shall not be denied or abridged by the United States or by any State on account of race, color, or previous condition of servitude.

The ratification received a one-hundred-gun salute and a parade in Washington. It wasn't enough. The intransigence of the South, the hankering for a restoration of the "Lost Cause," was in evidence. The death of Robert E. Lee on September 28, after he suffered a stroke, brought those feelings to the surface. The South mourned its hero, who had retired to a quiet existence as president of Washington College. In death, the former Confederacy lovingly restored him to his pedestal.

A new rebellion was happening in secret. Some Southern men returned from war with roiling psyches, bursting with anger, resentment, frustration, and a thirst for revenge. Some were farmers, others the sons of privilege, but in many respects they shared a common plight. With commerce temporarily in shambles, they had room to let the unhealthy spirits rise to the surface. They believed that the Black freedmen were poised to rob them of their land, their safety, and their majority. A few of them gathered one evening in 1865 in the small town of Pulaski, Tennessee, and decided to form a club. Its name, drawn from the Greek *kuklos*, meaning a "band" or a "circle," would be Ku Klux, completing the alliteration with Klan.

They decided that they would be a secret society. They wore costumes as disguises—not yet the white robes and hoods of the twentieth-century iteration, but face masks, animal horns, and elaborate body paint.

At first the KKK was just a bunch of Confederate veterans licking their wounds and making noise. But it soon became emboldened as a vigilante organization and spread rapidly throughout the South. Its members were from all social classes and educational levels, and some were public officials. Their cause was white power. Hoping to regain a semblance of the influence lost in war, the KKK terrorized Southern Blacks and their white defenders. KKK members burned down Black churches, schools, and meeting halls as fast as they could be erected. Unlucky individuals caught in the KKK's net were beaten. Lynchings served as a warning to Blacks to mind their place.

The KKK became even more active during the 1868 election, when the threat of the Black vote shifted its goals to politics. Political activism greatly increased Klan numbers and spread. Grant's slogan in the election was "Let us have peace," but in large pockets of the South there was anything but peace. Intimidation, assault, and even murder blocked Blacks' access to the polls.

In this climate, the ratification of the Fifteenth Amendment made little difference in quelling the violence. In Washington, Grant sought to increase the legal arsenal against the terrorism. Attorney General Hoar had been at best indifferent to Black rights, and when Grant forced him out of office in November 1870, the office turned toward seeking justice. The new AG, Georgia state attorney Amos T. Akerman, was a fierce advocate for civil rights, and with the creation of the Department of Justice he had greater resources at his disposal.

But Grant wanted the power to use a military solution—to send the Army after the Klan. In this context, murder and assault would be elevated above state crimes to become federal crimes. It was a controversial idea. On March 23, 1871, Grant made a personal appeal on Capitol Hill, hoping to sway Congress. After he received a skeptical response from Republicans, he sat down and wrote a message:

> A condition of affairs now exists in some of the states of the Union rendering life and property insecure, and the carrying of the mails, and the collection of the revenues dangerous. The proof that such a condition of affairs exists in some localities is now before the Senate. That the power to correct those evils is beyond the control of State authorities, I do not doubt. That the power of the Executive of the United States, acting within the limits of existing laws, is sufficient for present emergencies, is not clear.

Grant's inclusion of a threat to mail delivery and the collection of tax revenue was a clever ploy, meant to appeal to those who might not be swayed by injury to Blacks. And the appeal worked. In April, Congress passed "An Act to Enforce the Provisions of the Fourteenth Amendment," known as the Ku Klux Klan Act. Grant instantly signed it into law. This bill gave the federal government the power to intervene, and Grant sent troops to disperse the Klan.

It was, of course, controversial. Even some Republicans who had been the most passionate about Black civil rights suddenly turned on Grant, decrying his alleged abuse of states' rights. Perhaps they'd grown weary of the fight and were throwing up their hands. Perhaps they'd stopped believing that it was possible to quell the anti-Black sentiment in the South and were just hoping to keep things as calm as possible without military interference.

Resistance didn't matter to Grant. Although he was precluded from pursuing a massive campaign across the South, he decided to target a particular area where the Klan was especially rampant, hoping to create an example. He asked General Alfred H. Terry, Commander of the South, to suggest such a location, and Terry named the northwest counties of South Carolina. As Mark Bradley explains in *The Army and Reconstruction*, two incidents in that area made it the right target. One was an October 1870 riot at Laurens that left several hundred Blacks wounded. The second was a January 1871 lynching by night riders of eight Black militiamen at Unionville.

Grant appointed Army Major Lewis Merrill to conduct an investigation. Merrill, who had served bravely in the war, had been appointed to command in York County, South Carolina. His survey of northwest South Carolina yielded shocking details of the extent of Klan activity—what he called "a carnival of crime not paralleled in the history of any civilized community." Merrill found that in the northwest counties about three-fourths of white men were Klan members. They included some law enforcement officers and at least one judge. The local judiciary would not convict night riders when they were indicted for crimes.

Grant was moved by Merrill's report, and he sent AG Akerman to confer with him and bring back his judgment. Akerman encouraged action, and Grant moved swiftly to issue a proclamation, targeting nine northwestern counties. Those involved were ordered to disperse and surrender their weapons. A second order suspended the writ of habeas corpus, a protection against unlawful imprisonment, opening the way for arrests to be made.

With one thousand federal troops in position, under the direction of Merrill, the action began. Merrill's troops arrested some six hundred KKK suspects in the first month alone. However, three months in, few of them had been convicted and sentenced in the district courts. The federal infrastructure was not up to the task. Anguishing about the failure, Merrill recounted, "The machinery for the execution of these [laws] . . . is wholly inadequate to the task. The United States courts are choked with a quantity of business which amounts practically to a denial of a hearing of four-fifths of the cases."

The subsequent trials, when they occurred at all, yielded few convictions. In many cases, disguises made it impossible to identify perpetrators. However, the federal government's unrelenting effort was a signal to the Klan that the nation would use every legal avenue to halt its activity. By 1872, Grant's act had effectively ended the KKK, at least for the time being. It would reconstitute itself forty-three years later, in 1915, like a hardy weed springing to life from a barren ideology.

However, from the standpoint of Blacks it mattered little whether the official KKK was active or not. Violence found them in other ways. Bold new white militias were forming in every state.

By some measures, early Reconstruction efforts were successful. Within two years of Grant taking office, eleven seceded states had returned to the Union, reestablishing their representation in Congress. But the occupation of troubled areas by government forces created a lot of bad blood. Southerners felt *invaded*, abused. When would the government consider *their* rights? They felt justified for being angry, even violent. They had been robbed of their power, their land, their autonomy. Their anger was increasingly incendiary.

Grant didn't see it that way. He was an avid supporter of states' rights and believed that the federal government should allow states their freedom of governance. However, violence against Blacks forced his hand.

At times it seemed to Grant that the South was just trying to wear him down, to wait out the public support for Reconstruction, while gnawing away at its foundations in its towns and villages, outside the public eye. Blacks lived in fear across the South, and they heard often enough to believe it that slavery would be restored one day.

The deeper, mostly unexamined issue was the way the nation as a whole, both North and South, was going to regard the African American citizens. Even in the North, it was a sad and barely noted fact that Blacks were not always welcome in ordinary society. Benjamin Perley Poore wrote poignantly of the Blacks who came by the thousands to the capital, seeking a new life in freedom.

> They knew little, but they dreamed much of what would be the result of the sudden and unprovided-for change in their condition. It was a leap in the dark, but they imagined it a leap from darkness into light—from a state of bondage into a glorious condition of freedom—and they naturally considered that they would be recipients of the blessings that such a change should produce.
>
> Alas! Alas! For the awakening from this delusion! They found themselves at last in Washington homeless and friendless. . . . No feast was offered them, they were invited to no hospitable homes. They found themselves strangers in a strange land, destitute and despised and pinched by hunger.

Although Blacks in the North suffered little of the abuse Blacks faced in the South, they were still locked out of positions of influence. Ironically, that normalcy was often more evident in the South as Blacks began to take their place in Congress, elected in districts with Black majorities. The first Black man to be elected to the US House of Representatives was Joseph Rainey, in 1870, representing the First District in South Carolina. Others followed, including several more from South Carolina and representatives from Georgia, Alabama, Florida, North Carolina, and Mississippi. For a short time, there was a sense that the large population of Southern Blacks would justly take their places among the governing class and Congress would look more like the nation. This promise would not survive the end of Reconstruction.

Hiram Rhodes Revels became the first Black man elected to the US Senate in 1870, representing Mississippi. A second Black senator, Blanche K. Bruce, was elected in 1875. He would be the last Black elected to the Senate until 1967, when Edward Brooke of Massachusetts was elected. (To date, only eleven Black men and women have served in the US Senate.)

Approaching the 1872 reelection campaign, Grant's decisive action in the South had increased his popularity in some segments of the party while upsetting others. Even those liberals who might have agreed with him in principle despised his tactics. A week before the Republican convention, Senator Charles Sumner, a frequent critic, gave a four-hour speech, packed with accusations about Grant's corruption, greed, authoritarianism, and abuse of the Constitution. He concluded, "With sorrow unspeakable have I made this exposure of pretensions which for the sake of Republican institutions every good citizen should wish expunged from history, but had no alternative."

Liberal Republicans like Sumner, seeing no chance to defeat Grant from within, simply left the party temporarily and organized their own competing convention in Cincinnati. They nominated *New York Tribune* publisher Horace Greeley, a bullish figure somewhat past his prime. He advanced a position that had support in both parties to ease off the protections for Blacks and the restraints on Southern independence. Blacks had had their fill of government coddling, he claimed, and the states must regain their autonomy. Greeley called Grant's current policy "bayonet rules."

Who was Horace Greeley? Historian H. W. Brands captures Greeley's eclectic range: "He did have a record as a reformer, but it was a record that roamed widely across the landscape of American politics and culture, touching socialism, vegetarianism and spiritualism, in addition to such mundane causes as abolition and temperance." Brands didn't add that Greeley had once served as a congressman for three months.

It was a bizarre feature of the election that the Democrats chose not to nominate their own candidate, instead falling into line behind Greeley. So now Republicans were colluding with Democrats to end government interference in the South. The whole Republican split seemed unprincipled and inexplicable. By all measures, the liberal Republicans should have been behind Grant and in favor of his Reconstruction policies. Alignment with the Democrats seemed particularly fraught with peril. It could only be that antagonism to Grant, spurred on by men like Sumner, had overwhelmed all other considerations, so that many loyal Republicans found themselves voting against their principles. There might have been plenty to criticize in Grant's administration, but his pursuit of justice for Blacks and peace in a united nation could hardly be faulted by members of his party. And yet it was. Crook had a simple explanation for Sumner's agitation: "He was an idealist, who had grown into a chronic state of disgust with everything."

Sometimes Sumner could seem like a crackpot. Such was the case in his dispute with Grant over the British *Alabama* claims.

During the war, Britain had continued to do business with both sides of the American conflict, which meant lending commercial support to the Confederacy. Most egregiously, Britain had colluded with the Southerners to build a warship, the *Alabama*, which was used by the Confederacy. Once in office, Grant announced claims against Britain for the harm the *Alabama* had caused the Union. While Grant's intention was to make a point, largely symbolic, Sumner interjected an outrageous demand. He stated that the damage was so great that Britain should pay $2 billion and cede Canada to the United States as compensation. Grant ignored him, and a more fitting price of $15 million was negotiated.

As usual, Grant did not personally participate in the campaign. Even though an entire block of his party had abandoned him, he was not troubled by any doubt. This worried his friend George Childs, the publisher of the *Philadelphia Public Ledger*, who thought Grant was taking the result for granted, although his presidency was in jeopardy. Childs traveled to the White House and shared his worries with Grant.

Grant responded by producing a map of the United States. Unfolding it on a table, he began to mark each state: "We will carry this state, that state, that state," and so on, Childs recalled. "When the election came, the result was that Grant carried every state that he had said he would."

On election day, Grant won by a landslide, with an electoral vote advantage of 286 to 66. The election turned out to be a last stand for Greeley. Beset by exhaustion, illness, and despair, Greeley died on November 29. His meager electoral votes had not yet been officially cast.

Grant came to New York City to lead Greeley's funeral procession, bringing his cabinet along. He was honoring the man whose national contribution had been much larger than his last act—a generosity of spirit that was typical for Grant. Not everyone was so kind. Poore wrote, "Greeley's Presidential campaign would have been a farce had not his untimely death made it a tragedy." Crook surmised that Greeley's campaign was such a disaster that "he was killed by ridicule." Yet the crowds came out to honor Greeley. In death he was restored to his dignity as the champion of democracy and freedom—a larger-than-life figure in the American press.

Inauguration day on March 4, 1873, was a harbinger to a painful year. It was blisteringly cold: the temperature during the noon ceremony was 16 degrees, with brutal wind gusts adding to the suffering. The large crowds that turned out huddled against the bitter wind, and a parade before the ceremony left many military cadets suffering frostbite. Fred Grant, down from West Point, was sent to his bed with a chill afterward.

Once again, Chief Justice Chase administered the oath of office. Grant placed a hand on the Bible, opened to Isaiah, chapter 11:

> And the spirit of the Lord shall rest upon him, the spirit of wisdom and understanding, the spirit of counsel and might, the spirit of knowledge and the fear of the Lord.

He looked much older than his years. His heft had aged him, as did the weight of the office. He reaffirmed his commitment to Black civil rights:

> The effects of the late civil strife have been to free the slave and make him a citizen. Yet he is not possessed of the civil rights which citizenship should carry with it. This is wrong, and should be corrected. To this correction, I stand committed, so far as Executive influence can avail.

At the end, he could not resist speaking from the depths of his injured pride in a way that didn't really sound like himself. He spoke of the great responsibility he'd carried, having had no respite from the moment Fort Sumter was fired upon in April 1861—and how he'd had little in the way of gratitude as compensation.

> I performed a conscientious duty, without asking promotion or command, and without a revengeful feeling toward any section or individual.
>
> Notwithstanding this, throughout the war, and from my candidacy for my present office in 1868 to the close of the last Presidential campaign, I have been the subject of abuse and slander scarcely ever equaled in political history, which to-day I feel that I can afford to disregard in view of your verdict, which I gratefully accept as my vindication.

On that sour note, Grant's second term commenced. That evening, in a makeshift facility that was mostly unheated, Grant's second inaugural ball took place. Most of the attendees remained bundled in heavy coats throughout the celebration.

Soon after Grant began his second term, violence in Louisiana forced him to send federal troops to settle an election dispute. The ongoing debate about who won the governor's race was tearing the state apart.

The 1872 race had served as a warning that the Reconstruction peace was not holding in the South. The election between Republican William Pitt Kellogg, a carpetbagger senator who had resigned from the Senate to seek the governor's office, and the Democrat John F. McEnery, a Louisiana lawyer and political figure, was contentious, and it ended in uncertainty. McEnery claimed victory, citing thousands more votes. Kellogg declared the votes fraudulent. For a time there was a standoff, with two self-anointed governors and two self-anointed legislatures. Kellogg, the "winner," had the support of Grant and the Army, while McEnery, protected by the newly organized militia of the White League, refused to concede. In the end, the Republican judiciary declared the election for Kellogg, a result that seemed fraudulent to most Democrats. (It might have been. On the other hand, there was plenty of shady vote counting on both sides.) Grant ordered federal troops to Louisiana to enforce the order.

Many Louisiana whites were outraged at the idea that this election would be stolen from them by Kellogg, who, though he'd served as their senator, was viewed with suspicion as an outsider who didn't understand or respect the people he served. They refused to accept the result. Hopelessly embittered, they believed that no matter what they did, the Reconstruction Republicans always won.

That rage boiled over. There were repeated physical challenges to Kellogg's legitimacy. And then the worst happened. On April 13, Easter Sunday, a white paramilitary group, numbering in the hundreds, attacked a Black militia that was protecting Kellogg's control over the Grant Parish Courthouse. The Blacks were overwhelmed by the assault, and in an hour of fighting most of them were driven back into nearby fields. As they fled, white militia members on horseback chased them and shot them in cold blood. At the end of the assault, at least sixty Blacks were dead and forty others were captured by the paramilitary. That night the prisoners were taken to a field and executed.

Grant invoked the Enforcement Act—popularly known as the Ku Klux Klan Act—which allows the president to send military and federalized National Guard forces to states in limited instances when there are severe civil disturbances or insurrection. (This same act was applied nearly a century later by presidents Eisenhower and Kennedy to enforce desegregation in the South.)

Federal prosecutors brought charges against the insurrection-
ists, to little effect. There was a trial, and three of them were
convicted of conspiracy (not murder), but the judge dismissed
the indictments, declaring the Enforcement Act unconstitutional.
The Supreme Court ultimately agreed, ruling that the Enforcement Act applied only to state behavior, not to private conspira-
cies. As a result, white militias in the states grew stronger, with
the tacit backing of the Constitution.

The hard reality on the ground was that the nation—and not
just the South—was growing tired of Reconstruction. Even many
Republicans found the carpetbagger regimes in Southern states
unseemly and untenable. The Louisiana intervention was a debacle, yet the violence could not be tolerated. Grant was seeing his
options shrinking.

Was this a harbinger of doom for Reconstruction? As Mark
Wahlgren Summers, author and professor of history at the University of Kentucky, put it bluntly: "Governments that could not
keep order without outside aid, states that chose governors in
twos, authorities dependent on force, technicality, and judicial
caprice—none of this fit the promise of Radical Reconstruction."

Grant's second term would be filled with trials, and he would
have to fight for every success. Almost immediately the financial
system collapsed. As he presided over the postwar boom years,
Grant had always been proud of the healthy economy. In particular, railroad expansion signaled the transformation of the nation. Money and human resources were pouring into the railroad
business, making it the largest nonfarm employer in the nation.
Banks were rushing to invest in railroads. But much of the investment in railroads was in paper money not backed by specie (gold).
Debt skyrocketed right along with the railroad boom, and banks
that couldn't raise the money began to fail. When Jay Cooke and
Company, the government's most heavily invested bank agent,

collapsed, the stock market fell and the Panic of 1873 ensued. The nation was driven into a major economic depression that would last for more than five years.

The sharp economic downturn further exacerbated the tensions in the South. Southerners complained that they felt constricted by Reconstruction rules, right at a time when they were suffering the most. Grant was frustrated as he saw the national mood continue to shift away from Reconstruction and back toward "normalcy." The Supreme Court was chipping away at the precious rights of Blacks, so hard-won, including a surprise assault on the Fourteenth Amendment.

The case at hand wasn't even about civil rights. It was about slaughterhouse regulations in New Orleans. Animal slaughter was a dirty business, and also a health crisis for the city. According to one graphic portrayal, when the Mississippi River was at low tide, "intestines and putrefied animal matter lodged [around the drinking pipes]." In 1869, after the city failed to regulate the industry, the Louisiana state legislature stepped in and passed a law to create a centralized slaughterhouse corporation to prevent the contamination of the water supply. The Butchers' Benevolent Association sued, and the case went all the way to the Supreme Court.

The plaintiffs argued that the regulations were a violation of the Fourteenth Amendment's due process, equal protection, and immunities clauses, which had been designed to protect Blacks and former slaves. In a five-to-four ruling, the Supreme Court decided against the butchers, but in the process decimated the scope of the Fourteenth Amendment. Writing for the majority, Justice Samuel F. Miller concluded that the Fourteenth Amendment was meant to apply to the "newly freed race" and the immunities clause applied only in matters related to national citizenship, not against state powers. By deferring to the states in matters of rights, the court crippled the ability of Blacks to seek redress from the courts.

Professor and historian Michael Ross speculates that the decision might have reflected the growing dissatisfaction with Reconstruction and served as a way to restore a semblance of white control to Southern communities. Justice Miller, he proposed, could have ruled against the butchers, stating that "the right to operate a slaughterhouse in the midst of a crowded city was not one of the fundamental rights protected by the amendment." By ruling more broadly, Justice Miller placed the civil rights of beleaguered Southern Blacks at risk. After Reconstruction, the slaughterhouse ruling was frequently used against Blacks who challenged state Jim Crow laws.

Against the gloomy backdrop of an economic slowdown and growing civil unrest in the South, the White House briefly took time off for a lavish celebration—the wedding of the Grants' only daughter, Nellie. As a high-spirited teenager in the White House, known to be something of a party girl, Nellie had been regularly featured on the society pages. When her parents sent her abroad as a maturing experience, she fell in love with a British sophisticate, Algernon Sartoris, who was a decade older and far more worldly than the young girl whose heart he captured.

Nellie brought Sartoris back to Washington, where he and Grant engaged in a very uncomfortable first meeting. Sartoris nervously asked for Nellie's hand. Grant balked. Nellie was only eighteen, far too young. But Nellie begged her father, who had never been able to deny her a single thing. He finally agreed.

The wedding on May 21, 1874—the seventh in the White House, the first being Dolley Madison's sister's in 1812—was an extravagant floral wonder that transformed the modest East

Room into a fragrant chapel. As "The Wedding March" played, Grant walked his daughter down the aisle and handed her over to Sartoris. She was glowing with youth and beauty, her elaborate gown trimmed in lace and purportedly costing thousands. Her brother Fred, in uniform, stood as best man.

The newspapers and magazines covered the event in force. Walt Whitman penned a poem, "A Kiss to the Bride," for the *New York Daily Graphic*: "O youth and health! O sweet Missouri rose! O bonny bride!"

The only one who seemed not to be enjoying himself was Grant. Knowing his daughter would soon be moving across the ocean for good, Grant struggled to control his surging emotions. Observers couldn't take their eyes off the president, who was clearly devastated. Jesse described his father as "silent, tense, with tears upon his cheeks that he made no movement to brush away." Later, during the reception, Grant disappeared and couldn't be located. An aide found him in his daughter's room, sobbing. (Perhaps he was prescient. Although they had four children, the Sartoris marriage was unhappy due to his drinking and womanizing. Nellie would divorce him many years later, after her father's death.)

Back in the political world, Republicans were struggling. The party limped into the 1874 midterms in a weakened position. For years Republicans had been beating the drum that the Democrats were the party of anti-Americanism, suppression of Black freedom, and economic collapse. Now the voters, disgruntled by their circumstances and hungry for change, were no longer willing to blindly follow the standard Republican campaign line.

Democrats launched what they called the Redeemer movement—a plan to regain the power they'd lost during Reconstruction. Redeemers were mostly former slave owners, many of them businessmen and landowners who had never accepted the end of slavery or the elevation of former slaves to equal status. In particular, they loathed the idea that Blacks should be equally represented at the polls and even serve in office. Their campaign of intimidation against Black voters had the clear purpose of sending Blacks back into subservience. Being "redeemed" meant being without federal interference.

Ironically, even while this was going on, savvy white politicians were also making appeals to Blacks, who were just as dissatisfied as everyone else with the poor economy and the sluggish pace of progress. Increasingly, Republicans were struggling to hold on to their base. The conflict was obvious in Congress. At one point, Blanche K. Bruce of Mississippi, the US Senate's only Black member, was chastised by one of his Republican colleagues, who reminded him to stand with the party and not to waver, saying, "We are your true friends." Bruce snapped back, calling him a Grant bootlicker. "Go and lick your master's boots," he said, "but don't call on me to do it."

Republican troubles were especially frustrating to Grant, because the problems in the South still demanded such urgent attention. In the weeks before the midterm election, there was a disturbing rise in voter intimidation in Louisiana. White rifle clubs were riding through the streets, looking menacing. Grant wasn't having it. Believing the threat of violence at the polls was real, he issued a presidential proclamation on September 15, 1874, making it entirely clear that the federal government had the authority to intervene:

Whereas it has been satisfactorily represented to me that turbulent and disorderly persons have combined together with force and arms to overthrow the State government of Louisiana and to resist the laws and constituted authorities of said State: and

Whereas it is provided in the Constitution of the United States that the United States shall protect every State in this Union, on application of the legislature, or of the executive when the legislature can not be convened, against domestic violence; and

Whereas it is provided in the laws of the United States that in all cases of insurrection in any State or of obstruction to the laws thereof it shall be lawful for the President of the United States, on application of the legislature of such State, or of the executive when the legislature can not be convened, to call forth the militia of any other State or States, or to employ such part of the land and naval forces as shall be judged necessary, for the purpose of suppressing such insurrection or causing the laws to be duly executed . . .

Grant's critics saw his actions as military overkill and accused him of behaving like a general at war rather than the president of a nation at peace. But Grant did not relish the idea of sending troops into the states. Far from it. He knew that doing so would increase his unpopularity and sow distrust in the South. He believed that the majority of Southern citizens were law-abiding and wanted to do the right thing. They were victimized by their violent brethren, just as so many Southerners had been victimized by the war that took place in their own backyards. At one point, in a churlish mood, Grant directed his frustration to the complaining Southerners. "You have had the most trying governments to live under; but can you proclaim yourselves entirely irresponsible for this condition?"

However, as long as there was violence, he had an obligation to act. The vote was sacred. It had to be protected.

On election day, the Republican postwar firewall was obliterated, with Democrats winning a healthy majority in the House and adding nine seats in the Senate. Many prophesied the end of Reconstruction, but that was something Grant wasn't willing to concede. He vowed that as long as the White House remained in Republican hands, the rights of Black Americans would be protected.

Grant had reason to boast about some accomplishments, particularly the passage of the Civil Rights Act in 1875. Introduced by Sumner back in 1870, the Civil Rights Act had been struggling to get through Congress ever since.

The act was radical for its time. It proposed that all public institutions, such as railroads, hotels, restaurants, churches, and schools, be available equally to Blacks. Such social equality, Sumner believed, was just as important as political rights. The Senate rejected Sumner's bill in 1870, and he continued to introduce it every year. "Again the barbarous tyranny stalks into this Chamber," he cried when it was voted down in 1872.

But then something dramatic happened to give the Civil Rights Act another chance. Sumner fell unexpectedly ill and was reported to have pleaded to a Senate colleague, from his deathbed, "Don't let the bill fail." Frederick Douglass received a similar plea when he visited Sumner. After Sumner died, on March 11, 1874, the Senate, "in respect to Sumner's memory," finally moved the bill, which Grant signed into law the following year.

That would have been a happy story for Sumner and Grant had not the Supreme Court declared the act unconstitutional in 1883. Eighty-one years would pass before a new civil rights bill would be passed, during Lyndon Johnson's administration.

Looking back, it's a shame that Grant and Sumner were often so bitterly at odds. Their clash was a matter of degrees, as Grant was a moderate; their ultimate goals were in sync. Grant's success in securing ratification for the Fifteenth Amendment should have solidified his stature. But his constant skirmishes with the liberal wing of his party weakened his presidency.

With all the trials of his second term and the accusations hurled against him, his enemies might have expected Grant to wither under the assault. But Crook saw no evidence of that. "Of course, his decline in popularity was evident to himself as to those by whom he was surrounded," Crook acknowledged. "But he took it all apparently as one of the fortunes of war. . . . During the worst of the attacks on him he never looked worn, as he did when I saw him during the battle of Petersburg. He believed in himself too much to be shaken by abuse."

But he knew his time in office was nearing its end. Grant was particularly contemplative on a summer visit to Long Branch, where he would ride his buggy alone down the miles of beach. When the Grants returned to Washington, the reason for his pensive mood was clear. The question of whether he would run for a third term had to be answered. Calling together his cabinet, Grant told them that he planned to inform the Republican Party chairman that he was not going to run again.

After the meeting, Grant sat down immediately and wrote a letter to the chairman, which he then personally took to the postbox. On return, he steeled himself to break the news to Julia. She didn't take it well and argued with him fiercely. Not only did she love being in the White House and want to continue, but she had a somewhat naive view of her husband's greatness and popularity.

Julia refused to take Grant's answer as final. Later, she tried to insinuate herself into the matter, taking charge of the letters that poured in from across the country urging him to run. When Grant found out how involved she was with this correspondence, he chastised her. "You ought not have done that . . . Mrs. Grant, I think you are a—what shall I call you—mischief!" He made it clear that he would not change his mind, and she would have to accept it.

The centennial year of the American Republic began with the customary New Year's ritual at the Grant White House. They opened it up to the public, and people flooded in to gawk at the pretty rooms, perhaps catch a glimpse of the First Couple, and, if lucky, speak with them. All of the city's public officials—from cabinet members to court officials, congressmen and senators, and foreign ministers—arrived to pay their respects, but it was the common folks with their pleased and genuine greetings of "Happy New Year!" who gave the Grants the most pleasure.

It was a special occasion: 1876 marked the one-hundredth birthday of the nation, which had suffered so many growing pains. But it had also thrived in important ways. One hundred years had seen a nation prospering in spite of war, internal conflicts with the Native Americans, and economic calamities. Commerce was booming, sparked by technological advances that would once have been unimaginable—railroads swiftly connecting the far outposts, the telegraph transporting information in a flash, the cotton gin changing the economics of the plantation. In his annual message, Grant highlighted the advances of one hundred years and urged the country to continue its growth by recommending a constitutional amendment to provide free public schools for all citizens.

The Centennial Exposition of 1876—the nation's first World's Fair—opened at Fairmont Park in Philadelphia on May 10. This hundred-year celebration, which was spread over twenty-one and a half acres and would draw some nine million visitors to the seat of the country's beginnings, put the glory of America on full display. For an entrance fee of ten cents, visitors could marvel at new inventions such as the Corliss steam engine, Alexander Graham

Bell's telephone, and Remington's typographic machine (typewriter). The site was also crammed with food, entertainments, and other delights, with exhibits featuring the usual pleasures of American carnivals. Food exhibits introduced new delicacies, such as Hiram's root beer and Heinz catsup.

Grant was on hand to open the exhibition, but he was clearly distracted and unable to summon up great enthusiasm. His welcoming remarks fell short of a rave review: "Whilst proud of what we have done, we regret that we have not done more." In the *New York Sun* description, "he read sulkily." However, Grant's friend George Childs, with whom he was staying in Philadelphia, defended Grant's prose. "I have had a wide acquaintance among gifted men of letters, and yet I can say that General Grant is one of the most facile writers I have ever known. This address is certainly a dignified and polished piece of work, but the General composed it in about an hour as he sat at my desk, not long before the opening ceremonies of the Exhibition began."

Meanwhile, Grant's administration continued to be plagued by the scandalous deeds of its players. While no one ever suggested a hint of impropriety or greed on Grant's part, he was determinedly blind when it came to his friends and so got tarred with their actions. That was the case with a close aide involved in an illegal plot called "the Whiskey Ring," which was originally a campaign financing scheme that involved collusion with US Treasury agents to sell more whiskey than was reported for tax purposes. The excess tax proceeds went to a variety of players, including political campaigns.

The Whiskey Ring was quietly functioning undiscovered until 1874, when Grant appointed Benjamin Bristow as his new Treasury secretary, replacing William Richardson, who had resigned in scandal. Bristow was like a bloodhound going after corruption. Hearing rumors of the Whiskey Ring, which were circulating around

Washington, he began an investigation. Among other players, the investigation uncovered an inside fixer—Grant's personal aide Orville Babcock. In 1875, Babcock was indicted for engaging in a conspiracy to defraud the Treasury.

Babcock was so close to Grant that he was practically a member of the family. He lived in the White House and often joined the Grants for meals. He was Grant's chief gatekeeper outside his office. When Babcock was indicted, Grant simply didn't believe it. He took the rare step of agreeing to sit for a deposition, in which he firmly defended Babcock. As historian and archives specialist Timothy Rives wrote about it, "Grant's legendary photographic memory consistently failed him throughout most of the deposition, but it did not fail him when it came to Babcock. The President had no trouble remembering his aide's fidelity and efficiency nor in testifying to his universally good reputation among men of affairs." Babcock was acquitted—perhaps thanks to his loyal boss—but he was forced to resign.

If Babcock's Whiskey Ring was a pathetic episode, the tabloid-driven escapades of William Worth Belknap and the trading post scam had everything—sex, deceit, war profiteering, and even General Custer!

Belknap, a close Grant ally and former general who had assumed the position of secretary of War after Rawlins's death, was a colorful man about town, very different in manner than his friend Grant. Handsome and charming, he lived a lavish lifestyle with his beautiful wives—Cara, who died in 1862; his second wife, Carita, who died in 1870; and his third wife, Amanda, who was Carita's sister. The wives are important because at least the last two were involved in the scandal. In fact, according to some of Belknap's supporters, they had duped their hapless husband in order to enrich the family—a doubtful charge, as he had to wonder where all the extra money came from when he was making a modest cabinet salary of $8,000 a year.

Indian trading post rings were becoming a national scandal. These lucrative operations were much sought after, and their procurement involved fraud, price-gouging, and kickbacks. Belknap (or his wives) was said to be in on a trading post scam that involved a healthy amount of kickback money. The evidence against Belknap was so strong that it was clear he could not survive in his cabinet position. As talk of impeachment grew louder, Belknap chose to save himself the indignity by resigning.

Crook, who was present when Belknap left, described the defeated aide arriving at the president's office and announcing, "I have come to offer my resignation, Mr. President." Crook was struck by Belknap's anguish. "He was a fine, large man, with military carriage and a long patriarchal beard, which was considered a mark of distinction in those days," Cook wrote. "But now nobody could have helped feeling sorry for him. He looked heartbroken. The President met Belknap's eyes and there was pity in his; 'I am sorry, Belknap,' was all he said. But the two men shook hands."

Belknap's resignation did not save him from impeachment. In what would become a hot topic 145 years later, during the second impeachment trial of President Donald Trump in 2021, Congress chose to pursue its constitutional course, believing that, as the floor manager, Representative George Hoar, put it, "the effect of this decision will be that for a century to come there will not be in the history of this country a repetition by a Cabinet officer or other high official of such offenses."

Perhaps the high point of the trial was the testimony of the famed General Armstrong Custer himself, who testified that both Belknap and Grant's brother Orvil were involved in the trading post scams. Congress was dazzled to have the magnetic general in its midst, although most of his testimony was hearsay and did not withstand scrutiny.

Ultimately, the Senate vote fell short of the two-thirds needed to convict Belknap. The issue for many of those who voted "no" was one of jurisdiction. They believed it was improper for Congress to impeach a private citizen. (The same argument was instrumental in Trump's acquittal in 2021.)

Grant was furious with Custer for breaking a soldier's code of loyalty, but especially for hurling accusations against his brother. After Custer's testimony, Grant removed him from command. Only a desperate entreaty by Custer restored him to his place as head of the Seventh US Cavalry. He set off for the Little Bighorn in Montana that June to clear out the Lakota and Cheyenne tribes. The battle resulted in his death, along with the deaths of over 250 men. Known as "Custer's Last Stand," the battle burnished Custer's hero status but also exposed his reckless nature. He'd gone in believing he had something to prove, and the mission ended in tragedy.

The Belknap scandal cost Grant dearly in many ways. As Badeau, who knew him so well, wrote, "The greatest mistakes in his career, the greatest misfortunes of his life, came from his mischoice of friends."

PART FOUR

A GRAND
BARGAIN

CHAPTER 10

THE BITTER DIVIDE

As the election-year conventions approached, Grant felt no inner conflict about not seeking a third term. It was time for someone else to wrestle with the great demons of the era. It was time for someone else to try to summon the better angels. He was done, or so he thought. The late historian Dee Brown succinctly identified the reality of Grant's complicated reputation with the American people: "The truth is that Grant was a Hero, who happened to live in a myth-making age which could not tolerate human weaknesses in its idols." Even so, he would have one last critical role to play before he left office.

The 1876 election ushered onto the stage two men, innocuous in their lives, without controversy or scandal. They would be at the center of an election drama that threatened to bring down the nation. Their names were Rutherford B. Hayes and Samuel J. Tilden.

A man of his times, Rutherford Birchard Hayes was born in 1822, the same year as Grant, and like Grant, he found that his life and ambitions were defined by the Civil War. Until history tapped him on the shoulder in 1876, he had lived a life of both struggle and success. It got off to a rocky start in his Delaware, Ohio, birthplace. His father died while he was in the womb, and he was born a fatherless child. But Rud, as he was called, was fortunate in the way his loving family gathered round. He was especially close to his older sister Fanny, who was like a little mother to him; and to an uncle, his mother's younger brother, Sardis Birchard, who served as a guardian and male role model. Sardis made sure Rud got into Harvard Law School and was set up for a meaningful career—first as a lawyer and then as a public official.

Hayes was blessed with a long and happy marriage, which produced eight children, five of whom lived—four boys and a girl. He met Lucy Ware Webb while she was a student at Ohio Wesleyan in Hayes's hometown, and he was captivated by her spirited personality, her beauty, and her intellect. Lucy was also a devoted abolitionist. Her parents had been staunch antislavery activists. When her father, who was from Kentucky, inherited fifteen to twenty slaves, he vowed to free them. But he fell ill with cholera and died before he had a chance. Left penniless with three small children, Lucy's mother announced that she would go ahead and free the slaves anyway, vowing that before she would sell a slave, she'd take in washing to support her family. Prior to meeting Lucy, Hayes had been mostly indifferent to the cause of abolition. With her influence, he became more engaged in the issue, using his law practice to defend runaway slaves.

Hayes had no military experience, so when Lincoln sent out his call for volunteers at the beginning of the Civil War, it wasn't a natural choice for him to join up. But he thought it over and decided that he could not abide staying out of the fight. He told a friend, "I would prefer to go into it if I knew I was going to die than to live through and after it without taking any part in it."

He almost didn't survive the war. As a lieutenant colonel at the

Battle of South Mountain in Maryland on September 14, 1862, Hayes ordered his men of the Twenty-third Ohio into battle. Suddenly, he felt "a stunning blow." A musket ball had entered his arm just above the elbow. He described it in his diary:

> Fearing that an artery might be cut, I asked a soldier near me to tie my handkerchief above the wound. I soon felt weak, faint, and sick at the stomach. I laid down and was pretty comfortable. I was perhaps twenty feet behind the line of my men, and could form a pretty accurate notion of the way the fight was going. The enemy's fire was occasionally very heavy; balls passed near my face and hit the ground all around me. I could see wounded men staggering or carried to the rear; but I felt sure our men were holding their own. I listened anxiously to hear the approach of reinforcements; wondered they did not come.

At last, feeling abandoned, Hayes called to his men, "Hallo Twenty-third men. Are you going to leave your colonel here for the enemy?" Thus alerted, his men rescued Hayes from the field, and his brother-in-law, Dr. Joseph Webb, an army surgeon, treated his injury. At first, Webb didn't expect Hayes to live, but he recovered and returned to the battlefield in December.

In 1864, Hayes was still serving when friends from Cincinnati nominated him for a congressional seat. When they urged him to seek a furlough so he could return home to campaign, they received this indignant response: "An officer fit for duty who at this crisis would abandon his post to electioneer for a seat in Congress ought to be scalped. You may feel perfectly sure I shall do no such thing." His friends discovered that perhaps his reply was a more valuable campaign tool than his physical presence. They made sure the voters heard about it, and Hayes was elected. His term would start the following March, but he stayed with the Army until the war ended in April. His first session of Congress opened in December 1865. It was the contentious session that began after President Johnson had attempted to do an end run during the recess and restore seceded states. On the question of when and how the seceded states should be restored, Hayes stood squarely in the middle.

Hayes served until 1867, when he resigned to run for governor of Ohio. He won that election on a platform proposing an amendment to the Ohio constitution to give voting rights to African Americans. Though he won, the Democrats took the state legislature, where the amendment had no chance. However, in his second term Hayes proudly saw the Fifteenth Amendment ratified in Ohio.

In 1872, Hayes ran for Congress as a Grant supporter and lost. He briefly retired from politics until friends persuaded him to run for governor again in 1875, this time against a sitting Democrat. Almost as soon as he achieved a narrow victory and took office, people started talking about Hayes as a potential presidential contender.

In early 1876, Hayes wasn't at the top of anyone's list as a front-runner in the presidential election. He was one of those steady political figures—well regarded and reliable, but forgettable too. Once Grant had made it clear that he would not run, the safe money was on James Blaine, a Maine congressman and Speaker of the House. Blaine, whose nickname among his supporters was "the magnetic man," provided a charismatic contrast to Grant's subdued style. He'd been preparing for years to step into the highest office and had built a power base more impressive than that of any other contender.

However, it's a truism of politics that early front-runners are more vulnerable to slipping, and that's what happened to Blaine. As the nominating convention approached, rumors began to circulate about suspicious financial transactions involving railroads. Suddenly Blaine, who was preparing to accept the mantle of the party, was consumed with a congressional investigation.

Through sheer force of personality and political showmanship, Blaine survived the early investigation. But there were lingering questions. Many Republicans worried that the party couldn't afford to have yet another scandal hanging over it. Even if the allegations against Blaine were unwarranted, the scandal would have an impact. But a startling incident had a further impact on Blaine's suitability. The Sunday before the convention, as he was on his way into church, Blaine passed out, supposedly from the heat. He was carried away and was said to be in a dire condition. There were rumors that he might not survive. He recovered, but he was weakened as a candidate.

Suddenly, the other candidates for the nomination saw hope, and one of them was Hayes. He looked the part, handsome and dignified. He was everything Blaine was not—steady, statesman-like, and untainted by any hint of scandal. He was a heroic war veteran. (Blaine had never served.) And as governor of Ohio, he was the Cincinnati convention's favorite son. Hayes was one of those candidates who come along every so often who lack excitement but look perfect on paper. Such candidates are objectionable to few and seem to offer a little something for every supplicant. They often get mentioned as ideal vice presidential candidates, and that's where Hayes started as well: he had been talked up as a strong running mate for Blaine. But with Blaine's star looking tarnished, Hayes let it be known that he was only interested in the top spot.

The convention was the first since before the war that was totally up for grabs, and there was no lack of candidates throwing in their hats. Benjamin Bristow, Grant's Treasury secretary, who was on the verge of stepping down, was favored by reform-minded

Republicans who had appreciated his firm hand against corruption in the Grant administration. Other candidates were Indiana senator Oliver P. Morton and New York senator Roscoe Conkling. A couple of perfunctory candidates, such as Pennsylvania governor John Hartranft, scraped the bottom and stayed there.

Despite Blaine's clear lead, Grant favored Conkling, who had become a friend during the Johnson administration and had continued to be a reliable supporter during his administration. Conkling had been instrumental in the founding of the Republican Party in New York State back in the 1850s, and he stood behind Lincoln and later became a Radical Republican. Unfortunately, Conkling always left a whiff of corruption in his wake. Despite paying lip service to President Grant's talk of civil service reform, he was deeply embedded in New York machine politics and was a master of the patronage system. He could be personally outrageous in his manner and dress, and by 1876 Conkling was the antithesis of a reformer. Still, Grant felt he owed Conkling quiet allegiance.

However, Conkling was never in the top tier in the nominating process. Bristow was much more popular. Fresh from his takedown of the Whiskey Ring, he'd earned his stripes as a reformer. Morton, too, had a solid following, but he had some drawbacks. He represented the hearty Hoosier backing in Indiana. He was a leader of the Stalwarts, a centrist faction in the Republican Party, but was not well known nationally. It didn't help that Morton was in poor health.

When the convention opened June 14 at the Exposition Hall in the center of Cincinnati, there was tremendous excitement. A glowing sense of a new American century beckoned. Speakers ranged from Frederick Douglass to suffragist leader Sarah Spencer. However, many speeches and the platform itself preferred to reference past glories rather than future uncertainties, especially the biggest glory of all—winning the Civil War. The Democratic Party was rhetorically dispatched as the party of racial violence and questionable national loyalty.

The delegates soon grew restless with these pro forma speeches. They were eager for the main event—the balloting.

Three hundred and seventy-nine votes were needed for the nomination, and on the first ballot Blaine won 285 of them. The others didn't even come close. Morton got 124, Bristow 113, and Conkling 99. Hayes trailed badly with only 61 votes. It might have seemed that the momentum was back in Blaine's camp, but old hands would warn that the first ballot meant nothing. It was merely a prelude to the horse trading that would deliver a victor. (We don't see much of this dynamic of multiple ballots, often well into the double digits, in modern conventions, but in those days the drama was nothing short of operatic.)

Some backstage maneuvering among the campaigns had already helped them decide who'd get their votes if they didn't measure up in later balloting. Their thinking was that the delegate split would come down to Blaine versus everybody else, and "everybody else" needed to coalesce behind one candidate.

On the second ballot, Blaine's vote count edged higher by eleven votes; the others rose and fell by a smattering of votes. The third and then the fourth ballots showed little change. Blaine was far ahead, but still well short of the number he needed to secure the nomination.

Finally, on the fifth ballot, there was movement. Michigan, which had been divided and squabbling, shook loose from the impasse and delivered all 22 of its votes to Hayes. Now the count was Blaine 286, Bristow 114, and Hayes 104. It was hardly decisive numerically, but the symbolic effect was electric. Michigan was the first real shot across Blaine's bow.

At last the idea of a coalition among minor candidates took

on some momentum. The compromise discussions began. Hayes confided to his diary that "it seems something more than a possibility that he [Blaine] will fail. If he fails, my chance, as a compromise candidate, seems to be better than that of any other candidate."

On the sixth ballot, Blaine edged higher, to 308 votes, and Hayes was now in second place with 113. In the Blaine camp, there was an excited certainty of victory. The gap seemed unbridgeable and was growing wider with each vote. Unfortunately, this confidence ignored a numerical reality. Among them, Bristow, Morton, Conkling, and Hartranft had enough votes to deliver victory to Hayes.

One by one, they began to withdraw their names, sending their votes to Hayes. And then it happened. The seventh ballot delivered a narrow victory to Hayes of a mere five votes above the number needed. The final count was Hayes 384 and Blaine 351. Hayes was in. For vice president, the convention nominated New York congressman William A. Wheeler, who had been instrumental in devising a compromise that settled the disputed Louisiana gubernatorial election in 1872. Perhaps the party suspected that such wisdom would be needed again.

The reaction in the party was elation. Hayes was a strong candidate, and the worrisome Blaine had been dispatched. Grant was subdued but pleased. "Governor Hayes is a good selection and will make a good candidate," he said in his understated way. He chose to ignore what many of his allies considered a swipe at his administration in Hayes's acceptance statement—a pious call for a civil service "organized upon a system which will secure purity, experience, efficiency, and economy."

The *New York Times*, however, was overflowing with excessive praise. "In 1876 as in 1860 the Republican party has found its Lincoln to lead it on to victory," the paper enthused. Few people would go quite that far, but Hayes was deemed to be a solid candidate.

Two weeks later, the Democrats met in St. Louis and quickly nominated Samuel J. Tilden as their candidate. At sixty-two, Tilden was eight years older than Hayes, and he had been a party fixture since before the war. Short and thin, with fair hair and pale, sickly features, he was a lifelong hypochondriac who shunned social pleasantries and had never married. He was said to be cold as ice. But what he lacked in charm Tilden made up for in political skills and motivation. During his legal career, he had amassed considerable wealth.

Born and raised in the upstate New York town of Lebanon, Tilden had a privileged upbringing. His father was a wealthy merchant and gentleman farmer who provided his bright son with every opportunity to succeed. Smart as a whip, Tilden chose the law, but his true passion was politics. Rather than become a Republican—the typical choice for a Northern progressive— Tilden joined the antislavery wing of the Democratic Party, bluntly explaining his choice as a matter of opportunism. He pointed out that a party less crowded with progressive challengers could be more easily shaped. That strategy seemed to work well for him.

During the war, Tilden was pro-Union but also pro–states' rights, a tricky balancing act in a time of secession. However, he played no role in the war and just tucked himself away in New York for the duration. After the war, he became New York Democratic Party chairman, served in the state legislature, and was elected governor of New York in 1874. He used that position to launch his presidential campaign. A crusader against corruption, Tilden ran on a platform of reform and was immediately a frontrunner.

Tilden's claim to fame was the stance he took against the corrupt Tammany Hall—the Democratic political machine in New

York City—and especially against William M. Tweed, known as Boss Tweed. Tweed had run Tammany Hall and effectively controlled politics and commerce in New York. After Tilden's successful run for the State Assembly in 1870 on an anti–Tammany Hall platform, he launched investigations against Tweed that ultimately brought him down. Tilden's position as an anti-corruption crusader—even though the corruption had been in his own party—made him well suited for the times.

Democrats were determined to take back the national stage in 1876. It was their first real chance since before the war. Tired of being called the party of secession and then the party of the KKK, Democrats were eager to rebrand themselves as a true national party that, unlike the young upstart Republicans, had stood the test of time. Tilden was the perfect avatar, and despite having five opponents for the nomination, he never fell out of the lead. At the convention, Tilden was unanimously nominated on the second ballot. Because he was a moderate pro-Union Easterner, the convention chose as his vice presidential running mate Indiana governor Thomas Henricks, a Westerner who believed in the right of Southerners to be free of federal interference.

It was ironic that a Northerner, and a New Yorker no less, was the standard-bearer in an election that was effectively a battle of North versus South. Indeed, Tilden's New York roots briefly caused some consternation, when the convention was reminded that the last two losing Democrats—Horatio Seymour and Horace Greeley—were from New York. The Democratic platform stood firm on the demand that the federal armies withdraw from Southern states and that carpetbaggers, who had stolen Southern prosperity and insinuated themselves into political power, be forced to return to their homes in the North. From the Democrats' standpoint, all the ills of the nation could be summarized by this plague called "Grantism."

The solution to the country's ills, Tilden told supporters from his front porch, "is comprised in one word—reform."

President Grant and George Childs sat on the porch of the Grants' two-and-a-half-story beach house in Long Branch, New Jersey, a chalet-style getaway that was effectively the Summer White House. Childs, whose wealth and relationship to Grant had made the purchase possible, had a house right next door.

The two men had met in 1863, at the height of the war, when the Grants had gone to Philadelphia with the hope of registering their children at a school in nearby Burlington, New Jersey. They hit it off and became close friends. "General Grant was one of the truest and most congenial friends I ever had," Childs recalled after Grant's death. He added, "In his life three qualities were conspicuously revealed—justice, kindness, and firmness."

Long Branch was a favorite beach retreat for Philadelphians, and the Grants had found a haven there from the constant masses that demanded attention in Washington. Each morning Grant drove a buggy along the oceanfront, sometimes riding as far as twenty miles, clearing his head and breathing in the bracing ocean air. Upon his return, he would settle on the porch with the newspaper, a book, or correspondence, quite content. He couldn't completely escape from visitors. They found him there. His favorite pastime was sitting and chatting with Childs, and they saw each other every day when they were both at the beach.

It has been well established that every president needs a retreat from the burdens of office. Long Branch served that purpose for Grant. Like a number of his successors, he enjoyed painting, and it's a little-known fact that he was quite good at it. One painting that has survived depicts a noble-looking Indian chief at a trading post in the Northwest, with traders and trappers in the background conducting business. The striking figure of the chief is clear evidence of Grant's regard for the Indian people he met while stationed there.

At Long Branch, the hard feelings of war were far behind them. Childs noticed that rarely did a former Confederate officer visit the town that he did not stop and pay his respects to Grant. On one occasion, Childs was delighted to host a dinner party that included General Johnston along with Grant, Sherman, and Sheridan. The locals were beside themselves!

Grant's good-natured neighborliness was well known to the locals. Out in the world, he conveyed such an ordinary demeanor that people didn't at first realize who he was. Badeau recounted an incident on the steamer going from New York City to Long Branch. A woman came on board with two small children. She needed to send them to Long Branch, but she could not accompany them. Friends would meet them there. Seeing her dilemma, Grant offered to watch the children until they arrived at their destination. The woman was uncertain. How could she entrust her children to a strange man? To ease her mind, Grant said, blushing, "I am General Grant." She peered at his face and then exclaimed, "Why, so you are!"—and left her children in his care.

The summer leading into the election, Grant and Childs's conversations were full of politics. Grant had invited Hayes to visit Long Branch that summer so he could relax for a bit and enjoy the beauty and hospitality of the setting before the work of the campaign began in earnest. Hayes had declined, likely not wanting to tie himself too closely to the president. Indeed, although Hayes had always been completely proper and cordial in his dealings with Grant, he was privately quite critical of the president and believed that he could do a much better job of uniting the nation and appeasing the South.

As he sat on his Long Branch porch and chatted with Childs,

Grant felt an unfamiliar sensation of liberation at not being on the ballot. But this was quickly replaced by anxiety about the coming election and the obligations of his office. He shared his troubled thoughts with Childs. Hayes, he believed, was an adequate candidate, but there were signs in his acceptance speech that he was willing to abandon the hard work of Reconstruction if it suited the voting public. Grant had a soldier's mind, not a politician's, and he'd never set a course of action because it was the most popular. In war you don't take a vote before you march. After the war, the South needed a firm hand, and while progress had been made, as long as there was violence against Blacks and unresolved issues of human rights, it was the federal obligation to intervene. Looking ahead to the fall, Grant worried that the forces of intimidation would be out in greater numbers during this critical election. Childs had been concerned for some time that the Republican case had weakened, and both Grant and Childs recognized that Reconstruction was running out of steam. It had been a little over a decade since the Civil War ended. Was the nation ready to move forward, or was it hopelessly trapped in the division that led to war in the first place?

Unquestionably this would be a different kind of campaign. For the first time, Republicans and Democrats would be standing for election as *equals*, and there was a sense that people wanted it that way. The highly respected historian of the 1876 election, Paul Haworth, wrote of the intense desire for change across the land—a pure impulse of patriotism in the nation's hundredth year: "In the minds of many a sincere patriot, proud of the record of a hundred years but humiliated by the fact that the Centennial of the nation's birth must witness so much corruption in high places, there inevitably arose a desire for a political change."

Even so, it was fair to question whether the Democratic Party, so recently on the side of the rebels, was a fit alternative. "Would it be safe," Haworth wondered, "to trust the nation's affairs with men many of whom had once raised their hands against her life? Would it not, after all, be better to keep in power a party which, whatever its faults, had always stood unflinchingly for the preservation of the Union?"

That was the central question facing voters.

As in most political campaigns of the era, the candidates themselves were rarely on the stump, but instead were pulling the strings from their residences, each with an army of surrogates. Although the stakes of the election were high, both campaigns were muted on the national stage. Neither Hayes nor Tilden had the stomach for cutthroat rhetoric. Inflamed passions might be found among their supporters, not within the campaigns. And those passions were mostly being expressed in the South.

Tilden's headquarters was his New York mansion at Gramercy Park. From there he created the Literary Bureau, which organized an extensive print campaign, including a hastily written 750-page book about Republican corruption and Tilden's plan for reform. A bevy of writers was also employed to pen editorials, news releases, and massive quantities of printed matter for public consumption. In a similar manner, Tilden created a speakers' bureau and organized rallies.

What Tilden had going for him was a combination of deep pockets, an unerring strategic mind, and the hunger of the South for a Democrat in the White House. Democrats in the North found common cause with that desire. They believed that only a Democratic president could end the stain of war and make the South whole.

That said, Tilden had the most challenging balancing act of the two candidates. As a New Yorker, he engendered natural suspicions among Southerners, especially the more hot-blooded in their midst. He refused to condone any violence or extralegal activity on his behalf, and he was dismayed when he heard reports that white armies in Louisiana, South Carolina, and other states were prepared to "protect" the vote from Black voters. Southerners seeking a candidate they could rally behind on a whites-only premise were disappointed in Tilden. Was he just another untrustworthy Northerner?

Tilden tried valiantly to sidestep discussion of Black-white politics in the South. Hayes had no issue with decrying the violence in the South, although historically he was more moderate in his views than the old-style Radical Republicans. He wanted to reach out, hoping to appeal to Southerners on the basis of a common desire for peace and unity, which would also mean independence and normalcy in the South. However, Hayes's surrogates weren't so civil. In big, blustering rallies of Northern veterans, they claimed a Tilden victory was tantamount to a Confederate overthrow of the government.

The Hayes camp had its own literary operation churning out materials, including a massive distribution of anti-Tilden pamphlets. The text was fiery, rendering the mild Tilden almost unrecognizable. Whatever it lacked in accuracy, it succeeded in playing to the anti-Democratic base—a strategy as old as campaigning.

It took a toll. "Month after month, Tilden knew, he was being called a hypocrite, a thief, a drunkard, a liar, a perjurer, a swindler, a counterfeiter, and worse," wrote Lloyd Robinson in his history of the election. "A storm of similar abuse had broken Horace Greeley's heart in 1872 and killed him within weeks of Election day, but Tilden, though he suffered and was saddened by the propaganda, endured it and kept up his own fight."

At the same time, Hayes, who should have been reviled in the South, was making overtures—suggesting it was time to end military intervention and allow the South to be fully restored. It was a nice enough idea, but there was little discussion of what the terms of such a removal of forces would be. It was easy to promote a hands-off approach, but the question still had to be answered—what would the federal government do if there was violence?

There was another issue. Like many Republicans, Hayes was squeamish about the idea of a strong and united South. He never said so openly, but his surrogates on the stump were not afraid to say it. They painted a picture of a Southern bloc that would ignore constitutional rights and give local militias the power to roam freely. Under such a reign, Blacks would have little recourse. Most Northerners, especially those who had fought in the war, still saw Southerners (and by extension Democrats) as rebels. Privately, however, Hayes had his doubts that a continued military presence in the South was warranted.

In Washington, the federal machinery was grinding into motion, ready to go in the event of violence or disenfranchisement in the South. General Sherman was directed to keep all troops on standby in case they were needed. Yet even as these preparations were being made, some in the South were eager to flaunt the federal authority and appoint themselves the law.

South Carolina governor Daniel H. Chamberlain was a carpetbagger, what Democrats regarded as a scourge from the North. Born and raised in Massachusetts and educated at Harvard Law School, he served in the Fifth Massachusetts Cavalry during the war. After the war, he moved to South Carolina, allegedly to take care of the business of a deceased classmate, but actually as a carpetbagger. Within two years of his arrival, he was involved in politics. In 1874, he was elected governor.

Carpetbaggers—those Northerners who moved South to seek

political power and profit during Reconstruction—were reviled by native Southerners as opportunists who had no business insinuating themselves into Southern politics. At the time of the 1876 election, three Southern states—South Carolina, Louisiana, and Florida—were headed by Republican carpetbagger governors, and these states were being watched closely for any signs of election-related trouble. In South Carolina, white rifle clubs were forming throughout the state. Their mission was to terrorize Blacks and repel the Black vote.

Chamberlain was never a beloved chief executive. There was too much turmoil in his state, and he was held in suspicion. Complicating Chamberlain's problems governing during the 1876 election was his own bid for reelection that year. Both his state and his job were on the line. His Democratic opponent was Wade Hampton, a former Confederate general. During the campaign, Hampton unexpectedly reached out to Blacks, vowing to protect their rights and asking for their votes. He had little hope of gaining the trust of Blacks, who still viewed Democrats as the party of their enslavement. But Hampton's outreach acknowledged an important reality: enfranchised Blacks comprised huge numbers, and in some areas even majorities of the voting public. There were only two courses of action for Democrats: win them over or suppress their vote.

The latter strategy was in full force through the white militias. In some communities, it was a known fact that Blacks voting Republican were risking their lives. The tiniest spark lit the timber that erupted into a bonfire. It began on America's most sacred anniversary, July 4, in the small town of Hamburg, South Carolina, whose citizens were primarily Black. Like most African American communities, it was a solid Republican stronghold.

The July 4 incident seemed like a small-time misunderstanding at first. Two white farmers from a nearby town tried to drive a carriage through Hamburg at the same time that the all-Black militia was conducting an exercise. There was a modest delay, and the men were then allowed to proceed, but they were incensed. Two days later, they returned to Hamburg to lodge a formal complaint in the local court. They charged obstruction of a public road, and the hearing was set for July 8.

The day of the hearing, hundreds of armed white agitators, many of them from rifle clubs, crowded into the tiny town. The flame-colored outfits of the violent Red Shirts were evident in the crowd. They were not there for a court case; they were there to fight. As Dock Adams, the head of the Black militia, would later tell a congressional committee, "Even before it begun you could hear, 'We are going to redeem South Carolina today!' You could hear them singing it on the streets, 'This is the beginning of the redemption of South Carolina.'"

The Black militia members and some of the townspeople were forced to barricade themselves in a stone warehouse that served as an armory. The mob was ready for that. Positioning a cannon in front of the building, they blew a wide hole in the structure. As Blacks began to flee, they were shot at and many were wounded. The mob then dragged the remaining men from the armory.

At the end of the day, there were seven dead—six Blacks and one white farmer. Although ninety-nine men were indicted for the attack, they were never prosecuted.

The massacre further inflamed passions in the Black community and hardened the white resistance. Chamberlain sent an urgent appeal to Grant: "It is not to be doubted that the effect of this massacre has been to cause widespread terror and apprehension among the colored race and the Republicans of the state," he wrote, adding his belief that this was only the beginning of the terror.

Grant responded carefully. He replied that the Hamburg debacle was "cruel, bloodthirsty, wanton, unprovoked. . . . There has never been a desire on the part of the North to humiliate the South. Nothing is claimed for one State that is not fully accorded to all the others, unless it may be the right to kill negroes and Republicans without fear of punishment and without loss of caste or reputation." However, he also realized that if he sent federal troops into the states so close to the election, it would certainly be viewed as an attempt to interfere with the vote. He urged Chamberlain to firmly assert the rights of his citizenry—to challenge the assumption taking hold that the violent rifle clubs had the right to kill Blacks and Republicans without fear of reprisal.

By October, the situation was getting much worse. After a deadly encounter at a church in Cainhoy, which left five whites and one Black dead, Chamberlain appealed once more to the federal government for help. He worried that an election would be impossible with so much violence. "Insurrection and domestic violence exist in various portions of this state," he wrote. "I am unable with any means at my command to suppress the same."

This time Grant issued a presidential proclamation ordering all persons to cease their lawlessness and return home. Nearly 1,500 federal troops were sent to back up the proclamation, and they restored peace for the time being. But it was a stopgap measure. As Democrats woke to the realization that this election was their best chance since the war to win the White House, the mood among Southerners grew increasingly aggressive. They weren't about to stand back and allow Black Republicans to take that away from them.

Writing to his wife days before the election, General Sherman expressed the deep fears of many of his Northern countrymen. In their minds and hearts, they were still back in the war. It was far from over for them. "There is no use concealing the fact that the country is not free from danger," Sherman wrote. "Should

Tilden be elected the Southern politicians, who are strong passionate men, will demand a full share of the honors and emoluments of a government, and may lord it over us who were their enemies. The passions and sorrows of war are not healed enough for us to bear too much." By that point, Sherman believed that every indicator pointed to a Tilden victory. He shuddered to think where that would leave the Army, telling Sheridan that it could mean "a four year struggle for existence."

There was indeed a sense approaching the election that Tilden had an edge. "And all eyes were turned upon President Grant, as November came on," Garland wrote, "to know what he would do with regard to preventing violence and wrong in the South, and whether he would sustain the Republican candidate if he should receive a majority of votes cast." The wheels were already turning, in expectation of trouble.

On November 7, when eight and a half million voters went to the polls, it was widely believed that Tilden had an insurmountable lead. Even Hayes felt it. He wrote in his diary that day, "*Dies irae*"—day of wrath. For his part, Tilden began election day with a statement from his campaign manager that they expected a landslide. In spite of the driving rain, Tilden was cheered. He cast his vote wearing a red carnation in his buttonhole.

Most people agreed, in the early accounts of the election, that Tilden had almost certainly won. A. M. Gibson, the Washington correspondent for the *New York Sun*, wrote colorfully of election night:

> On the night of Tuesday, November 7th, 1876, tidings of disaster came from every quarter to the rooms of the National Republican Committee in the Fifth Avenue Hotel, New York City. Long before the dawn of the succeeding morning the members of the

Committee and the throng of anxious inquirers had sought repose with the conviction that their party had met its Waterloo.

Although some newspapers came out on November 8 declaring Tilden victorious, others, such as the *New York Times*, remained cautious.

The day after the election, Grant left for Philadelphia, where he would preside over the end of the Centennial Exhibition on November 10. He would be staying with Childs. On the ninth, he accompanied Childs to his newspaper office, where prominent men were gathering to talk about the election. Several leading Republicans were present, including a senator, and they were discussing the returns. All of them believed that Hayes was the winner. Grant listened to them silently, saying nothing until they had reached their conclusion. Then he said, in that quiet, firm way he had, "Gentlemen, it looks to me as if Mr. Tilden is elected."

His evidence was partly the unprecedented results in some Northern strongholds. Tilden's New York credentials seemed to pay off as New York, New Jersey, and Connecticut all went for him. So did Indiana. Assuming a solid South in the Democratic column, this would seem to be a decisive edge.

Hayes himself was in agreement with this calculation. Meeting with reporters, he was frank. "I think we are defeated," he said. Later, he wrote to his son at Cornell, trying to put a positive spin on the loss. He wrote philosophically, "We escape a heavy responsibility, severe labors, great anxiety and care, and a world of obliging by defeat. We are now free and independent and at peace with all the world, and the rest of mankind."

But a Hayes defeat was far from certain. There were rumblings in the South, specifically in the carpetbagger states of Florida, Louisiana, and South Carolina. For one thing, a quirk in the electoral system (which still exists today) allowed electors to vote for a candidate who did not win a state's popular vote. Technically, the three Republican Southern state governors could pressure electors to vote for Hayes. The numbers in those three states were still in doubt. The Republican governors could declare the votes for Hayes, based on an argument that the Democrats had cheated by resorting to underhanded strategies and violence to prevent Blacks from voting.

Behind the scenes, the *New York Times* was engaged in mischief to this end, even publishing a banner headline: "The Battle Won. A Republican Victory in the Nation—Gov. Hayes Elected President and William A. Wheeler Vice President." It wasn't even close to true at that point. Neither was the *New York Sun*'s declaration, "Tilden is Elected."

Both of these verdicts were inaccurate. Here's the way the vote broke down:

Three contested states, Florida (four electoral votes), Louisiana (eight electoral votes), and South Carolina (seven electoral votes), were not yet in the count. Without them, Tilden had 184 electoral votes and needed only one more vote for victory. Even if Tilden lost all three disputed states, one of Oregon's Republican electors was deemed ineligible because he was a public official, and he would be replaced by a Democrat, potentially putting Tilden over the top.

Hayes had 166 electoral votes, without Florida, Louisiana, or South Carolina being finalized. He needed all 19 of the disputed votes in order to win. He also needed the Oregon vote to stay in his column.

So what was holding up the three states? In South Carolina, Hayes appeared to have a majority of votes, but there was a troubling inconsistency in the governor's race. The numbers showed Chamberlain losing to Hampton by a significant margin, but Chamberlain refused to concede. As the man in charge of sorting it all out, Chamberlain wasn't exactly trustworthy.

In Florida, Tilden squeaked to victory by ninety-one votes, but there were loud accusations of foul play. Election day had seen various shenanigans. Governor Marcellus L. Stearns reported that it was no accident when a train carrying ballots was derailed. He said it was "ku kluxed" by Democrats. This claim was later found to be untrue. There was also an incident where a judge was said to have thrown out half the returns in a county because of a rumor that one voter had been denied the right to vote.

The Florida situation was complicated by the state's history of election corruption. Elections there were typically close, and the state had seen plenty of dirty tricks and outright illegality in the past. Neither party had clean hands in trying to steal elections.

Florida Republicans appealed to Black voters to "vote early and often" or risk being returned to slavery. In some instances, their opponents made this fear seem real. According to one account, a group of white men accosted a group of Blacks on a back road in Columbia County in the north-central part of the state. They threatened the Blacks with hanging and went so far as to put a rope around one of their necks. As the terror grew, the attackers began to calmly discuss making a deal. They'd let the men go if they dropped out of the Republican Party and actively campaigned for the Democrats. They agreed.

On the other hand, Democrats believed that they were the ones in jeopardy. A group of them visited Governor Stearns and told him, "We have come, sir, to put you on notice that if a single white man is killed in Leon County on election day, there are three hundred of us who have sworn that your life shall pay for it."

Tilden's margin of victory in Louisiana was fairly substantial, but the state had a colorful history of upending election results, and Republicans were counting on that history and general confusion to turn the result toward Hayes.

Suddenly, Tilden's certain victory seemed to be disappearing.

Abram Hewitt, a congressman and chairman of the national Democratic Party, came to see Tilden. Hewitt was one of Tilden's most fervent supporters, and he was ready to fight, but from the outset he and the candidate were at odds. Hewitt favored an aggressive public demand of fairness. He wanted to hold mass meetings.

Tilden disagreed. He felt that a contested election was a constitutional issue whose resolution would be found in the law books. He had no stomach for a street fight.

Hewitt brought in Allen G. Thurman, an Ohio senator and one of Tilden's former opponents for the nomination, to consult about the next steps. A small group of advisers sat and talked, and Thurman finally summed up their options in a succinct manner. "We can fight; we can back down; or we can arbitrate," he said.

Tilden spoke instantly. "It will not do to fight," he said. "We have just emerged from one Civil War, and it will never do to engage in another Civil War." He thought the only option was to arbitrate. It was an attitude that demoralized his supporters.

On November 9, Hamilton Fish came to Philadelphia and joined Grant and Childs for dinner. Of course, the topic was the election. During dinner a message arrived for the president that there were severe disturbances in the conflicted states. He and Fish left the table and rushed to the Western Union office, where they heard troubling news of "the wrecking of trains, tearing up of telegraph wires, and general disturbances." Since there were already forces available in those states, Grant knew he would have to act. The idea depressed him. He'd hoped to avoid military action. He knew it went against what the people wanted. But what choice did he have?

The following morning Grant wrote orders to General Sherman and his commanders to travel to the disputed states and restore order. "Instruct General Augur, in Louisiana, and General Ruger, in Florida, to be vigilant with the force at their command to preserve peace and good order, and to see that the proper and legal Boards of Canvassers are unmolested in the performance of their duties. Should there be any grounds of suspicion of fraudulent count on either side it should be reported and denounced at once."

In conclusion, he established the basic principle that would guide him during this crisis. "No man worthy of the office of President should be willing to hold it if 'counted in' or placed there by fraud. Either party can afford to be disappointed in the result tainted by the suspicion of illegal or false returns."

That day Grant was scheduled to preside over the end of the Centennial Exposition in Philadelphia. The event should have been a high point for Grant, an avowed modernist who had championed the exposition and presided at its opening. But he could not enjoy himself. The greatest contribution of America to the world—democracy and the smooth and peaceful transition of the presidency—was in jeopardy.

On November 11, Grant returned to Washington, where there was an ominous electricity. Troops were gathering throughout the greater metropolitan area, ready for action if it was needed. The train station was packed with party representatives heading south to monitor the election returns. "Everything now depends upon a fair count," Grant said to reporters who were gathered at the White House. But what constituted fair? Privately, Grant believed that the Republican election boards in the disputed states could ensure a victor, but if Democrats produced their own result, it would have little validity in the minds of Southerners. He'd long dreaded that fatal rift that could tip the nation back into war. Would this be the moment?

Grant was well aware of the public discontent. In spite of his best efforts, he had not won the trust of the South or of Democrats at large. Now, as they sensed the nearness of victory, they loudly accused him of wanting to put a hand on the scale—to behave like a dictator and anoint Hayes.

Writing about it eighteen years later, Hewitt recalled, "It is almost impossible to form any adequate idea of the excitement and the apprehension which prevailed throughout the country. Business was arrested, the wheels of industry ceased to move, and it seemed as if the terrors of civil war were again to be renewed."

The one-story house in Point Pleasant, Ohio, where Ulysses S. Grant was born is a historic site now. When the Grants lived there, it had only one room.

Bultema-Williams Collection, Ulysses S. Grant Presidential Library.

Jesse Grant was opinionated and sometimes bombastic, while Hannah was quiet and even-tempered. Together they created a stable, loving family life for their children.

Wikimedia Commons.

A young officer Grant.

Ulysses S. and Julia D. Grant Papers,
Ulysses S. Grant Presidential Library.

Julia Dent Grant was the love of Ulysses's life. They had a successful marriage, which endured separations, financial hardships, war, political turmoil, and his final battle with cancer.

Ulysses S. and Julia D. Grant Papers, Ulysses S. Grant Presidential Library.

White Haven, the Dent family's farm plantation.

Ulysses S. and Julia D. Grant Papers, Ulysses S. Grant Presidential Library.

The Grants. *Left to right:* Nellie, Ulysses, Jesse, Fred, Julia, and Ulysses Jr. (Buck).

Bultema-Williams Collection, Ulysses S. Grant Presidential Library.

President Lincoln confers with Allan Pinkerton (*left*) and Major General John A. McClernand (*right*) during the Battle of Antietam in Maryland in the fall of 1862. *Library of Congress.*

A depiction of the brutal, bloody Siege of Vicksburg (May 18–July 4, 1863), which cemented Grant's reputation as a military leader. *Library of Congress.*

Confederate soldiers lay behind a stone wall at Fredericksburg after the Sixth Maine Infantry Regiment overwhelmed them in May 1863, a sign of the horrible toll the war took on both sides. *National Archives.*

General Grant at his headquarters in Cold Harbor, Virginia, in June 1864. He was quiet and unassuming even at his greatest moment. *Library of Congress.*

A critical meeting at Grant's City Point headquarters. Abraham Lincoln, William Tecumseh Sherman, Philip Henry Sheridan, and Ulysses S. Grant (*left to right*) study a map and plot a strategy to finally end the war.

Library of Congress

Let Us Have Peace by Jean Leon Gerome Ferris (1920), depicting the surrender of General Robert E. Lee to General Ulysses S. Grant on April 9, 1865. *By VCG Wilson/Corbis via Getty Images.*

Andrew Johnson had been vice president for less than two months when Lincoln was assassinated. Johnson's turbulent single term had the nation longing for a hero, which they once again found in Grant.

Library of Congress.

President Abraham Lincoln's assassination, only six days after Lee's surrender, sent the nation into a state of shock and grief. Silk mourning ribbons bearing Lincoln's image were in high demand. They were pinned to clothing or displayed in homes.

Library of Congress.

HARPER'S WEEKLY

A JOURNAL OF CIVILIZATION

VOL. XII.—No. 620.]   NEW YORK, SATURDAY, NOVEMBER 14, 1868.   [SINGLE COPIES, TEN CENTS. $4.00 PER YEAR IN ADVANCE.

Entered according to Act of Congress, in the Year 1868, by Harper & Brothers, in the Clerk's Office of the District Court of the United States, for the Southern District of New York.

VICTORY!

This caricature demonstrates Grant's heroic stature at the time of the 1868 election. He is portrayed on horseback waving a US flag labeled "Union Equal Rights" and beheading his Democratic opponent Horatio Seymour, who is riding a horse branded "K.K.K."

Library of Congress.

Ulysses Grant's first inauguration, on March 4, 1869, brought huge crowds to the capital to see their war hero sworn into office. Not present was Grant's predecessor, Andrew Johnson, and Grant's mother, who thought all the hoopla was unseemly.

Bultema-Williams Collection, Ulysses S. Grant Presidential Library.

A cabinet meeting in the Grant administration, drawn by W. S. L. Jewett. *Left to right:* Jacob D. Cox, Hamilton Fish, John A. Rawlins, John A. J. Creswell, President Grant, George S. Boutwell, Adolph E. Borie. The original caption doesn't name the eighth person, who appears to be Ebenezer R. Hoar.

Library of Congress/Corbis Historical via Getty Images.

The first Black senator and members of the House of Representatives during the 41st and 42nd Congresses. *Left to right:* Representative Robert C. De Large, South Carolina; Representative Jefferson H. Long, Georgia; Senator H. R. Revels, Mississippi; Representative Benjamin S. Turner, Alabama; Representative Josiah T. Walls, Florida; Representative Joseph H. Rainey, South Carolina; Representative R. Brown Elliot, South Carolina.

Library of Congress.

This 1874 Thomas Nast illustration demonstrates the violence suffered by Blacks in the South. A smiling robed KKK member shakes hands with a member of the "White League" above a skull and crossbones as a Black couple cowers while holding their dead baby, with a Black man hanging in the background and a schoolhouse burning.

Library of Congress.

This drawing by C. S. Reinhart titled *Let Us Have Peace* depicts Grant greeting Red Cloud, Spotted Tail, and Swift Bear during a visit of the Indian delegation with Commissioner of Indian Affairs Ely S. Parker. *Library of Congress.*

Ulysses, Julia, and young Jesse at the Grant cottage by the sea in Long Branch, New Jersey. It was Grant's presidential escape and restorative during the blistering Washington summers. *Library of Congress.*

The 1876 election, in America's centennial year, pitted moderate Republican Rutherford B. Hayes and vice presidential nominee William A. Wheeler against Democratic reformer Samuel J. Tilden and vice presidential nominee Thomas A. Hendricks. Severe disputes in key Southern states would put the future of democracy to the test. As president, Grant felt an obligation to once again rescue the Republic.

Library of Congress.

Above left: Mark Twain was Grant's friend and then his publisher. Twain was surprised to find that Grant was a good writer, and he was dazzled by the "wonderful machine" of Grant's memory.

Library of Congress.

Above right: Bundled up and in failing health, Grant puts the finishing touches on his memoirs at Mount McGregor, New York. He has less than a month left to live. *Library of Congress.*

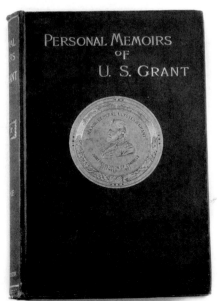

Grant's memoirs, published shortly after his death, were a critical and commercial success. To this day they are considered among the most important wartime accounts ever written.

NPS/David Newmann.

On August 8, 1885, more than a quarter million mourners lined the procession route on Fifth Avenue in New York City to bid farewell to General Grant. The procession extended seven miles and included veterans from both sides of the Civil War. Grant's pallbearers were Union generals Sherman and Sheridan and Confederate generals Buckner and Johnston.
Library of Congress.

The Ulysses S. Grant Memorial at the US Capitol in Washington, DC, where America's beloved soldier of democracy and man of peace watches over the nation's constant challenge to fulfill its promise. *Library of Congress.*

The author at the Ulysses S. Grant Presidential Library, located at Mississippi State University in Starkville, Mississippi. It's fascinating to read original documents such as campaign flyers from 1868 and 1876, a letter from President Lincoln to General Grant, and a scathing pamphlet diatribe from Grant's Senate nemesis, Charles Sumner.

Photograph by Daniel Swartz.

CHAPTER 11

AN ELECTION IN DOUBT

Sunday, November 26, was a cold and stormy day in Washington, and Secretary of State Hamilton Fish's rheumatism was flaring up. He decided to skip church and stay home in front of the fire.

It had been a rough period since the election, and it didn't seem as though the parties had made any progress toward a resolution. Cabinet meetings were obsessed with a threat of violence not seen since before the war. Grant worried about an unbreachable chasm forming in the population.

John S. Mosby, a former Confederate calvary leader who had become a Grant supporter, had warned Fish of the danger. "He told me," Fish wrote in his diary, "that the language of the Democrats now was more desperate and more threatening and violent than that of the Southern men on the election of Lincoln in 1860." Mosby cautioned Fish that there were threats to both Hayes and Grant if Hayes was declared the winner.

Now Fish's rare chance for rest was disturbed by the arrival of a messenger, summoning him to an emergency cabinet meeting at the White House. Pulling his aching body into action, Fish headed in and found Grant and his fellow members in a state of deep worry. Grant told them he'd received information that rifle companies were organizing in South Carolina, composed of seven or eight thousand men. They were planning to head for the capital in Columbia to challenge the Assembly when it gathered two days later. Predicting violence, Governor Chamberlain was asking Grant for federal protection. The cabinet was in agreement that troops must be sent. Grant ordered his secretary of War, Donald Cameron, who had been in office only since May, to send the troops.

Almost immediately, things went bad. Chamberlain viewed the troops as his private army and used them to push aside the Democrats. When the contesting delegations representing the Republican and Democratic counts arrived at the capital, Chamberlain admitted the Republican delegation and sent the Democrats away. But in the next couple of days the Democrats took possession of the Assembly Hall, and Chamberlain sent an appeal to the president.

On Thanksgiving Day, as Fish was enjoying dinner with his family, he heard from Cameron that there was an urgent matter in South Carolina. Governor Chamberlain wanted them to send orders to the troops who were standing by to remove the Democrats from the Assembly Hall. Cameron approved of the idea, but Fish thought it was outrageous—just the kind of inappropriate intervention that would come back to bite them.

Fish insisted that the only use of the military should be to put down violence. It was not the War Department's place to take sides in the establishment of a state legislature.

A frustrated Grant heard about the situation and was aggravated. Although it was Thanksgiving, he sent word that he needed the cabinet to gather after dinner. By that point, Cameron was quite agitated. He felt that they must order troops to take control of the statehouse. Others agreed. Alphonso Taft, who had briefly been secretary of War before switching to attorney general in the middle of 1876, agreed with Cameron. As they looked to Grant for his opinion, Fish broke in. He was angry. "I remonstrate and protest," he fumed, "against improper and unlawful employment of the military to suppress violence and preserve the peace." He gestured toward Grant. "The President is of the same opinion."

"This is war and revolution!" Cameron cried.

Grant recoiled. "No, no!" he said in horror. "It is no such thing."

No one mentioned the historical significance of the moment, not wanting to jinx the nation, but it was on Grant's mind. He still vividly remembered the moment fifteen years earlier when South Carolina became the first state to secede from the Union. In one way or another he'd been involved ever since—for more than a decade in a leadership role. He'd been commander of the Army before and after the war. He'd served two terms as president. Seeing South Carolina once again as the linchpin of dissent, he felt the chill of recognition.

Grant was further dismayed when he received a request from Louisiana governor Kellogg begging for the strong arm of federal troops. It was the most unpleasant kind of déjà vu—once again Kellogg was fighting the Democrats in a disputed election. This time Kellogg was a candidate for the US Senate, and he backed the Republican, Stephen B. Packard, for governor. Packard's Democratic opponent, Francis T. Nicholls, was declaring victory, and Kellogg was apoplectic.

Having pulled Kellogg out of the fire once before, Grant wasn't eager to risk more personal and political capital to do it again. "They are always in trouble there and always wanting the United States to send troops," he complained to Fish. The problem was, if Grant responded to every personal request to use the military to settle state elections, he could rightly be accused of political meddling. At some point, the states had to wrestle with these matters internally; otherwise the situation would just keep repeating itself.

As he deliberated on the right course of action, Grant asked himself how a republic could survive if its elections were forced by one party over another—or by a federal show of strength. Reconstruction had already sealed his reputation among many Southerners as a leader prone to excessive use of his authority. He didn't want to make matters worse. Still, he knew it was his duty as a leader to act decisively and to be objective.

At the same time, Grant wanted to soothe the fears of Democrats and assure them that he was committed to a fair vote. It was a delicate matter. If Democrats believed that he was trying to install Hayes, along with Republican statehouses, there would be bedlam. Similarly, if Republicans thought that Grant was trying to cut a deal in favor of Tilden to keep the peace, that, too, would be a crisis.

General Winfield Scott Hancock wrote to Sherman of his concerns about Army interference. "The army should have nothing to do with the selection or inauguration of Presidents," he wrote, sounding a sentimental note about the good old days of the Union. "I like Jefferson's way of inauguration. It suits our system. He rode alone on horseback to the capitol . . . tied his horse to a rail-fence, entered, and was duly sworn; then rode to the Executive mansion, and took possession. He inaugurated himself simply by taking the oath of office."

This was the result they sought.

Kellogg was a long way from accepting that simple transition. He was asserting fraud based on a seven-thousand-vote margin for Tilden. He said this result was impossible because it meant that a large number of Blacks had voted for the Democratic ticket.

They must have been terrorized into doing it! But were they? Subsequent investigations found that many Blacks *did* abandon the Republican Party, tired of broken promises and corruption. However, it was the Republican governor himself who was behaving in a fraudulent way—for example, by appointing an electoral board consisting only of Republicans.

According to the reporter A. M. Gibson, Kellogg was a real piece of work, a man not to be trusted. "Few shrewder and more adroit men have ever wielded such vast political power," he wrote. "He was utterly unscrupulous, thoroughly corrupt and full of wiles." Falsifying records and persuading others to lie was all in a day's work for Kellogg, and this was widely known.

Grant sent a number of Republican statesmen to New Orleans. The Democrats sent their own team. Analyzing the vote parish by parish, they found signs of voter intimidation and other irregularities, but most blatantly, what had been a Democratic lead by six thousand votes had turned into a Republican lead.

On December 3, Grant met with Democratic chair Abram Hewitt. It was in some ways a poignant meeting. Grant felt that he needed to defend his honor as a fair broker. He "thought it rather hard that any one should suspect him, who had given his best years to preserve the country, of any designs upon its liberties," Hewitt recalled. Grant told him with surprising candor that he had little confidence in the Louisiana election board, and he wondered whether the results in Louisiana should be declared invalid. This, of course, would throw the electoral count up in the air, possibly making the Democratic Congress the final judge. By the end of their meeting, Hewitt didn't know what to think. Did Grant believe Tilden was the winner in Louisiana? Was he willing to punt the decision to a Democratic Congress? He wasn't sure. Grant might just have been trying to appease Hewitt by appearing to be nonpartisan. Or he might have been preparing for the possibility that the unreliable Louisiana board would return a count for Tilden, and he wanted to get on the record as having questioned the board.

Hewitt didn't keep the meeting to himself, and his account made Grant sound more compliant toward Democrats than he was. When Hayes caught wind of Grant's remarks, he was concerned enough to send his friend and old war buddy, James M. Comly, the editor of the *Ohio State Journal*, to talk to Grant. Comly's role was essentially to butter Grant up—to convince him of Hayes's loyalty and friendship. There was also a personal matter to settle. Benjamin Bristow, who had so offended Grant in his pursuit of the Whiskey Ring, which had ensnared his friend Babcock, had gone on to become a critic of the president after he stepped down as secretary of the Treasury. In fact, he became a great ally of Hayes's, the presumption being that a Hayes administration would be much cleaner than Grant's. Now one of the carrots that Comly was prepared to offer Grant was an assurance that Bristow would not be invited to serve in a Hayes cabinet. By the end of the meeting, the two men were smoking cigars together. But however congenial their conversation, it didn't shake Grant's resolve to be fair.

In South Carolina, a bribery effort was uncovered. An election official was offered $80,000 in a hotel room to record votes for Tilden. When Tilden caught wind of the effort, he stopped it. Although the bribery attempts were unsuccessful and Tilden personally had no part in it, the incident exemplifies how muddy the election picture was in the disputed states. With both sides cheating, how could there ever be a fair result?

December 6 was the moment of truth for electors, and to no one's surprise, the disputed states turned in conflicting results. There were two sets of results from South Carolina; Chamberlain certified a set of results for Hayes, and Hampton certified a set for Tilden. There were also two sets of votes recorded for Florida. Things were even worse in Louisiana, with Kellogg at the helm. The unsettled governor's race surely meant violence ahead. Neither Packard nor Nicholls was willing to concede defeat. To top things off, there was the disputed vote in Oregon.

Democrats in Louisiana, Florida, and South Carolina were growing increasingly bullish, vowing to fight to the end for Tilden—"Tilden or Blood" was the rallying cry—and railing against a corrupt federal government that would so readily send troops to solve electoral issues. There were death threats against Grant as well as calls for impeachment. Organizers began to plan a massive march on Washington and dared Grant to defy them. Grant responded that they should not push him with such a threat. He was prepared to declare martial law if need be to protect the peace.

Former Confederate general Joseph Shelby was approached about taking command of an army of Democratic volunteers to march on Washington and get Tilden inaugurated, even if it happened at gunpoint. Across the country other militias were organizing. Some planned standard protests. Others planned to use force.

Upset, Julia urged her husband to *do* something. He saw panic as the worst response and was determined to use cool reason to find a solution, just as he had on those fearsome nights during the war when the enemy was encamped nearby and ready to strike. "It is lucky you are not the president," he told Julia. "I am afraid you would give trouble."

It was time for Grant to act, and to do so without any partisan leanings. Obviously, he wanted Hayes to win, but he stepped carefully around the pleadings of his party. Grant understood

274 • To Rescue the Republic

that Republicans felt justified in steamrolling over Tilden and in-
stalling Hayes because there had been so much voter intimidation
of Blacks. Surely, they argued, if all Black voters had been allowed
to vote freely and without harassment, Hayes's numbers would
have been much greater. As Grant liked to point out to reporters,
had all eligible Black voters been left free to vote their choice, the
totals in several other states, such as Mississippi, North Carolina,
and Arkansas, would also have produced victories for Hayes.

"Grant wanted to present himself as an honest broker," writes
Brooks Simpson in his analysis of the election. "This was essential to retain his power in the crisis. It was also the only way that
Hayes could survive. If Democrats sensed that Grant was out to
secure Hayes's election, they would cry fraud. Thus, Grant's pose
served the end of both statesmanship and politics."

However, Simpson adds, Grant had come to believe that the
Democrats had tried to do on the national level what they had
already been doing in individual Southern states—subvert the
electoral process through terrorism. So the course of action had
to be carefully considered. Because Republicans possessed the authority to install Hayes if they chose, but lacked any means of
proving the harm done to those attempting to vote for him, they
were entering a dangerous moment.

Alone with his thoughts, Grant feared for the Union he had
given his life to protect. He had no doubt that a victory by Tilden
would mean the end of Reconstruction and with it any federal
protection of Blacks.

If only it were as simple as declaring Hayes the winner and
moving on. There was a debate about the repercussions of such
a decision among Grant's advisers, but Grant himself firmly believed that if they were to anoint Hayes without the support of the
nation—and that meant the South as well—they would be standing on the cusp of a second civil war, which he did not believe the

country could survive. Somehow the Republicans and Democrats had to agree on the winner.

One day Childs received a message from Grant asking him to come to Washington. When Childs arrived and was settled across from his friend, Grant said, "This matter is very complicated, and the people will not be satisfied unless something is done in regard to it which will appeal to their sense of justice."

What would such a plan entail? "I have thought of an Electoral Commission," Grant went on, "but the leaders of the party are opposed to it, which I am sorry to see. They say that if an Electoral Commission is appointed, we might as well count in Mr. Tilden. I would rather have Mr. Tilden than that the Republicans should have a President who could be stigmatized as a fraud. If I were Mr. Hayes, I would not have the office unless my claim to it were settled in some way outside the Senate. This matter is opposed by the leading Republicans in the House and Senate and throughout the country."

To prove his point, Grant invited several Republican senators to dine with them that evening. As expected, they were almost unanimous in their objection to an electoral commission.

Childs suggested that they appeal to the Democratic Speaker of the House, Samuel J. Randall; if they could get Democrats on their side, perhaps it would clear the way for Republicans. Randall was known to be a man of integrity and a serious administrator. He admitted to feeling a sense of responsibility to help resolve the matter peacefully, and that might include a commission. As yet, however, there was little idea of how such a commission would operate.

Next Grant sent for Conkling and asked for his advice. Conkling told them that an electoral commission was a hard sell, noting that even Indiana senator Oliver P. Morton, a dedicated Hayes loyalist, was opposed to it. But Conkling promised to help as much as he could.

Grant recognized that it would do the nation no good if Hayes achieved a victory that was considered illegitimate. There had to be a consensus that it was the right result, but there was a great deal of disagreement about who would judge that result. Looking on, Childs noticed that the crisis of the election was reenergizing a weary man. Through his sensible, unbiased actions, Grant was redeeming himself in the eyes of many who had written him off.

Normally, electoral votes were certified by the president of the Senate. But there was no rule for when there were two sets of results. Republicans insisted that the president of the Senate (who happened to be a Republican) should still be the one to decide. Democrats countered that the power rested with the House (which was controlled by Democrats). As Congressman James Monroe so perfectly articulated the dilemma in an *Atlantic* piece a few years later:

> It was repeatedly stated on the floor of the House of Representatives, and apparently believed by the majority, that if the Republican party should proceed, through the President of the Senate, to count the votes of the disputed States, and declare them for General Hayes, the House would then proceed to elect Mr. Tilden, or to count the vote and declare him elected by the nation. There would then have been a dual presidency, a divided army and navy, a divided people, and probably civil war. What plan could be devised to save the country from the evils that threatened it?

To further complicate matters, there was no sitting president of the Senate. Grant's vice president, Henry Wilson, had died of a stroke a full year earlier, and Grant had not replaced him. Since the vice president is president of the Senate, that role was unfilled. There was only a president pro tempore, the second in command—Thomas W. Ferry, a Republican from Michigan. Many Republicans feared that if he were called upon to break a tie, there would be a bitter dispute about Ferry's legitimacy.

In another interesting wrinkle, since 1865 there had been a method of rejecting electoral votes called the "Twenty-second Joint Rule." This allowed the Senate or the House to reject electoral votes that were deemed to be invalid. It had actually been used in two prior elections. But in those cases, Republicans had a firm control of Congress, and after the 1874 election, when they realized that it could be Republican electors on the chopping block, the rule was discontinued.

Grant continued to broker a different path—the appointment of a commission, representing both parties. He pushed and prodded, until finally both parties came to see it as the only solution. Agreement came not a moment too soon. This was a matter of growing urgency, as the contested states were devolving into chaos.

In South Carolina, Chamberlain was intent on mischief. Although the governor's race was not settled and the state supreme court had ordered the parties to stand back, Chamberlain and the Republicans went ahead and inaugurated him for a second term. Predictably, this inspired the Democrats to inaugurate Hampton, and now the state had two vying governors to whip up the people.

The deteriorating circumstances made Grant even more eager for the commission to be up and running as quickly as possible. After weeks of discussion in both houses of Congress, resolutions were passed agreeing to the formula. The Electoral Commission would be composed of fifteen members: five members of the House (three Democrats and two Republicans), five members of the Senate (three Republicans and two Democrats), and five members of the Supreme Court. Two justices would be of Republican origin and two of Democratic origin, with a fifth being neutral—a determination that became very difficult to make.

The first justice named who seemed to fit this peculiar bill of being in essence half Republican and half Democrat was Justice David Davis from Illinois; he had been a close friend of Lincoln, but was also seen as open-minded. In 1872, he had been nominated for the Labor Reform Party. But simultaneous with his selection for the commission, the Illinois legislature elected Davis to the Senate. He decided to step down from the Court to serve in Congress, thus eliminating himself from eligibility for the commission. After some debate, Justice Joseph P. Bradley of New Jersey was selected. A lifelong Republican, he did not exactly meet the neutrality criteria, but the commission ultimately abandoned the notion that there was a hybrid individual who was equally favorable to each party.

Through it all, Grant remained calm. "The country is agitated," he said. "It needs and desires peace and quiet and harmony between all parties and all sections." The solution, he hoped, was a fresh start. Citing "the imminent peril of the institutions of the country," Grant signed the Electoral Commission Act into law on January 29.

CHAPTER 12

THE PRESIDENCY SAVED

February 1, 1877, was an auspicious day, as a rare combined gathering of the House and Senate, complete with members of the Supreme Court, began in the House of Representatives. The floor was crowded with all the players, and the visitors' gallery was bursting with high-level spectators, including foreign dignitaries and VIPs like General Sherman.

This would be stage one of the process, the presentation of the electoral counts. Speaker Randall and Senate President Pro Tempore Ferry sat side by side, a mahogany box in front of them containing the certified electoral votes. Each state's votes would be called and recorded. If there was a dispute, it would be sent to the Electoral Commission.

The count began, solemnly, in alphabetical order:

"Alabama . . ."

"Alabama casts its ten electoral votes for Samuel J. Tilden."

Arkansas: Tilden.

California: Hayes.

Colorado (newly a state): Hayes.
Connecticut: Tilden.
Delaware: Tilden.

Now the certificate for Florida was pulled and read: "Four votes for Hayes." But there was a second certificate for Florida: "Four votes for Tilden." Then, as if to emphasize the renegade certification, a third certificate was read, also showing four votes for Tilden.

The count ground to a halt as the disputed certifications were turned over to the Electoral Commission for review. On its face, it might have been an easy judgment, as only the Hayes certification ticked all the official boxes—dated December 6 and signed by Governor M. L. Stearns. The second and third certifications were signed by the Democratic attorney general and by the newly elected Democratic governor, G. F. Drew, respectively.

However, the position of the Democrats was that Stearns had fraudulently signed a certification for Hayes, even though the vote favored Tilden. The question on the table was how to prove or disprove that assertion. There was a strong feeling among the commission members that they might not have the authority to go behind the vote certification, as it was considered by law to be legitimate. To mess around in raw data would potentially exceed the legal scope of the commission. But others argued that this was precisely their job. New York congressman David Dudley Field, a longtime friend of Tilden's, argued forcefully that he believed the governor was the one who had falsified the certificate, not the Democrats. As he began to cite known instances of illegalities around the election, his Republican counterparts tried to drown out his complaints, asserting that the commission did not have the right to challenge a state's official vote count. It was not just a matter of states' rights, but a matter of pragmatism. How could they take the time to investigate every questionable vote when they had a hard deadline of March 4 to inaugurate the next president? It was already February 5, their fifth day of deliberation.

Justice Bradley realized that they had landed on the critical question of their duty as a commission. He told his fellows he needed time overnight to consider the proper course of action, and they adjourned until noon the next day. In Bradley's hands was essentially the ruling of whether the examination by the commission would be perfunctory or substantive.

The Tilden forces had reason to be cautiously optimistic, for although Bradley had Republican roots, he was believed to be scrupulously fair. What could be fairer than examining the election vote to make sure it was truthfully reflected in the certification?

Bradley contemplated the best course of action long into the night, well understanding his unique role as an unbiased arbiter. The next day he sat amid his fellow commissioners and read his opinion. In his judgment, the commission lacked the authority to examine the materials beyond the certified returns. "The two houses of Congress, in proceeding with the count, are bound to recognize the determination of the state board of canvassers as the act of the state and as the most authentic evidence of the state," he said. He concluded that Congress could not sit as a court of appeals in judgment of the state boards. There would be no investigation of any of the issues hanging over the procedure, and therefore no proof one way or another.

When the vote was taken, it was eight to seven. Bradley broke the tie by voting for Hayes.

Bradley's decision was stunning. For one thing, most observers had him figured for a Tilden vote. But also, his decision to bypass a review of supporting documentation seemed completely out of character for Bradley. According to a review by Anthony Champagne and Dennis Pope for the *International Society of Political Psychology*, Bradley was said to be "a terror" when it came to "testing every proposition" and would push the Court to consider areas that hadn't occurred to others. His decision on the Hayes-Tilden conflict made no sense. Whatever his motivation, "the ugly hint of corruption hung over him."

But there was another unspoken reason for dismay among Democratic leaders. Hewitt would later recount that they'd had evidence that Bradley was planning to vote for their side. The previous night, as Bradley deliberated, he was visited by a close friend, John G. Stevens. At midnight Stevens reported to Hewitt and others that he had read Bradley's opinion in favor of counting the Democratic electors.

They were elated. It would mean certain victory for Tilden. So they were shattered when Bradley ruled the opposite. What had happened after midnight to change his mind? It would later come out that after Stevens left, Bradley received two additional visitors in the dead of night. New Jersey Republican senator Frederick Frelinghuysen and Secretary of the Navy George Robeson pleaded with Bradley to accept the official certificate. Apparently, Mrs. Bradley, who was awake, weighed in as well, for the Republican side.

Bradley's conclusion did not just affect Florida. Looking ahead, everyone realized that it would play a significant role in each dispute. But for the time being, on the floor of Congress, the examination of the certificates continued in a steady alphabetical roll call.

Georgia: Tilden.
Illinois: Hayes.
Indiana: Tilden.

Iowa: Hayes.

Kansas: Hayes.

Kentucky: Tilden.

Louisiana. There were two certificates, one Republican, signed by Governor Kellogg, and the other Democrat, signed by John McEnery. There was also, bizarrely, a third, forged certificate, allegedly signed by Kellogg. Behind the scenes, of course, was the hotly contested governor's race, similar to the one in South Carolina, between Democrat Francis Nicholls and Republican Stephen Packard.

Since Tilden had won a majority in the popular vote, the whole scenario was puzzling. The Republicans asserted that their certification was absolutely on the up and up, even as Democrats argued that it was fraudulent. Given the likely corruption in the state board, it should have been a fierce debate, but with Bradley's decision on Florida, there was little that could be done. Without going behind the vote and doing a real examination, there was no way to tell. The Electoral Commission quickly ruled the eight electoral votes for Hayes.

The Electoral Commission simply rejected the idea that there was a Democratic majority in the popular vote, or that there were other improprieties. Kellogg was approved as the designated signatory, and his result was approved eight to seven.

When the vote was announced, a loud rumble went up on the House floor and in the gallery. "Fraud! . . . Fraud!! . . . Fraud!" But the Senate voted to accept the commission's judgment, and eight Louisiana electoral votes were added to Hayes's column.

Although it had no effect, an argument broke out on the floor, with several congressmen refusing to accept the decision and others arguing for Hayes. As each day passed, the hard feelings grew in that crowded, bitter chamber. It seemed to Tilden's supporters that the fix was in. The climate was so angry that some elected officials came to the sessions armed with pistols.

At the White House, Grant was staying out of the fray. He had vowed to remain neutral, to allow the constitutional process to continue, and he'd kept his word. Hayes and Tilden also remained silent. But their representatives were strategizing behind the scenes.

The vote went on.

Maine: Hayes.
Maryland: Tilden.
Massachusetts: Hayes.
Michigan: Hayes.
Minnesota: Hayes.
Mississippi: Tilden.
Nebraska: Hayes.
Nevada: Hayes.
New Hampshire: Hayes.
New Jersey: Tilden.
New York: Tilden.
North Carolina: Tilden.
Ohio: Hayes.

On February 21, the count stopped at Oregon. Hayes had originally received Oregon's three electoral votes. With John W. Watts, the postmaster, erroneously appointed an elector (no public officials could serve as electors), a replacement had to be found. Under heavy pressure by the Democrats, the governor selected a Democratic elector, E. A. Cronin. Suddenly, it seemed that one of Oregon's votes was up in the air. As a Democrat, would Cronin cast his vote for Tilden? In a late-breaking development before the commission, it was revealed that Watts *was* a valid elector because he had resigned as postmaster before December 4. The commission accepted his legitimacy and voted eight to seven to give the disputed vote to Hayes.

The count went on.

Pennsylvania: Hayes.
Rhode Island: Hayes.

All eyes were on South Carolina. If it was ruled for Hayes, he would be president. If it was ruled for Tilden, he would be president. No wonder emotions were so high in the chamber. Democrats had tried before to filibuster in order to delay the vote, to no avail. Randall would not allow it. But as the end grew near, the obstruction grew louder and more constant, with a bevy of manufactured procedural objections.

With the decision almost certainly in Hayes's favor, it appeared that many Democrats were determined to blow the whole thing up. At some points, the entire Democratic side of the aisle was on its feet, and one member even stood atop his desk, bombarding the Speaker with demands and questions that were at times so nonsensical that they could not be answered. It was bedlam.

Grant's worst fear was coming true—a massive lack of trust in the result. It was clear to anyone who thought about it that the declaration of a result by a commission would only be supported if both houses of Congress agreed that it had not been fraudulently given. The uproar among the filibustering Democrats seemed a worrisome precursor to the national reaction.

Grant was in a state of agitation. He had trouble sleeping, and at night he tossed in his bed unable to find comfort. In his darkest moments, he wondered if his policies had brought on this terrible crisis. He was haunted by the fallout from his years of trying to bring unity to the nation. He believed in Reconstruction, but he believed in the Union more. He had one week remaining in his presidency—a small window in which to assert some leadership. A compromise needed to be struck before Democrats brought down the house—and he let it be known that he would be in favor of such an effort.

On the particularly combustible Friday of February 26, with only a few days remaining until the inauguration, Congress chose to recess for the weekend. Perhaps cooler heads would prevail on Monday.

Monday morning at the White House, a lone figure made his way in to meet with President Grant. His name was Edward A. Burke, and he was a former Confederate soldier. Now a powerful and somewhat shadowy insider in Louisiana, Burke was a bitter enemy of Governor Kellogg; in one of their altercations, guns were drawn. Burke had helped run Nicholls's campaign to replace Kellogg, and he was interested in making a trade—the presidency for Hayes in exchange for putting Southern Democrats in the disputed governors' mansions. He promised Grant that such a deal would prevent an ugly filibuster among Democrats and the collapse of the whole system.

Grant was intrigued. He had privately believed for some time that Republican governance in Southern states was made possible only by the presence or threat of federal troops, and it had led to a form of corruption. That was certainly the case with Kellogg, who was now leaving the governor's mansion for the Senate. But Kellogg was fronting Packard as governor, when it was clear that Nicholls had beat him. Grant also believed that Tilden had won Louisiana.

He gave Burke a tentative assurance that this might be the path to a solution, as long as it could be inclusive of other states and issues that plagued the South. A collaborative group representing both sides would need to hammer out the details.

Grant knew the country no longer supported the use of federal troops. Yet he could not abandon the dream of true unity that Reconstruction was meant to usher in. Could a deal contain reliable assurances from Southerners? Could Hayes be counted on to pursue peace and equality in the South, even without reliance on troops?

The stately Wormley Hotel stood on the corner of Fifteenth and H Streets, minutes from the White House. It was a remarkable edifice, owned by James Wormley, a free-born Black man who had prospered in the hospitality trade and made many influential friends during and after the Civil War. On February 26, weary and alarmed by the heat of the Democratic filibuster on the floor of Congress, a group of men met in the hotel rooms of William H. Evarts, a lawyer for the Republicans of the Electoral Commission. Present were key Republicans in the Hayes camp and Southern Democrats. Their aim was to construct a deal that would persuade Democrats to stop the filibuster and ultimately support without debate or violence the legitimacy of a Hayes presidency, if that was the result of the final count.

The Republicans included Ohio congressman James Garfield, who would one day be president himself, only to be assassinated in his sixth month in office. Originally a Blaine man, Garfield had become one of Hayes's closest advisers, and he was a widely respected figure. He didn't really trust Grant, but Grant trusted him; early in the election crisis, Grant had sent him to New Orleans to seek a fairer vote. All along, Garfield had favored being more bullish. He didn't believe for a minute that Democrats were serious about another war. Originally opposed to the Electoral Commission, now Garfield was one of its members.

Also present was Ohio senator John Sherman, brother of

William Tecumseh. He had been with Garfield in New Orleans and was considered one of the most important voices in the Republican Party. Hayes aide Charles Foster was also said to be there (although he tried to keep his name out of it), as was Ohio governor William Dennison. (No written notes were taken, so any other attendees might not be accounted for.)

On the Democratic side was Edward A. Burke, fresh from his meeting with President Grant. Burke was joined by Henry Watterson, a new congressman from Kentucky who had been appointed to replace a member who had died. By profession Watterson was a journalist; he was behind the idea of a march on Washington to force the inauguration of Tilden. Kentucky congressman John Young Brown may also have been present.

Garfield arrived late to the meeting, tired from the strain of being crowded in a small room with the commission, poring over data by flickering candlelight. At commission deliberations, Bradley was at the center of the storm; his voice mattered most. Garfield wrote to a friend that each time Bradley began to speak, the tension was so high it was painful—until he cast his vote and they could all breathe again.

Sitting in the smoke-filled room at the Wormley, Garfield argued for the highest level of integrity in their discussions. The others insisted that they weren't engaged in cheap political horse trading. Garfield wasn't so naive. He warned them against political bargaining, insisting it would be self-defeating. The public would be revolted by the idea of it. With repeated assurances to the contrary, Garfield left early, somewhat mollified. But his warning stuck. Perhaps that was the reason no written record of the Wormley agreement was kept. Foster went to great lengths to deny that Hayes had any idea the meeting was taking place. As he would later tell a reporter, "The meeting was entirely informal.

There was no organization. It was not called to order. Nobody stated its object. There was no chairman. It consisted of a general talk about the room among the different gentlemen who were there."

Foster's insistence that Hayes had no knowledge of the meeting is not credible, as there could be no real agreement without the assurances of the man who would be in the White House. Furthermore, Garfield's note to Hayes after he left the Wormley is pretty clear. He wondered "if in some discreet way, these southern men who are dissatisfied with Tilden and his violent followers, could know that the South is going to be treated with kind consideration by you." All that was left was to articulate what the South would demand.

"What did the South want?" It was a question posed with scathing clarity by C. Vann Woodward, who wrote about the compromise. The answer was complicated and messy, and it went far beyond which of two sons of Northern privilege would win the White House. The South wanted the end of political carpetbagging, which had turned some parts into mere colonies of Republican rule. (Southerners wanted to cooperate with *economic* carpetbaggers, Woodward noted, and benefit from investment in the South, but not political carpetbaggers.) The South wanted the end of military interference, which had kept it in a stage of siege. It wanted control of its own prosperity, instead of the insult of having property and resources robbed as compensation for slavery and the war. It wanted the same kind of economic opportunity that the North enjoyed. With the war more than a decade in the past, the South wanted to stand on its feet again.

And what of the Blacks, and their needs? What of Reconstruction? Woodward referred to the "curious combination of advanced social reform and vindictive persecution" that characterized many

Reconstruction acts—a status the South had grown weary of. At the same time, as the incendiary nature of the election had shown, there was still a strong strain of anti-Black violence coursing through the South. Could the nation now trust the South to guarantee the rights of Blacks without oversight?

Those conferring at the Wormley eased into the compromise, hoping to tick off the biggest boxes. The justification was that a united country, with both North and South finally operating in sync rather than in opposition, could transcend the worst difficulties. In this context, the Republicans and Democrats in the hotel room smoked their cigars and traded their assurances.

From the Republicans: There was a promise that Hayes would permanently withdraw federal troops from the South, putting an end to Reconstruction. In addition, the federal government would recognize the legitimacy of the two Democratic governors who were engaged in disputes with carpetbaggers: Wade Hampton would be legitimized as governor of South Carolina, and Francis Nicholls would be legitimized as governor of Louisiana. Although the federal government did not have the authority to install a governor, by recognizing the Southern candidates and withdrawing federal troops, it would have the same effect. Chamberlain and Packard, both of whom were inaugurated in January despite contested results, would be unable to hold on to their offices without the backing of the military. This concession might not have been made were it not for Grant's intervention earlier in the day, when he'd struck a deal with Burke.

From the Democrats: They agreed to bring an end to the filibuster and allow the Electoral Commission to finish its job. Then they would openly acknowledge that Hayes was the duly elected president and give him their allegiance. With the withdrawal of federal troops, they would give assurances that Black citizens of the South would be treated with respect and would not be abused.

Violence against Blacks and against Republicans would cease. Programs for Blacks, such as schools and social services, would continue.

Essentially, Republicans retained control of the federal government, while the South regained control of its state governments. The Republicans added a couple of sweeteners, such as providing funds to rebuild the Southern economy and to build the Texas and Pacific Railroad. They also agreed that Hayes would appoint at least one Southern Democrat to his cabinet. (He did. David M. Key of Tennessee was named postmaster general.)

It was late when the meeting broke up, sealed with a handshake. As the word reached President Grant, Hayes and Tilden, the House Speaker and the Senate President, and the Electoral Commission members, then down the line to the saber-rattlers on the House floor, the federal troops in the disputed states, and all the players, major and minor, the nation breathed a sigh of relief.

Most of the losers were temporarily comforted by the concessions they gained and began to think ahead to how they would fight the next battle. There seemed nothing to be gained by protesting now, although some had trouble accepting the verdict. Until the bitter end, Stephen Packard in Louisiana was begging the federal government to save his office, refusing to believe that it had been bargained away in the compromise. He pleaded with Grant to protect him with federal might. Grant assigned a secretary, Culver C. Sniffen, to send a telegram: "In answer to your dispatch, the President directs me to say that he feels it his duty to state frankly that he does not believe public opinion will longer support the maintenance of State government in Louisiana by the use of military." It was the final blow to Packard's ambitions.

When Speaker Randall next called Congress to order, the members calmly took their seats, the filibuster having ended. The count continued. Soon after, South Carolina was declared for Hayes. The six remaining states were almost perfunctory.

Tennessee: Tilden.
Texas: Tilden.
Vermont: Hayes.
Virginia: Tilden.
West Virginia: Tilden.
Wisconsin: Hayes.

There was a brief dustup over the Wisconsin results, which landed like a final cry of pain and then submission. It was over.

At 4:10 A.M. on March 2, Senator Ferry rose to his feet and commanded the attention of the chamber. He spoke. "Wherefore I do declare: That Rutherford B. Hayes, of Ohio, having received a majority of the whole number of electoral votes, is duly elected President of the United States for four years, commencing on the 4th day of March, 1877. And that William A. Wheeler, of New York, having received a majority of the whole number of electors votes, is duly elected Vice President of the United States for four years, commencing on the 4th day of March, 1877."

Hewitt, who had sat through the whole grueling mess, did not make it to the end, claiming, "My nervous system yielded to the strain of many days and nights of excessive anxiety passed without sleep. I was taken from the House by my friends in a state of collapse . . . from which I did not recover until after Hayes had taken the oath of office."

Perhaps he was suffering from the reality that historian John Bergamini writes of: "Tilden simply lacked the courage of his convictions that he had been duly elected."

The sad and inescapable truth is that there was no way of

knowing the right verdict. Was Tilden robbed? As Bergamini so succinctly describes the situation:

> With so much fraud and harassment perpetrated against the voters in the three Southern states by both parties, it is impossible for historians to say with final accuracy what the true results were, even though some have taken the trouble to examine the records in minute detail. The consensus of best guesses was that Tilden clearly won in Florida, he probably won in Louisiana, and he lost in South Carolina. All he needed was one of them. As for the Democratic claims to Oregon, they rested only on a legalism.

Even today people debate the legitimacy of the outcome. For those who believe the count was biased, did the end justify the means? Tilden's presidency would likely have differed little from Hayes's. It remained unclear what they were fighting for, beyond satisfying basic partisan instincts. Those who felt betrayed by Grant's failure to fight for Reconstruction might have been reminded that Grant's priority was always the Union—and that he had already realized that he couldn't sustain military rule in the South.

In the minds of some, the very fact that a deal could be made was evidence that a new, more peaceful era was upon them. Mark Wahlgren Summers perfectly sums up the reality:

> By 1875, it was plain to any thinking person—which is to say just about anyone who was not a newspaper editor—that the Union would not be undone, that, however much they prided themselves on their southernness, white southerners would never go out of the Union, would never seek a new war.

Every dedication of a Confederate war memorial added to that sense. Nostalgia was not a danger, and there was nothing more soothing than ceremonies, all done in the spirit of elegy, for a Lost Cause—a cause recognized as lost beyond recovery.

Life went on, but unsettling nicknames stuck to Hayes—"Old Eight to Seven," for instance, and "His Fraudulency."

While the final votes were being counted, Hayes boarded a train in Columbus headed for Washington and joked with well-wishers that he might be back sooner than expected. But by the time he arrived in Washington on the morning of March 2, his election was official.

Grant had invited Hayes to stay at the White House, but he declined, not wanting to look presumptuous. He would stay with Senator Sherman until the inauguration. However, his first evening in town Hayes dined with Grant at the White House. Beforehand, they drove from the White House to Capitol Hill, where Grant graciously presented Hayes to members of Congress and the cabinet.

Because March 4 fell on a Sunday, Grant suggested that Hayes have a private swearing-in on Saturday just to make it official, with a public inauguration on Monday, March 5.

Julia was tearful and somewhat distraught to be leaving and turning what she viewed as *her* house over to Lucy Hayes. She declined to go to the inauguration because she could not bear it. But she did arrange to give a luncheon for the Hayes family at the White House after the ceremony. When the luncheon was over, the Grants would make their farewells.

When her daughter asked Julia what she would say to Mrs. Hayes by way of goodbye, Julia replied, "I will say just what

Buckner said to General Grant when he surrendered Fort Donelson, 'My house is yours.'" She didn't say it, though. In the moment she forgot. Instead, she said, "Mrs. Hayes, I hope you will be as happy here as I have been for the past eight years."

How did Grant feel about leaving? General Christopher Columbus Augur, who had been such a reliable support, had dinner with the president at the White House a few days before the end of his term. As they smoked cigars after dinner, Augur commented that Grant must be looking forward to a return to civilian life, when he would be free from all the burdens and attacks of the presidency.

"To my dismay," Augur recalled, "the President said, with deep feeling, that he welcomed the change, because his confidence was badly shaken. He added that it was the saddest hour of his life, not that he was to end his term as President, but because he had come to realize that he did not know where to go, outside of his family, to find a man to be his confidential secretary, in whom he could put entire trust. I knew what a blow this was to him, as he had always placed the utmost confidence in the fidelity of those he had admitted to his friendship."

Augur's account seemed like an odd note to strike about a man who had twice achieved the highest office of the land, and before that was commanding general of the Army. But it speaks to Grant's peculiar character. He might have looked forward to being out of the presidency, but without an official purpose, be it the Army or government, he did not really know who he was or whom he could depend on. Maybe at his core he suffered low self-esteem—a fear that no one would respect or defend him if he was not in command. Or maybe he simply realized that his errors in judgment had compromised his capacity for greatness in the White House.

He'd admitted as much in his final statement to Congress on

December 5. "Mistakes have been made, as all can see and I admit," he said, describing his errors in selecting assistants, but he added, "It is impossible, where so many trusts are to be allotted, that the right parties should be chosen in every instance."

Perhaps he was trying to find an excuse, or perhaps by admitting his flaws he was exhibiting a quality of humility that demonstrated strength of character. Garfield recognized a deeper truth about Grant. No fan of the general, Garfield now looked at the receding figure with fresh appreciation. In the viper pit of Washington politics, Grant remained unique. Garfield wrote, "No American has carried greater fame out of the White House than this silent man who leaves it today."

PART FIVE

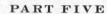

THE FINAL
BATTLE

CHAPTER 13

THE SEARCH FOR PURPOSE

"Oh, Ulys," Julia wailed melodramatically, "I feel like a waif, like a waif on the world's wide common." On the train to visit Grant's childhood home after they left the White House, Julia could not resist spilling out her misery. Tears poured from her eyes as she thought about the future. She was inconsolable.

Grant smiled at his wife affectionately. "Oh, is that all?" he said. "I thought something had happened. You must not forget that I, too, am a waif. So you are not alone."

Grant did not share Julia's unhappiness. Indeed, for the first time in years he found himself surrounded by cheering crowds as he made his way across the country. It was as if the nation had forgotten its regrets about him and only remembered his finest hours. Stopping in Galena, the Grants were embraced with such warmth and love by their neighbors that it felt like a true home-coming.

But the Grants were planning to leave town in a big way—with a world tour, "the wanderings of Ulysses," Badeau called it. They set sail in Philadelphia on May 17, along with nineteen-year-old

Jesse, aboard the *Indiana*, which would dock in Liverpool, England. The day before, Grant had participated in a moving event at Philadelphia's Independence Hall where he greeted 1,200 veterans. He still felt a glow from that occasion, and before sailing, a large breakfast given by Childs and packed with luminaries and friends provided a hearty send-off. The festivities continued in their stateroom when they boarded the *Indiana*.

On May 23, a message was issued from the State Department to the diplomatic corps and the consular offices alerting them that the Grants were embarking on a tour, "the object of his journey being to secure a few months of rest and recreation after sixteen years of unremitting and devoted labor in the military and civil service of this country." As it turned out, the tour would become an unprecedented diplomatic feat, and it would last two and a half years. John Russell Young, a journalist with the *New York Herald*, would join the trip and send reports back home so that Americans could enjoy an inside view of the journey. Young would become very close to the Grants on the trip.

It should be noted that presidential pensions did not exist in Grant's day, and his assets included only the properties that had been gifted to him and a rare good investment. It was money from that investment that funded their travels.

They were cheered everywhere they went and feted by international figures. They met with Queen Victoria at Windsor Castle, where Jesse, spoiled by his indulgent parents, created a scene when he wasn't seated at the queen's table. They had an audience with the pope in Rome and were hosted by the czar of Russia and the emperor of Japan. Grant was amazed by the outpouring, which reminded him of the way it was just after the war. It had not occurred to him that he would be so popular abroad, and that the ordinary people of every nation would turn out on the streets to catch a glimpse of him. "I know this reception is intended more for my country than for myself," he said with typical self-deprecation, although that was not the least bit true. They wanted to see the man, the war hero.

On a more serious note, world leaders sought Grant's interpretation of the meaning of the war and America's attitude toward slavery. In one fascinating account that made it home via Young, Grant frankly shared his views in a conversation with Otto von Bismarck, the first chancellor of the German Empire. Bismarck was curious about the hardship of the Civil War and the necessity of fighting one's own brothers.

"But it had to be done," Grant said.

"Yes," said the prince, "you had to save the Union just as we had to save Germany."

"Not only save the Union, but *destroy slavery*," Grant clarified.

"I suppose, however, the Union was the real sentiment, the dominant sentiment," the prince said. This was a smart observation, because it was certainly true early on, for both Lincoln and Grant. But Grant took the opportunity to provide a deeper understanding of what was at stake.

"In the beginning, yes," he agreed, "but as soon as slavery fired upon the flag it was felt, we all felt, even those who did not object to slaves, that slavery must be destroyed. We felt that it was a stain to the Union that men should be bought and sold like cattle. . . . There had to be an end of slavery."

On his trip Grant was unexpectedly forced to do what had always made him the most uncomfortable—speak to crowds, sometimes spontaneously. Resistance was futile, and he actually improved his oratorical skills.

Meanwhile, in Washington, Hayes was struggling with how to orchestrate the end of Reconstruction. The problem, as Andrew L. Slap, professor of history at East Tennessee State University and author of *The Doom of Reconstruction*, has put it, "was that twelve years of federal occupation had not convinced white Southerners to accept the realities of the Fourteenth and Fifteenth Amendments, and probably little short of military occupation for generations would have dramatically changed conditions and attitudes in the region. . . . The liberal republicans were caught in a dilemma they could not solve, as they wanted republican governments in the South that were fair to both blacks and whites, yet they were not willing to use force indefinitely to create and uphold such governments." Thus the compromise that put Hayes in the White House.

It would be wildly optimistic to expect the nation in such turmoil to easily right itself with a new president. Hayes quickly found that keeping the promises of the compromise was not such a simple matter. One of Hayes's first acts in office was to remove the troops from South Carolina, which he did on April 10. Then he removed troops from Louisiana on April 20. On April 22, he wrote in his diary:

We got through with the South Carolina and Louisiana [difficulties]. At any rate, the troops are ordered away and I now hope for peace, and what is equally important, security and prosperity for the colored people. The result of my plans to get from those States by their governors, legislatures, press, and people pledges that the Thirteenth, Fourteenth, and Fifteenth Amendments shall be faithfully observed; that the colored people shall have equal rights to labor, education, and the privileges of citizenship. I am confident this is a good work. Time will tell.

Hayes was right that it would take time to decipher the fallout. Initially, a sense of calm fell over the nation, as if it were settling into itself at last under the direction of a steady civilian leader who reminded no one of a warrior. Even the Blacks felt it. As C. Vann Woodward pointed out, while the mass of Southern Blacks might have felt uneasy, their leaders were enjoying the appearance of public acceptance. For example, Douglass was appointed marshal of the District of Columbia and was living in a spectacular home. His status bore little resemblance to the plight of most Southern Blacks, but it was a start. Hayes believed firmly that the way to reconstruct the South was to give it the freedom to exercise its independence and seek a route to prosperity that was no longer dependent on slavery.

On the whole, life was peaceful, and that was a relief. No one knew that the unraveling would not be widely visible for a decade. For while the nation's leaders, from the president on down, spoke of Black opportunity and the promise of equality, the scar tissue from the Civil War was more lasting, and it found expression in the farthest corners of the rural South.

As Grant's acclaim abroad grew and the stories of his diplomatic and personal feats reached the United States, his friends had begun to plot a political future for him. Specifically, they were preparing the way for Grant to enter the presidential contest in 1880, telling people, "He is better fitted to be President of the United States than any other American citizen."

Running for a third term was far from Grant's own mind. His son Buck viewed the political comeback as the inspiration of his father's friends—not something Grant would ever have sought or necessarily wanted for himself. Their plans were so far along by the time Grant returned from overseas that he felt obligated. "The Presidency was not a thing to be sought, neither was it a thing to refuse if the people felt he ought to have it," Buck said by way of explaining his father's thinking. "But when it came to him, he felt it was his duty to accept it if he could fill the place. He was also incapable of supposing his friends to be dishonest."

Grant was invited to use the office of Judge William R. Rowley as his Galena headquarters. Rowley had served as brigadier general in the war and had been Grant's military secretary for part of it. He had moved to Galena afterward and been elected a county judge.

The Republican convention opened with three candidates. In addition to Grant, there was Blaine (again!) and Secretary of the Treasury John Sherman.

Many who were opposed to breaking the two-term tradition established by George Washington supported either Blaine or Sherman over Grant. Acknowledging this bias against a third term, Julia begged Grant to go to Chicago in person and address the delegates. He told her he'd rather cut off his right hand.

"Do you not desire success?" she demanded.

"Well, yes, of course, since my name is up, I would rather be nominated, but I will do nothing to further that end."

"Oh, Ulys," Julia said with exasperation, "how unwise, what mistaken chivalry. For heaven's sake, go . . . I beseech you."

Grant shook his head. "Julia, I am amazed at you," he replied, and walked out of the room.

Grant was in Galena with Rowley during the convention, receiving wire bulletins. At one point, Rowley's son rushed in announcing with great excitement, "There is a rumor that Hamilton Fish's name will be sprung on the Convention!"

Grant exclaimed, "Rowley! As undignified as it might seem in me to do it, if the Convention will agree to nominate Fish, I'll agree to stand on my head right here. Fish is one of the best men in the country." But the rumor didn't pan out.

When the roll call came to New York, Conkling rose and gave the full-throated nomination of Grant he had long wanted to give, crying out:

And when asked what State he hails from,
Our sole reply shall be,
He hails from Appomattox,
And its famous apple tree.

That "famous apple tree" referred more to myth than reality. There had been a story that while waiting for General Grant to accept the white flag of surrender, General Lee had rested beneath an apple tree at Appomattox. In some versions, the actual surrender took place beneath the tree. It was said that the tree was then cut down by Union soldiers and chopped into pieces for souvenirs. The story doesn't square with firsthand accounts of that day, but it became a beloved fable. At Conkling's mention of the tree, the delegates cheered wildly. Conkling's voice rose above them: "New York is for Ulysses S. Grant. Never defeated—never defeated in peace or in war, his name is the most illustrious borne by living men."

Buck had come to Galena to join his parents during the convention. He was afraid his father would be defeated and the loss would crush him, and he wanted to be there to console him. On the evening of the nomination, he was with his father in Rowley's office.

Buck recalled:

As the account of Conkling's speech came on, and reports of the applause lasting twenty minutes, and then coming again and again, father began to feel uneasy and either from dislike or from modesty, determined to go home. So, he said good evening to those in the office and we walked off together. As we got a little way up the walk, he said in a peculiar tone of voice, a little sad it seemed to me, "I am afraid I may be nominated." When I heard him say this, I immediately felt free to go home, and I took the train at once. It became perfectly evident that he would not take defeat as a calamity.

For most of the convention, it appeared that Grant might just prevail. He started off strong, with 304 of the needed 379 votes on the first ballot, Blaine nipping at his heels at 285, and Sherman far behind at 93. Thirty-five ballots later, the delegates were no closer to breaking the deadlock. At that point, both Blaine and Sherman withdrew and gave their votes in support of a dark-horse candidate, James Garfield. He won on the thirty-sixth ballot with 399 votes to Grant's 306.

The convention chose Chester A. Arthur, chairman of the New York Republican Party, as the vice presidential candidate.

As Buck had recognized, Grant didn't seem to care that he'd lost. He told his friends, "I can't say that I regret my own defeat, by it I shall escape four years of hard work and four years of abuse; and gentlemen, we can all support the candidate." Julia, however, was quite disappointed.

The Garfield-Arthur ticket won the presidency, defeating the Democrats' Winfield Scott Hancock and former Indiana congressman William Hayden English. Once again, the Republicans were in the White House.

Grant had campaigned for Garfield, exhibiting his newfound confidence with public speaking. As he put it, "My knees don't knock together like they did at first." There was some talk once Garfield took office of Grant joining his cabinet, but Grant put an end to the idea. He wasn't interested in a political position. He did, however, feel troubled by the struggles of Southern Blacks, knowing that they had not fared well amid all the talk of equality. On June 14, 1881, he spoke at a benefit for the

Colored Citizens' Association of New York and Brooklyn, expressing his hope for the Black community and his confidence in them.

> I sincerely hope with you that the time is not far distant when all the privileges that citizenship carries with it will be accorded you throughout the land without any opposition . . . and I have no fear myself but what they will be exercised as well and fully by you as by any other race enjoying the blessings and privileges of this country.

As it turned out, Garfield's presidency lasted only a few months. On July 2, as Garfield was entering the train station accompanied by Blaine—who was now secretary of State—a man came up to him and fired two shots, one hitting him in the arm and the other in his back. He fell to the ground.

The assassin was Charles J. Guiteau, from Illinois. He'd been a fervent supporter of Garfield and had even written a speech in praise of him during the campaign. In his twisted view, Garfield owed him his presidency and should have considered him for a plum position. Plagued with resentment, he awoke one night with an inspiration that God wanted him to kill the president so that Arthur could step into the office.

It had to occur to Grant that perhaps he'd dodged a bullet for a second time. The prior year Guiteau had made a nuisance of himself with Grant as well, pestering him for an audience when Grant was temporarily living at the Fifth Avenue Hotel in New York City. Grant asked his son Fred if he knew anything about this guy who wanted so much to talk to him.

"He is a sort of lawyer and deadbeat in Chicago," Fred said. "Don't let him come up. If you do, he would bore you to death."

Guiteau did manage to get in once, though, and Grant had a hard time convincing him to leave.

Garfield lingered for two and a half months, and he probably would have survived were it not for massive infections caused by his treatment. He died on September 19. Found guilty of murder, Guiteau was hanged a year after the shooting.

Chester Arthur, a Republican Stalwart and friend of Conkling, took office and quickly replaced most of Garfield's cabinet. Arthur, who was an experienced administrator committed to civil service reform, was considered a solid if unshowy president, but by the end of his first term he was in poor health, suffering from kidney disease. He didn't mount much of a campaign for the nomination in 1884 and lost it to Blaine. At last achieving the prize he had long coveted, Blaine went on to lose the election to Grover Cleveland, a Democrat who finally broke the Republican presidential winning streak.

For the first time in twenty-some years, Grant faced a life without purpose. What would he do? How would he earn a living? He thought back to the time in his life before the Civil War when he experienced deep insecurity and failure. Although he was now more worldly, he still lacked an understanding of business and was a poor manager of his own money. For so long he had floated safely above these concerns. Now he had to face them. At least he and Julia would have a lovely home from which to do so. After their world trip, which had nearly exhausted the family savings, friends of the Grants, with Childs in the lead, had created a fund so that they could secure a mortgage to purchase a brownstone in Manhattan, at 3 East Sixty-Sixth Street, right off Fifth Avenue and Central Park. Decorated with the many treasures and artifacts they had received as gifts on their tour, the interior had an international flavor. It was—and remains—one of the best addresses in Manhattan, although the Grant brownstone was eventually replaced by an apartment building.

Grant still needed an income, though. He was impressed when Buck went into partnership with a promising young financier named Ferdinand Ward. Their firm, Grant & Ward, had offices at 2 Wall Street, a prestigious location. Placing full confidence in his son, Grant invested all of his liquid assets—about $100,000—in the brokerage. The investment paid off handsomely. By 1884, the Grants were nearly millionaires and for the first time in their lives could imagine what it meant to be truly wealthy. Buck and his wife, Fannie, moved in with them, and soon the happy prospect of grandchildren was upon them. The Grants doted on their grandchildren every bit as much as they had on their own children.

It was a very happy, comfortable time. The only sour note came on Christmas Eve 1883. Stepping down from his carriage, Grant slipped on the ice and seriously injured his leg. He was in great pain and spent the winter hobbling on crutches.

Then, one afternoon in May 1884, Ward visited Grant and Buck at Sixty-Sixth Street and told them a troubling story. Marine Bank, which had more than $700,000 of Grant's money on deposit, was suffering from a temporary liquidity problem. All it needed was a bridge loan and the situation would be righted. Ward wondered if Grant would appeal to his friend William Vanderbilt for a $150,000 loan. Grant agreed, and Vanderbilt was happy to make the loan, no questions asked.

Days later, Marine Bank closed, and Ward dropped out of sight. It was discovered that Ward and the president of the bank had colluded to use bank funds to speculate in real estate, and everything was lost. Not only was Grant broke, but he was also in debt. Vanderbilt tried to refuse repayment of the loan, but Grant insisted. He sold some of his property and also gave Vanderbilt valuable souvenirs from his travels. He was deeply humiliated and destitute.

In their poverty, the Grants were moved by the kindness of others. Julia wrote of being "literally without means" when a New York man—a stranger—sent $500 with the note, "General, I owe you this for Appomattox." When Grant replied with gratitude, the man sent a check for $1,000, and said it was a loan to be repaid when it was convenient.

In the midst of an intensely stressful period, Grant faced another crisis. As Julia recalled it, the incident started in the most innocuous way. Grant was eating a delicious peach on a June day when he jumped back and exclaimed, "Oh my. I think something has stung me from that peach." He washed his throat repeatedly, but it continued to burn "like liquid fire." As Grant's throat problem continued, it seemed less likely to be related to the peach. When Grant finally saw a doctor in August, he was alarmed and urged Grant to see his personal physician. However, Grant's doctor, Fordyce Barker, was in Europe for the summer, and Grant didn't see him until October. Given that Grant was a longtime and enthusiastic smoker of cigars, there wasn't much surprise about his scratchy throat. The doctor recommended that he gargle frequently and use salves. Grant temporarily stopped smoking cigars and told Julia he didn't think the problem was serious. Besides, he had other things on his mind.

The final years of great men often feel bittersweet, and their failures seem to loom as large as their successes. In the ninth year after he left the White House, Grant had found himself in a desperate situation. But in the midst of this crisis, and even because of it, he finally found something he could do in his post-presidency. He could write.

CHAPTER 14

GRANT'S OWN STORY

The editors of *Century* magazine, a popular periodical, had watched Grant's tale of financial ruin with great sympathy but also opportunistic interest. The magazine, which had begun publishing in New York City in 1881 as a successor to *Scribner's Monthly*, was the nation's leading source of entertainment and personal narrative, and articles about the war were always a big draw. Grant had previously declined suggestions by *Century*'s editor-in-chief, Richard Gilder, that he write about his war campaigns, but after Grant's highly publicized financial fall, Gilder thought he might be persuaded. Gilder assigned an editor, Robert Underwood Johnson, to put the case to Adam Badeau, who had Grant's ear.

Johnson wrote, "The country looks with so much regret and sympathy upon General Grant's misfortune that it would gladly welcome the . . . publication of material relating to him or by him, concerning a part of his honored career in which every one takes pride. It would be glad to have its attention diverted from his present troubles, and no doubt such diversion of his own mind would be welcome to him."

Grant was in Long Branch for the summer, and when Badeau showed him the letter, he was touched by Johnson's kind tone, as well as the possibility of income. He agreed to talk to Johnson, but he was still doubtful that he had what it took to write about his experiences.

It so happened that Johnson was spending the summer at Point Pleasant, which was near Long Branch. So one day he traveled to Grant's town for a conversation. The Grant beach house was a bustling place that summer, as Fred's family was with them. But when Johnson sat in the cottage waiting for Grant to join him, he felt that it had "a lonely air."

To Johnson's astonishment, Grant immediately launched into a full account of the collapse of Grant & Ward. He said that he felt it was important to clear the air of any suspicion of wrongdoing on his part. Johnson was struck by the deeply personal nature of Grant's words. "He had been hurt to the quick in his proud name and in his honor, and the man who, we had been told, was stolid and reserved showed himself to me as a person of the most sensitive nature and the most human expression of feeling," Johnson later wrote in his own memoir. "No man-of-letters could more openly have worn his heart."

Grant then acknowledged what was already apparent. His new state of poverty—he barely had money to pay the butcher—had led him to reconsider the idea of writing a series of articles about the war. Delighted, Johnson described his vision for a four-part series covering Shiloh, Vicksburg, the Wilderness, and Lee's surrender. The magazine was willing to pay $500 apiece for the articles. Grant agreed to write the first one about the Battle of Shiloh, and they would see how it went.

It did not go well. "Every editor will sympathize with our dismay," Johnson wrote later about his response to Grant's first effort. It was as dry as a military report, completely stripped of the vivid portrayal of battle that readers longed for. In fairness, Johnson realized, Grant had no experience in the form, and little understanding of what a magazine audience wanted to hear. It was ignorance, not inability, that froze his pen.

Johnson traveled to Long Branch, where he gently engaged Grant in a conversation without expressing a hint of disappointment in the first draft. He asked probing questions, and before he knew it Grant was describing the battle in the most compelling way. Johnson was struck by Grant's extreme sensitivity; he brought no bluster to his account of military events. He made one confession about the aftermath of Shiloh that particularly struck Johnson: "I couldn't stand the amputations and had to go out in the rain and sit for most of the night under a tree."

After they had talked for a while, Johnson gave Grant his most important lesson in writing for the public. "I told him," Johnson would recall, "that what was desirable for the success of the paper was to approximate to such a talk as he would make to friends after dinner, some of whom should know all about the battle and some nothing at all, and that the public, who could easily discover the geography and the movements of the engagement—which of course could not be omitted—was particularly interested in his point of view, in everything that concerned him, in what he planned, thought, saw, said, and did."

Grant had not thought of it that way, and he was intrigued by Johnson's final piece of advice. Johnson told him not to try too hard. In other words, just tell the story as it happened and as he experienced it. The guidance worked. When Grant resubmitted the article, it was exactly what Johnson had in mind. *Century* would publish it in February 1885.

Grant found that he relished the work. Immersed in accounts of the past, he was partially distracted from his looming health crisis—a different kind of invasion than the one he was writing about. The diagnosis had finally come. Grant had agreed to visit Dr. John Hancock Douglas, a prominent otolaryngologist (ear, nose, and throat doctor), whom he trusted because of their prior relationship. Douglas had run the field hospitals at Shiloh and in the Wilderness. He was shocked at the condition of Grant's throat and gently pronounced the damning verdict: It was throat cancer. The prognosis was poor.

Faced with a death sentence, Grant would occasionally allow despair to overwhelm him. Staring hopelessly at the page, he would wonder about the point of it all. Badeau felt emboldened to speak his mind more honestly than ever before. "There came moments and crises when he allowed me to say things to him such as few men ever say to each other; and I ventured now to beg him to throw aside this strange depression—the result of his illness; to be himself; not to give way, even to fate."

Thus encouraged, "his apathy was not long-lived," Badeau reported. Grant managed through sheer force of will to transcend his sorry state of health and to write.

One evening in early November 1884, Samuel Clemens—aka Mark Twain—and his wife, Livy, came upon Gilder, whom they knew well. On the spot Gilder invited them to come home with him for a late supper, and they accepted. Over the meal, Gilder could not contain his enthusiasm at having scored a real literary coup for *Century*. General Grant was in the process of writing three—possibly four—war articles for the magazine. Nothing could be a bigger draw than a firsthand account of the war by its top general. According to Gilder, Grant was thrilled at the opportunity. He needed the money and was delighted to accept a payment of $500 for each article.

Twain left the dinner fuming. Five hundred dollars! He was

appalled by the meager amount of the fee and saw it as a scandalous treatment of a hero. It was, he wrote in his diary, "not only the monumental injustice of the nineteenth century, but of all centuries." And Twain believed that Gilder knew it as well as he did.

"He ought to have known that if he had given General Grant a check for ten thousand dollars, the sum would still have been trivial; that if he had paid him twenty thousand dollars for a single article, the sum would still have been inadequate; that if he had paid him thirty thousand dollars for a single magazine war article, it still could not be called paid for; that if he had given him forty thousand dollars for a single magazine article, he would still be in General Grant's debt." (When he discovered that Grant's first article had yielded the periodical fifty thousand new subscribers, he was more indignant than ever.)

Not only that, Gilder had bragged about Grant agreeing to write a full memoir. The contract for his book was in the process of being drawn. Not only was Twain alarmed, but he was disappointed. Why had Grant not spoken with *him* about a memoir?

Twain and Grant were friends, and as far back as 1881, Twain had appealed to Grant to consider a memoir, writing him what he hoped was a persuasive letter. Grant waited a week to answer, which at that time was a lengthy delay. He explained, "I had delayed answering it until this time not because of any doubt as to how to answer it but because of the principal reason I have for not doing what you suggest, namely laziness." Grant wrote honestly that he didn't have what it took to embark upon such an ambitious literary work. "In the first place I have always distrusted my ability to write anything that would satisfy myself, and the public would be much more difficult to please. In the second place I am not possessed of the kind of industry necessary to undertake such a work."

Twain disagreed. He had every confidence in Grant and was willing to help him. He knew the public would greet a Grant memoir with great excitement. Most of all, he wanted this success for a man he admired.

The two men were strange bedfellows. During the war Twain had briefly served in the Marion Rangers, which was an outlier Confederate unit from his hometown of Hannibal, Missouri. But he soon found he couldn't stomach the fight. He abandoned the war in 1861, after three weeks. His first meeting with Grant occurred while Grant was president. Introduced at a White House event, the two men shook hands and then fell into an uneasy silence, neither knowing what to say. Finally, Twain said, "Mr. President, I am embarrassed. Are you?" It was a strange remark and Grant did not reply.

Their next meeting took place in 1879, after the Grants returned from their world tour. A parade and great dinner were given in Grant's honor in Chicago. Twain was invited to be the last in a long line of speakers at the dinner. When the Chicago mayor introduced the two men at the parade earlier in the day, Grant twinkled at Twain and said, "Mr. Clemens, I am not embarrassed, are you?" Twain was completely charmed and impressed by Grant's memory.

At the dinner, fourteen speakers, one after the other, rose to praise Grant in the dull manner of proper dinner toasts. Twain was the last speaker. Standing atop a table, he delighted in breaking up the interminable boredom of the toasts with humor—he roasted Grant! It would become known as "the Babies speech" because of its hilarious finale, in which Twain described a baby Grant, determined to suck his toes: "Giving his whole strategic mind at this moment to trying to find out some way to get his big toe into his mouth—an achievement which, meaning no disrespect, the illustrious guest of this evening turned his entire attention to some fifty-six years ago; and if the child is but a prophecy of the man, there are mighty few who will doubt that he succeeded."

His words brought down the house, and no one laughed louder than Grant. As Twain boasted to a friend, "I shook him up like dynamite & he sat there fifteen minutes & laughed & cried like the mortalest of mortals."

After that, the two men became friends, and Twain allowed himself to dream of the possibility that he would one day publish the great general's memoir. His meeting with Gilder shook him to the core, though, and the next day he went to see Grant. Was it true what Gilder had told him? Grant said it was. Twain asked if there was a contract, and Grant said it had been drawn up but was not signed yet. At that point, Twain's chief interest was in protecting his friend from making a terrible financial deal. He asked if he could look at the contract and share his expertise.

Grant pulled out the contract, which was in draft form, and read it aloud. When he heard it, Twain's worst fears were realized. "I didn't know whether to cry or laugh," he recalled. First and foremost, the *Century* was seriously undercutting Grant on royalties. The standard at the time, and in Twain's experience, was to pay 10 percent to a new author who was expected to sell no more than a few thousand copies. But when an author was expected to sell a few *hundred* thousand copies, as Grant was sure to do, the standard royalty was 20 percent.

Twain didn't consider the *Century*'s offer a deliberate effort to cheat Grant. Rather, he gave them the benefit of the doubt, assuming they made their offer in ignorance given their lack of experience in book publishing. Twain patiently explained to Grant why he should reject the offer and detailed the counteroffer he should make. He stressed that any of the great publishers would be happy to have this book, and Grant was in a perfect position to secure a good deal. If all else failed, Twain said, Grant could publish with him.

Twain didn't really expect Grant to do that, and Grant seemed shy about breaking up with *Century*. As Twain left town for a lengthy tour, Grant continued his magazine writing for the paltry wage. Meanwhile, other publishers had picked up the scent, and Grant was being barraged daily by solicitations for his memoir. Most of them made clear that he could name his price.

Suddenly, Grant's eyes were opened. He realized that he'd barely escaped making a bad deal. He asked Childs to visit him and give his advice, and Childs quickly saw that Grant was leaning toward publishing with Twain. And that's what happened.

There was still one more detail to settle. Twain was so confident in the sales potential of the memoir that he offered to give Grant a $25,000 advance for each of two volumes. Grant was horrified. He explained that he couldn't possibly accept money that Twain might never recoup. He also felt that the 20 percent royalty arrangement was not as good for Twain, and he insisted on a profit-sharing plan. "This was just like General Grant," Twain wrote, with some exasperation. "It was absolutely impossible for him to entertain for a moment any proposition which might prosper him at the risk of any other man."

Ultimately, the deal the two men struck was for a profit-sharing subscription sale—a common bookselling method of the day. Twain would publish the book through his company, Charles L. Webster & Co., named for his niece's husband, who was in charge of business and sales.

Still uncertain about his prospects, Grant wondered if Twain thought they could sell twenty-five thousand copies. That was the number the *Century* had given him. Oh, yes! Twain reassured him.

Because of his cancer, Grant knew the project would be a race against time.

Julia wanted to feel elation over the prospect of the book deal, but she was too stricken with terror about Grant's medical condition. She struggled with acceptance and clung to her faith, although "down in my heart, I could not believe that God in his wisdom and mercy would take this great, wise, good man from us."

In many ways, Grant was elevated by his illness. He was able to set aside his fears and agonies, as he had once done on the field of battle, and focus on the mission at hand. Watching Grant write his memoirs was a revelation for Twain, who was dazzled by the "wonderful machine" of Grant's memory. "He told me one day that he never made a report of the battles of the Wilderness until they were all over and he was back in Washington," Twain recalled. "Then he sat down and made a full report from memory, and, when it was finished, examined the reports of his subordinates, and found that he had made hardly an error. To be exact, he said he had made two errors."

Even as Grant's condition grew much worse, he never gave up. Julia would later recall, with some bitterness, "with what perseverance he continued to the end this writing, writing, writing for bread."

In excruciating pain that made lying flat impossible, Grant propped himself up in his chair and wrote from morning until night, fearing death would take him before his book was finished and his wife's financial future secured.

In the process, he found a voice that would long survive his passing.

The perennial question of who wrote the memoirs remains, but most historians believe that Grant wrote the book himself. Badeau, who helped him with research, sued the estate after Grant's death, claiming that he should have received more credit. According to McFeely, however, Badeau "arrived [at Grant's side] hoping to win immortality by putting into literary form the words of the dying general. It did not occur to him that Grant could write a book." But he soon found out. Perhaps

Badeau's unhappiness stemmed from envy, or he may have just wanted a cut of the money.

There was speculation that Mark Twain was the author of Grant's memoirs, but Twain debunked those suspicions by stating that he'd barely edited them except for form. Reading the *Memoirs*, it is Grant's voice one hears—unadorned, dispassionate, with none of the grandiosity with which great generals tend to embellish their stories. Seated at a large table in the sitting room of his New York City house, with the warm babble of his grandchildren in the background, Grant worked for hours on end, his power of concentration greater than his pain. His son Fred, in a great labor of love, was by his side, having usurped the disgruntled Badeau as his father's primary researcher.

By the spring of 1885, Grant was nearing the final chapters, even as his condition worsened. Throat cancer is an ugly disease, and Grant would often be overtaken by uncontrollable coughing fits and vomiting. He confessed to Childs that drinking water was so agonizing that it was "what molten lead would be" going down his throat. It was difficult for him to eat solid food, and finally to speak. The pain was so severe that his doctor injected morphine straight into his throat. Yet through it all he kept writing. And he did it in public view, such as it was at the time. News of his illness had leaked out, as had publicity about his upcoming book, and the newspapers were full of rumor and speculation. The high drama of Grant's final act left the nation breathless.

His son Buck witnessed his agony and also his determination. One night he relieved his father's aide and slept on a small Dutch bed next to him. His father tossed and turned, groaning in his sleep, and Buck gently rewrapped the woolen cap around his throat when he shook it loose. After this happened several times, Buck recalled, "my great dear father said, 'I see, Buck, you are not going to get any sleep so we will talk. The doctors are much interested in my case and are making a study of it. No Grant was ever afraid to die and we can talk freely about my cancer and all my symptoms. My only apprehension is that your mother is unprepared for my death and it will shock her. That and the fact that I leave her so poor off financially.'"

As summer approached, Grant's doctor was concerned that the heat would increase his suffering. A friend offered a cottage on the grounds of his hotel at Mount McGregor, located in upstate New York near Saratoga Springs. There, in the cool air of the Adirondacks, Grant might find some relief.

He knew he was dying, and that the end would come soon. The signs were clear. In a note to Dr. Douglas, asking for no heroic measures, he detailed the three ways in which his body was preparing for the end: "One by hemorrhages, one by strangulation, and the third by exhaustion. The first and second are liable to come at any moment to relieve me of my earthly sufferings; the time for the arrival of the third can be computed with almost mathematical certainty."

He told Childs in their last conversation before he left for the Adirondacks, "I have been twice within a half a minute of death. I realize it fully, and my life was only preserved by the skill and attention of my physicians. I have told them the next time to let me go."

A steady stream of visitors came for brief moments to deliver their best wishes. Grant did not have the time or strength to see them all, and Fred filled in when he could. But some visitors moved him deeply. One day Simon Bolivar Buckner, whom he had defeated at Fort Donelson early in the war, arrived with a pressing matter on his mind. In "A Blue and Gray Friendship," John R. Procter wrote of the visit in 1897:

General Buckner said that, aside from the gratification of a feeling of personal friendship, he had a special object in view

in paying this visit. It was to assure General Grant that every Confederate soldier held him in kindly remembrance, not only for his magnanimity at the close of the war, but for his just and friendly conduct afterward.

They sat together for a time, and when Buckner rose to go, they clasped hands.

"Grant," Buckner said, looking into his eyes with intensity.

Grant returned the steady gaze. "Buckner."

Sherman came to visit, and both men were struck as always by how much there was between them. "We were as brothers," Sherman said, and like brothers they had their spats and jealousies. Sherman was high-strung where Grant was placid. Sherman was also more interested in glorification. When he'd written his own memoirs a decade earlier, he'd emphasized his personal heroics. Some of Grant's friends were offended by that. Once, at a gathering in Philadelphia arranged by Childs, one of the attendees asked Grant if he'd read Sherman's book. He said that he hadn't. "Why, general," the man said, "you won't find much in it about yourself. Sherman doesn't seem to think you were in the war." Grant shrugged it off and said he'd wait to form a judgment until he'd read the book. In truth, he was proud of Sherman for having written it, and he generously told him it had been a fine source of research for his own book—which pleased Sherman.

His friends were saddened to see him so weakened, and some could not help but remember that time on the battlefield long ago when Grant's strength was so certain. "The hand which had seized the surrendered swords of countless thousands could scarcely return the pressure of a friendly grasp," Horace Porter lamented. "The voice which had cheered on to triumphant victory the conquering legions of America's manhood could no longer call for the cooling draught that slaked the thirst of a fevered tongue."

Finally, on July 19, curled in a chair, his frail body weighing less than one hundred pounds, Grant pressed the lead of his pencil firmly onto the page and wrote his final words. For the ending, he had summoned a strong reserve of faith in the goodness of the nation. In a sentiment that would resonate for every troubled time, he wrote of the basic unifying quality of America. It was something he had witnessed anew during his illness:

> I feel that we are on the eve of a new era, when there is to be great harmony between the Federal and Confederate. I cannot stay to be a living witness to the correctness of this prophecy; but I feel it within me that it is to be so. The universally kind feeling expressed for me at a time when it was supposed that each day would prove my last, seemed to me the beginning of the answer to "Let us have peace."
>
> The expression of these kindly feelings were not restricted to a section of the country, nor to a division of the people. They came from individual citizens of all nationalities; from all denominations—the Protestant, the Catholic and the Jew; and from the various societies of the land—scientific, educational, religious or otherwise. Politics did not enter into the matter at all.
>
> . . . The war between the states was a very bloody and a very costly war. One side or the other had to yield principles they deemed dearer than life before it could be brought to an end. I commanded the whole of the mighty host engaged on the victorious side. . . . It is a significant and gratifying fact that Confederates should have joined heartily in this spontaneous move. I hope the good feeling inaugurated may continue to the end.

He felt at peace. Days earlier, Twain had visited and assured him that subscription sales were already strong. Julia would be protected.

Now he could rest. He lay in bed surrounded by the family that adored him. In his conscious moments, he saw their stricken faces, but he also saw their love. That love had made him a very lucky man. On July 23, he slipped away.

After his death, a note was found pinned to Grant's robe, addressed to Julia. "Look after our dear children and direct them in the paths of rectitude," he'd written, adding simple instructions to that effect. He closed, "With these few injunctions and the knowledge I have of your love and affection, and of the dutiful affection of all our children, I bid you a final farewell until we meet in another and I trust a better world." Julia would live on to see a new century, dying in 1902. And not a day would pass when she did not reach out for him in her heart and find him there, his love still warming her.

More than one million people attended Grant's funeral in New York City, a testament to his enduring popularity. His pallbearers included two Union generals, Sherman and Sheridan, and two Confederate generals, Buckner and Johnston. Veterans from both armies lined the streets and wept.

Mark Twain was on a mission. He and Charles Webster had hired ten thousand canvassers to travel the country selling subscriptions to Grant's *Memoirs*. They composed a thirty-seven-page manual, titled "Selling U. S. Grant's Memoirs: The Art of the Canvasser," to teach them the ropes. It began with a proposed opening line: "I called to give you an opportunity to see General Grant's book, of which so much has been said in the papers." Many of the canvassers were military veterans, and their honest labor was also a sacred cause. Webster told them to wear their Grand Army badges to make them more appealing.

The canvassers had been taking orders since March, during the final months of Grant's life. They were selling as he was writing.

The emotional appeal was key. The manual advised, "Get the prospect seated, in a fence corner, behind a stump, on the plow beam. Put the book right in his lap, but *you* turn the pages." Twain's style was evident in the written advice. "In leaving a house be careful not to turn your back to the family; retire sideways, keeping your eye on the good people, and let your last glance be full of sunshine."

The campaign was a success. The book sold itself. In the first months of canvassing, orders piled up—sixty thousand two-volume sets sold in the early months, and two hundred thousand by the end of 1885. Julia received a check for $200,000 in 1886 and would eventually receive a total of around $450,000, making her a very wealthy woman. Grant had cared little for wealth, but he would have been gratified to see her live her remaining years in comfort.

Grant had never really understood why Americans loved him so much. He was far from being the noble ideal of a soldier. The leadership skills he possessed on the battlefield did not translate well to civilian life. He had tried to be a good and faithful president. He had tried to heal the wounds of slavery. He had fallen short. But he knew that in times of great national conflict there are only two choices—to stand for division or to stand for peace. He chose peace.

CHAPTER 15

THE MEANING OF GRANT'S
LIFE . . . THEN AND NOW

JUNE 19, 2020

It was a cool Friday night in June at San Francisco's Golden Gate Park. The crowd of about four hundred people started getting rowdy and loud, confronting police, throwing bottles, and spray-painting statues, fountains, and benches in the park. Then it happened.

Just as a police officer shouted, "You've made your point! We're not going to let you take this statue down!" the crowd's screams reached a crescendo and the statue of Ulysses S. Grant toppled to the ground. The takedown of the Grant statue was quickly followed by the felling of three other statues, including that of Francis Scott Key.

The group had been marching and protesting for hours, calling for an end to police brutality. June 19, known as "Juneteenth," is a holiday celebrating the emancipation of slaves in America. But this year Juneteenth took on greater significance for the people gathered. They were part of a national protest movement that had arisen in the wake of the killing in Minneapolis of George Floyd, a Black man, by a white police officer. Floyd's death, recorded on video, set in motion demonstrations against racism—passionate but largely peaceful—across the nation. In some cities, the protests were accompanied by looting. Frequently, the protesters targeted statues erected to honor Confederate war figures: General Stonewall Jackson came down in Richmond, Virginia; Confederacy president Jefferson Davis came down in Richmond and Frankfurt, Kentucky; statues came down in Raleigh, North Carolina, and Houston, Texas; Robert E. Lee was scheduled for removal in Richmond.

But the toppling of Ulysses Grant's statue in Golden Gate Park that night was met by great confusion. *Ulysses Grant?* How did Grant, the hero of the Union Army and the champion of Reconstruction, end up on the ground? How had the Civil War narrative grown so twisted that Grant, the man who led the charge against the Confederacy, would become the enemy of emancipation?

The protesters were in no mood to consider Grant's virtues. Forget the courage and sacrifices he had demonstrated in the Civil War. Forget his dedication to the Reconstruction of the South and the rights of emancipated Blacks. In their view, he was tarnished by a brief association with slavery long before the war.

As described earlier in this book, Grant's father-in-law gave him a slave as a gift when he was struggling to make it as a farmer. Grant was uncomfortable owning a slave, and he freed him soon after.

That's pretty much all there is to know about Grant as a slaveholder. On the other hand, we know a great deal about Grant as an emancipator and a champion of African Americans. Grant was the general who won the Civil War, and he went on to devote the next twelve years to securing the peace and the freedom of former slaves through Reconstruction. *That's* his legacy. In the lexicon of our times, destroying his statue sounds a lot like "cancel culture."

When news of Grant's statue toppling reached me, I was deep into writing this book. I knew the history. I thought I was beginning to understand Grant, with all of his complexities. I had come to feel great admiration for his physical courage, his emotional intelligence, and his selfless patriotism at a time when the nation was being tested as it never had been before. It offended me to think that protesters would rewrite civil rights history to condemn him. I've never supported purity tests, and I know if we were to impose them on American presidents, not a single one would survive rebuke. Not only does it make no sense, but it is actually un-American.

The truth about Ulysses Grant? He went down in history as a hero, and yet his legacy has been plagued by his flaws. As Ron Chernow explains, "He got the big issues right during his presidency, even if he bungled many of the small ones." Ranked second from the bottom of US presidents by historians in 1948, Grant had risen to twenty-first by 2018—an acknowledgment that in the long view of history, his principled stand on civil rights and a unified nation has meaning for our times.

Grant entered the public sphere at the moment of the nation's greatest peril. When everyone around him was bowed with despair, he lifted them all up. A man of great comity, Grant knew that he could not do it alone, and he inspired his soldiers—even the lowliest among them—to believe in their cause and to give their all to the fight. No one ever heard a hint of doubt from him that he would succeed. And when he did, there was no spirit of revenge in his victory. In this way he rescued the Republic a second time.

After the war, Grant dedicated himself to bringing the nation together. He was the voice of calm during President Andrew Johnson's bitter, vengeful presidency, and when he assumed the presidency himself, Grant declared to the nation, "Let us have peace." By that he meant systematically mending the terrible wounds of the war, bringing the former Confederate states back into the fold, welcoming the emancipated Blacks into commerce and citizenship, and creating a new national vision around progress and goodwill.

We are so accustomed to dwelling on the failures of Reconstruction that we often overlook its successes. During that period, African Americans voted in such high numbers that in many places they were in the majority. They were elected to public office, including the US Senate, built schools and churches, and established themselves as members of the community. The Fourteenth and Fifteenth Amendments were established as constitutional protections of the rights of African Americans. Laws such as the Enforcement Act helped protect against violence from groups like the KKK. But the constant resistance from white Southerners doomed Grant's plans. In the early years after the war, the nation had no idea how to solve its racial problem except by force. And force didn't work.

Which brings us to the third time Grant rescued the Republic, during the election of 1876. What if Grant had not supported the so-called grand bargain that brought the 1876 election to its conclusion? There is no shortage of Grant critics who would have preferred that result. They're ready to blame Grant for the rise of Jim Crow and for nearly a century of racial injustice and suffering. These critics argue that no matter how heroic Grant's actions were during the war, he screwed up the peace. By fronting the grand bargain, he undid the good of Reconstruction.

But is that really true?

By putting his stamp on a plan to settle the 1876 election, Grant saved the nation from a potentially catastrophic upheaval. He preserved the Union, as flawed as it was. For Grant, it was always about preserving the Union, above all else. His calculation no doubt rested on the analysis that, with no Union, there could be no justice for African Americans—or for anyone else. The Union had to be saved to make all else possible.

History shows that by 1876 Reconstruction had grown untenable. The Supreme Court had watered down some of the most important rights gained through the efforts of Grant and others, leaving Blacks in an increasingly vulnerable position. The South was openly rebelling against ongoing federal interference, and it's unclear what more could have been done by the president and Congress short of permanent military occupation. As long as many Southern states and most members of the Democratic Party were opposed to forced Reconstruction, it would never work. Even Northern support of Reconstruction was declining. People on both sides of the aisle were ready to give the Southern states a chance to do the right thing on their own—and that helped make the grand bargain happen. Remember, one of its key tenets was the agreement by the South to foster equality and peace. Early on, Grant had imagined a growing postwar unity. He had received a warm welcome when he traveled in the South. But the nation's fracture wasn't so easily healed.

All this is not to deny that the rollback of civil rights during the decades-long Jim Crow era was a national tragedy. Jim Crow was a caste system based solely on race and enforced by myriad state laws in the South. It gave rise to a culture of oppression and violence against Blacks. Nearly every aspect of daily life was segregated, and Blacks lived as second-class citizens. The belief that Blacks were less-than, which harkened back to the slave era, was the justification for constant indignities imposed on them. Those Blacks who dared to step outside their "proper place"—for example, by trying to vote, sitting in the "whites only" section of a restaurant, or speaking disrespectfully to a white person—were harassed, beaten, arrested, and even killed. The NAACP reports that between 1882 and 1968 a staggering 3,446 Black Americans were lynched in the United States.

We as a nation need to face this shameful history collectively and understand how its legacy shapes the present. But to blame one man, Grant, for the collapse of Black civil rights is a lazy interpretation of history. It's a fallacy to believe that our country had only one shot at building a social order that fully embraced the emancipation of Blacks and that, if it failed, it was doomed to a century of racial struggle. Grant did not condemn Blacks for a century—those decisions were made repeatedly in each administration and down through the generations. Historian Eric Foner points this out in his analysis of Reconstruction:

> Reconstruction poses a challenge to Americans' historical understanding because we prefer stories with happy endings. Unfortunately, the overthrow of the South's biracial governments, accomplished in part by terrorist violence, was followed by a long period of legally enforced white supremacy. Yet this itself offers a timely lesson—that there is nothing inevitable or predetermined in the onward march of freedom and equality. Reconstruction and its aftermath remind us that rights in the Constitution are not self-enforcing, and that our liberties can never be taken for granted.

Foner's message is that vigilance is needed to keep our Republic. The freedoms we cherish aren't automatically given. They have to be pursued and won repeatedly. In that respect, every election becomes a new opportunity to express our common understanding. In times of great division, this presents a challenge. In 1876, there were two opposite interpretations of the election results in several states. Whether one was "true" and the other wasn't ultimately didn't matter. The two sides were so entrenched that some kind of reconciliation had to be fashioned out of a common agreement. Everyone was well aware that the last time tensions had been that high around an election, secession had followed.

We have witnessed a similar crisis in our modern elections, culminating with a violent attack on the Capitol by those who could not accept the results of the 2020 election. Elections are very much the same as they were in Grant's time, although they are much greater in size and complexity today, with 3,006 counties and 210,000 precincts. In hyperpartisan times, when victories are razor-thin, there are bound to be disputes. Disputes arise even when there is a wide margin. The last true landslide election was won by Ronald Reagan, and his critics were out in force from day one. Conflict doesn't necessarily mean our democracy is in crisis or on the brink of disaster.

I wonder what Ulysses Grant would think of our modern Republic. Would he be heartsick that so many of the struggles among people are still evident, or would he marvel that so much progress has been made? I'm sure Grant would not have cared about his statue being toppled. He wouldn't have wanted a statue in the first place. Surely he'd have been bemused that there are so many statues of Confederate leaders. After the war, he often spoke of his respect for the Southern soldiers who were his opponents, and he would have been pleased that so many of them attended his funeral.

Seeing the tumult in our political system today, Grant might call upon us to rise above the immediacy of the crisis we face and view it more broadly. The origin of our democracy is self-rule, and these divisions are baked into our story. They feel cataclysmic in the moment because everyone is so emotional, but in the historical context these upheavals can be seen as part of an ongoing battle to be the nation we defined in our Constitution.

On his deathbed, as Grant wrote the final words of his *Memoirs*, he expressed gratitude for "the universally kind feeling expressed for me at a time when it was supposed that each day would prove my last." He hastened to add that his appreciation wasn't personal gratitude for the support of well-wishers, although he surely felt that. In a larger sense these expressions from people of all backgrounds were proof that the peaceful society he had fought for was at hand. Maybe that society wouldn't come overnight. Maybe it would emerge in fits and starts and need to be fought for again. In the long stretch of history, we can see both the majestic peaks and the deep valleys of our nation's journey. But like Grant, we have never stopped seeking union.

ACKNOWLEDGMENTS

This is my fifth book: *Special Heart*, *Three Days in January*, *Three Days in Moscow*, *Three Days at the Brink*, and now *To Rescue the Republic*. For the previous four books, I have had the distinct pleasure of working alongside my coauthor and friend, Catherine Whitney. Catherine is a true star who can cut through the enormity of historical documents and firsthand accounts to find the important nuggets in history, enabling us to capture the pivotal moments and characters of the past. Her dedication to this project and her ability to incorporate ideas is unsurpassed. The book would not have been done without Catherine.

Many great historical details have been uncovered by our intrepid researcher, Sydney Soderberg, who has been digging up historic treasures in libraries across the country, but primarily at the Eisenhower, Reagan, Bush, FDR, and Grant libraries. Her ability to find the historic pieces of our narrative quilt has been a key part of the success of these books as well.

In our research, we got a lot of help from a lot of people. I want to give a special thanks to the folks at the Ulysses S. Grant Presidential Library at Mississippi State University. Thank you for all of your friendly and courteous assistance: John Marszalek, executive director and managing editor of the Papers of Ulysses S. Grant; Louis Gallo, assistant editor of the Papers of Ulysses S. Grant; Professor David Nolan, associate editor of the Papers of Ulysses S. Grant; Assistant Professor Kate Gregory, political papers archivist; and Amanda Carlock, senior library associate. I also want to thank Professor Ryan P. Semmes, archivist, who worked closely with us on finding the photos in the U. S. Grant Collection for the book.

Special thanks to the team at William Morrow, led by our editor, Peter Hubbard. Peter has an amazing sense of history and an eye for significant details that keep us going in the right direction. Book after book, he has provided much-needed "tweaks" and edits to make the product better. Thanks to everyone on Peter's team for helping to craft a solid plan for launching this book.

I would like to thank my agent, Jay Sures with United Talent Agency (UTA). And my book agent, Byrd Leavell, also with UTA, who helped steer the project from the beginning.

Thank you to my employer, Fox News, for allowing me the leeway to spend time on this project, like the others, and for once again producing a one-hour documentary special about the book, scheduled to run around the launch.

And thank you to my family—my co-anchor in life, Amy Baier, and my two sons, Paul and Daniel. Thanks for letting Dad work on and then promote this project, which sometimes means time away from you. I hope in years down the road, in history classes somewhere, you may read one of these books and think it's pretty cool your dad did this. If not, maybe you'll read them anyway and think that.

And finally, I owe a debt of appreciation to President Ulysses S. Grant. Because he was such an excellent writer himself, we got to know what he was thinking at various moments in his life. It wasn't a daily Twitter message, but his writings offer us a lot of insight. This book would probably not have happened without his personal reflections. It definitely wouldn't have been as rich. I feel privileged to tell this part of his story and perhaps give people a broader picture of Grant, not just as the famous general on the field of war, but as the striving president on the field of peace.

NOTES

Prologue: A Dark Night in Philadelphia

2   "I want to know": Julia Dent Grant, *The Personal Memoirs of Julia Dent Grant* (New York: Putnam, 1975), 186.

4   "It looks to me": Brooks D. Simpson, "Ulysses S. Grant and the Electoral Crisis of 1876–77," *Hayes Historical Journal* 11, no. 2 (Winter 1992).

4   "Everything now depends": Ibid.

Chapter 1: The Making of Grant

9   "I liked the way": William S. McFeely, *Grant: A Biography* (New York: W. W. Norton & Co., 1981), 16.

10   "Grant has been subjected": Ron Chernow, *Grant* (New York: Penguin Books, 2017), xx.

10   "ill at ease": Robert I. Girardi, *The Civil War Generals: Comrades, Peers, Rivals—in Their Own Words* (New York: Zenith Press, 2013), 68.

10   "No, that was impossible": A. E. Watrous, "Grant as His Son Saw Him: An Interview with Colonel Frederick D. Grant About His Father," *McClure's* 2 (1884): 515.

11   "To me he is a mystery": John Y. Simon, "The Paradox of Ulysses S. Grant," *Register of the Kentucky Historical Society* 81, no. 4 (Autumn 1983): 370.

11   "Grant was the most popular man": Adam Badeau, *Grant in Peace: From Appomattox to Mount McGregor: A Personal Memoir* (Hartford, CT: S. S. Scranton & Co., 1887), 69.

11   "It is certain that": Jesse R. Grant, *In the Days of My Father General Grant* (New York: Harper & Brothers, 1925), 1.

12   "But the truth is": J. T. Headley, *The Life of Ulysses S. Grant* (New York: E. B. Treat, 1868), 1.

15   "I have often heard": Ulysses S. Grant, *Personal Memoirs of Ulysses S. Grant* (New York: Charles L. Webster & Co., 1885, 1886), 20.

15 "she would not hunt me": Ibid.

15 "What are you thinking about": Lloyd Lewis, *Captain Sam Grant* (Boston: Little, Brown & Co., 1950), 4.

16 "I discovered she was": Ibid., 14.

17 "Ulysses inherited many": Albert Deane Richardson, *A Personal History of Ulysses S. Grant* (Hartford, CT: American Publishing Co., 1868), 58.

17 "for it seems akin": Richardson, *A Personal History*, 68.

17 "never any scolding": Grant, *Personal Memoirs*, 26.

18 "At eight or nine he would ride": Jesse Grant, letter to Robert Bonner, January 18, 1868, reprinted in *Ulysses S. Grant Association Newsletter* 8, no. 1 (October 1970), and 8, no. 2 (January 1971).

19 "Papa says I may offer": Grant, *Personal Memoirs*, 29.

19 "Boys enjoy the misery": Ibid., 30.

19 "Ulysses Grant was one of": Lewis, *Captain Sam Grant*, 32.

20 "thirst for education": Grant, *Personal Memoirs*, 21.

20 "I remember that he": Ibid., 42.

20 "I can see John D. White": Ibid., 31.

21 "A noun is the name": Ibid., 25.

21 "progress enough to compensate": Ibid.

21 "My son, I don't want": Hamlin Garland, "The Early Life of Ulysses Grant," *McClure's* 8 (1887): 21.

22 "Ulysses, I believe you are going": Grant, *Personal Memoirs*, 32.

23 "We well remember the stir": Richardson, *A Personal History*, 60.

24 "the perfection of rapid transit": Grant, *Personal Memoirs*, 37.

24 "A military life": Ibid., 38.

25 "I have put asaid [*sic*] my Algebra": Lewis, *Captain Sam Grant*, 70–71.

25 "From five o'clock": Ibid., 63.

26 "You've grown much straighter and taller": Ben Kemp, "Like Mother, Like Son," Grant Cottage Historic Site, Wilton, New York, https://www.grant cottage.org/blog/2019/5/11/like-mother-like-son.

26 "neither classmates nor professors": Richardson, *A Personal History*, 74.

26 "the most daring horseman": Lewis, *Captain Sam Grant*, 82.

26 "So near the bottom": "Grant and Sherman at West Point," *New York Times*, June 13, 1865.

27 "A more unpromising boy": Lewis, *Captain Sam Grant*, 62.

27 "Grant was such a quiet": Horace Porter, *Campaigning with Grant* (New York: Century Co., 1897), 341.

27 "I had not the faintest idea": Grant, *Personal Memoirs*, 38.

Chapter 2: Conflicted Warrior

29 "Coming as I did": Grant, *Personal Memoirs of Julia Dent Grant*, 35.

29 "always had a dusky train": Ibid., 36.

29 "attained the dignity": Ibid., 40.

30 "Oh, no, Mama would": Ibid., 49

30 "I, child that I was": Ibid.

30 "I am a romantic": Julia Dent Grant interview with Hamlin Garland, c. 1897, Hamlin Garland Papers, Doheny Library, University of Southern California; available at Ulysses S. Grant Homepage, https://www.grant homepage.com/intjdgrant1.htm.

31 "A few of them": Ibid.

31 "Now, if anything happens": Ishbel Ross, *The General's Wife: The Life of Mrs. Ulysses S. Grant* (New York: Dodd, Mead & Co., 1959).

32 "Aligators [*sic*] and other revolting": Ulysses S. Grant, *My Dearest Julia: The Wartime Letters of Ulysses S. Grant to His Wife* (New York: Library of America, 2018), 14.

34 "For myself, I was bitterly opposed": Grant, *Personal Memoirs*, 53.

34 "a conspiracy to acquire": Ibid., 54.

34 "No soldier could face": Ibid., 100.

35 "The journey was hazardous": Ibid., 75.

35 "I came to the conclusion": Ibid., 76.

35 "the most unearthly howling": Ibid., 77.

36 "We were sent": Ibid., 68.

37 "Their bayonets and spearheads": Ibid., 94.

37 "There is no great sport": Grant, *My Dearest Julia*, 7.

37 "It took off the head": Grant, *Personal Memoirs*, 96.

37 "A great many men": Ibid., 92.

38 "By the time": Ibid., 106.

39 "My curiosity got the better": Ibid., 110.

39 "My pity was aroused": Ibid., 117.

40 "The Mexican war was": Ibid., 119.

41 "With his commanding figure": Ibid., 41.

41 "I tell you": James Power Smith, "General Lee at Gettysburg," in *Southern Historical Society Pages*, ed. Robert Alonzo Brock, vol. 33 (1905): 156.

42 "And besides . . . I intended": Grant, *Personal Memoirs*, 158.

43 "General Scott's successes": Ibid., 166.

44 "I at least hope": Grant, *My Dearest Julia*, 73.

Chapter 3: The Lost Years

47 "rich, soft, white": "Julia Dent Grant (1862–1902)": "Great General's Widow Tells of Her First Trip from Home," *New York Journal and Advertiser*, June 11, 1901, available at Ulysses S. Grant Homepage, https://www.grant homepage.com/intjdgrant2.htm.

47 "Lieutenant Grant—he was just": Julia Dent Grant interview with Hamlin Garland, c. 1897, Hamlin Garland Papers, Doheny Library, University of Southern California.

47 "Never shall I forget": Ibid.

48   "Our honeymoon was a delight": Ibid.

49   "The Captain's father": Ibid.

49   "I could not": Grant, *Personal Memoirs of Julia Dent Grant*, 58.

49   "Grant, I can arrange": Ibid., 21.

50   "I cannot make out": Ibid., 61.

51   "I look back": Julia Dent Grant interview with Hamlin Garland, c. 1897, Hamlin Garland Papers, Doheny Library, University of Southern California.

51   "Of course I was indignant": Grant, *Personal Memoirs of Julia Dent Grant*, 71.

52   "You know how loath I am": Ibid.

52   "All thought that fortunes": Grant, *Personal Memoirs*, 201.

53   "who had never done": Ibid.

54   "My dear wife": Grant, *My Dearest Julia*, 96.

56   "he was not a slavery man": Hamlin Garland, *Ulysses S. Grant: His Life and Character* (New York: Macmillan Company, 1920), xxiii.

56   "He raised crops successfully": Frederick Dent Grant, [untitled article], *Ulysses S. Grant Newsletter*, April 1969, available at Ulysses S. Grant Homepage, https://www.granthomepage.com/frederick_dent_grant.htm.

57   "the ghost of a soldier": Lewis, *Captain Sam Grant*, 358.

57   "You must take it": Ibid.

58   "Stranger here?": Ibid., 375.

59   "Mister, do you want": Grant, *In the Days of My Father*, 10.

59   "rare and fine personality": Ibid., 11–12.

59   "his usual method of correction": Frederick Dent Grant, [untitled article], *Ulysses S. Grant Newsletter*, April 1969.

60   "When I was your age": Grant, *Personal Memoirs of Julia Dent Grant*, 178.

60   "The General had no idea": Interview with Mrs. Julia Dent Grant, Washington, DC, 1899, quoted in "Grant the Family Man," available at Ulysses S. Grant Homepage, https://www.granthomepage.com/grantfamily.htm.

60   "The nonsense of this": Ibid.

61   "It made my blood run cold": Lewis, *Captain Sam Grant*, 368.

62   "With a Democrat elected": Ross, *The General's Wife*.

63   "happily, a matter": James Buchanan, inaugural address, March 4, 1857, available at the American Presidency Project, https://www.presidency.ucsb.edu/documents/inaugural-address-33.

63   "There are two clauses in the Constitution": National Constitution Center, "Dred Scott Decision Still Resonates Today," March 6, 2021, https://www.constitutioncenter.org/blog/dred-scott-decision-still-resonates-today-2.

64   "A house divided against itself": Abraham Lincoln, "House Divided Speech," June 16, 1858, Springfield, IL, available at Abraham Lincoln Online, http://abrahamlincolnonline.org/lincoln/speeches/house.htm.

64   "so plainly suicidal": Grant, *Personal Memoirs*, 218.

66 "Galena was throbbing with patriotism": Grant, *Personal Memoirs of Julia Dent Grant*, 89.

66 "elections in this country": Michael Burlingame, *Abraham Lincoln: A Life*, vol. 1 (Baltimore: Johns Hopkins University Press, 2012), 677.

67 "It is beyond the power": James Buchanan, State of the Union address, December 3, 1860.

Chapter 4: The Union Cause

71 "Sir, if you are as happy": Jean H. Baker, *James Buchanan*, American Presidents Series (New York: Times Books/Henry Holt and Company, 2004), 140. This is one version of what Buchanan reputedly said to Lincoln.

72 "Davis and the whole gang": Lewis, *Captain Sam Grant*, 393.

72 "In *your* hands": Jay B. Hubbell, "Lincoln's First Inaugural Address," *American Historical Review* 36, no. 3 (April 1931): 550–52 (emphasis added).

72 "In your hands": Ibid.

73 "I am loath to close": Ibid.

73 "Illinois can whip the South by herself": Jean Edward Smith, *Grant* (New York: Simon & Schuster, 2001), 98.

73 "I was greatly exercised": Lydia Holt Farmer, ed., *What America Owes to Women*, chap. 4 (Buffalo: Charles Wells Moulton, 1893), 59.

74 "I have been a Democrat": James Harrison Wilson, *The Life of General John A. Rawlins* (Neale Publishing Co., 1916), 30.

74 "I never went into our leather store": Grant, *Personal Memoirs*, 231.

74 "Whatever may have been my opinions": Jesse Grant Cramer, ed., *Letters of Ulysses S. Grant to His Father and His Youngest Sister, 1857–78* (New York: G. P. Putnam's Sons, 1912).

75 "She was brave": Bishop John H. Vincent, "The Inner Life of Ulysses S. Grant," in *The Chautauquan*, vol. 30 (1900): 634.

75 "Grant is often called": Vincent, "The Inner Life of Ulysses S. Grant," 635.

75 "He had learned patience": *Reminiscence of Ulysses S. Grant: First-Hand Accounts of the General, the President, and the Man from Those Who Knew Him* (Portland, OR: Wetware Media LLC, 2012), 18.

76 "Our trip was a perfect ovation": Ulysses S. Grant, letter to Julia Dent Grant, April 27, 1861, Ulysses S. Grant Papers, series 9–11.

76 "My regiment was composed": Grant, *Personal Memoirs*, 243.

77 "was always the complement": Wilson, *The Life of General John A. Rawlins*, 41.

78 "for the first time": Charles Bracelen Flood, *Grant and Sherman: The Friendship That Won the Civil War* (New York: Harper Perennial, 2005), 54.

78 "I found that my brigade": Ibid., 55.

79 "So it seems to be true": Brooks D. Simpson and Jean V. Berlin, eds., *Sherman's Civil War: Selected Correspondence of William T. Sherman, 1860–1865* (Chapel Hill: University of North Carolina Press, 1999), 121.

79   "I considered it a pleasant summer": Grant, *Personal Memoirs of Julia Dent Grant*, 92.

79   "we may have some fighting to do": Ibid.

80   "As we approached the brow": Grant, *Personal Memoirs*, 249.

81   "To-morrow will come": Grant, *My Dearest Julia*, 115.

82   "Sir: Yours of this date": Grant, *Personal Memoirs*, 311.

83   "Where is Pillow?": Arndt Stickles, *Simon Bolivar Buckner: Borderland Knight* (Chapel Hill: University of North Carolina Press, 1940), 171.

83   "I do not say he [Pillow] would shoot himself": Cramer, *Letters of Ulysses S. Grant to His Father and His Youngest Sister*, 65.

83   "I am in most perfect health": Grant, *My Dearest Julia*, 118.

83   "Buckner, you may be going": John R. Procter, "A Blue and Gray Friendship," *The Century* 53 (April 1897): 944.

85   "A rumor has just reached me": Wilson, *The Life of John A. Rawlins*, 53.

87   "saw the rebel lines": General William T. Sherman, *Memoirs of General William T. Sherman* (New York: D. Appleton, 1889), 159.

87   "Although his troops": Grant, *Personal Memoirs*, 343.

88   "Well, Grant, we've had": Flood, *Grant and Sherman*, 114.

89   "The scenes on this field": Simpson and Berlin, *Sherman's Civil War*, 202.

89   "I saw an open field": Grant, *Personal Memoirs*, 356.

89   "The following incident": Frank Moore, ed., *The Rebellion Record: A Diary of American Events*, vol. 5 (New York: G. P. Putnam, 1861–1863), 12.

90   "I am seriously thinking of going home": Linus Pierpont Brockett, *Our Great Captains: Grant, Sherman, Thomas, Sheridan, and Farragut* (New York: Charles B. Richardson, 1865), 162.

90   "I then begged him": Ibid.; see also Flood, *Grant and Sherman*, 125.

90   "some happy accident": Ibid.

91   "immense knowledge of military science": Ulysses S. Grant and John Russell Young, *Around the World with General Grant: A Narrative of the Visit of General U. S. Grant, Ex-President of the United States, to Various Countries in Europe, Asia, and Africa, in 1877, 1878, 1879, to Which Are Added Certain Conversations with General Grant on Questions Connected with American Politics and History* (New York: American News Company, 1879), 248. The conversations were separately digitalized and published as Ulysses S. Grant and John Russell Young, *Conversations with General Grant* (Amazon Digital Services, 2016).

92   "Hunger was the dominant note": Andrew F. Smith, "Did Hunger Defeat the Confederacy?" *North & South* 13, no. 1 (May 2011): 40.

92   "My paramount object": Abraham Lincoln, letter to the editor, *Daily National Intelligencer*, August 1862.

93   "Who would be free": Frederick Douglass, *Life and Times of Frederick Douglass* (Hartford, CT: Park Publishing Co., 1881).

94 "There was no time": Grant, *Personal Memoirs*, 227.

94 "Vicksburg is the key": Joan Waugh, *U. S. Grant: American Hero, American Myth* (Chapel Hill: University of North Carolina Press, 2009), 61.

94 "the nail head that holds": Ibid.

95 "a handsome and very comfortable": Grant, *Personal Memoirs of Julia Dent Grant*, 103.

96 "wanted someone to go to Grant's army": Charles A. Dana, *Recollections of the Civil War: With the Leaders at Washington and in the Field in the Sixties* (New York: D. Appleton & Co., 1902), 45.

96 "Grant was an uncommon fellow": Ibid., 85.

97 "The Mississippi at Millicent's Bend": Ibid., 52.

97 "I am killed": "Frederick Dent Grant Joins His Father on the Battlefield," National Park Service, https://www.nps.gov/articles/000/frederick-dent-grant -joins-his-father-on-the-battlefield.htm.

97 "My son accompanied": Grant, *Personal Memoirs*, 297.

98 "On the battlefield General Grant": Frederick Dent Grant, [untitled article], *Missouri Republican*, 1912, available at Ulysses S. Grant Homepage, https://www.granthomepage.com/frederick_dent_grant.htm.

98 "A dispatch now in my possession": Harry S. Laver, *A General Who Will Fight: The Leadership of Ulysses S. Grant* (Louisville: University Press of Kentucky, 2013), 63.

99 "More difficulties and privations": Ibid., 71.

99 "I think Grant has hardly a friend": Ibid., 82.

100 "Not a man is seen": Simpson and Berlin, *Sherman's Civil War*, 492.

102 "Take a drink": Gene Smith, *Lee and Grant: A Dual Biography* (New York: McGraw-Hill, 1984), 165.

102 "The Confederate chief": James Longstreet, *From Manassas to Appomattox: Memoirs of the Civil War* (Philadelphia: J. B. Lippincott Co., 1896), 292.

104 "While a battle is raging": Grant, *Personal Memoirs*, 521.

104 "I write this now": Laver, *A General Who Will Fight*, 88.

105 "From these honored dead": Abraham Lincoln, "Gettysburg Address," November 19, 1863, Abraham Lincoln Online: Speeches and Writings, http://abrahamlincolnonline.org/lincoln/speeches/gettysburg.htm.

105 "The art of war": John Hill Brinton, *Personal Memoirs of John H. Brinton, Major and Surgeon U.S.V., 1861–1865* (New York: Neale Publishing Co., 1913), 239.

105 "The General never talked": Julia Dent Grant interview with Hamlin Garland, c. 1897, Hamlin Garland Papers, Doheny Library, University of Southern California.

106 "The children often romped": Porter, *Campaigning with Grant*, 344.

106 "To the small boy": Grant, *In the Days of My Father*, 16.

106 "I hear of these": Julia Dent Grant interview with Hamlin Garland,

c. 1897, Hamlin Garland Papers, Doheny Library, University of Southern California.

107   "Dear Mary, I hope the enclosure": Grant, *Personal Memoirs of Julia Dent Grant*, 126.

107   "I was rendered insensible": Grant, *Personal Memoirs*, 581.

107   "All the rivers of alcohol": McFeely, *Grant: A Biography*, 55.

108   "General Rosecrans seemed to be": Dana, *Recollections of the Civil War*, 151.

109   "It is hard for any one": Grant, *Personal Memoirs*, 318.

110   "With bands playing": Benjamin P. Thomas, ed., *Three Years with Grant: As Recalled by War Correspondent Sylvanus Cadwallader* (New York: Alfred A. Knopf, 1955).

110   "The boys seem pretty good": Ibid.

110   "I never aspired but to one office": Richardson, *A Personal History*, 377.

110   "In an arm-chair": Porter, *Campaigning with Grant*, 28.

111   "The first three years of the war": Franklin Spencer Edmonds, *Ulysses S. Grant* (New York: G. W. Jacobs, 1915), 224.

Chapter 5: Lincoln's General

112   "Do you know what brand of whiskey": Grant, *Personal Memoirs of Julia Dent Grant*, 114.

112   "the quietest little fellow": Laver, *A General Who Will Fight*, 107.

113   "I have sent for you": Rufus Rockwell Wilson, ed., *Intimate Memories of Lincoln* (Elmira, NY: Primavera Press, 1945), 484–85.

114   "Really, it was very embarrassing": Grant, *Personal Memoirs of Julia Dent Grant*, 138.

114   "Mr. Lincoln never had": William H. Herndon, *Herndon's Lincoln: The True Story of a Great Life* (Chicago: Belford, Clarke & Co., 1889).

115   "What marked him": Young, *Around the World with General Grant*, 354.

115   "General Grant, the nation's appreciation": *Collected Works of Abraham Lincoln*, vol. 7 (Abraham Lincoln Association, 1953), 235.

115   "I feel the full weight": Grant, *Personal Memoirs*, 358.

116   "For God's sake and for your country's": Simpson and Berlin, *Sherman's Civil War*, 603.

117   "They (the President and others)": George McClellan, *McClellan's Own Story: The War for the Union, the Soldiers Who Fought It, the Civilians Who Directed It, and His Relations to It and to Them* (New York: C. L. Webster, 1887), 150.

117   "hair trigger temper": Shelby Foote, *The Civil War: A Narrative*, vol. 3, *Red River to Appomattox* (New York: Random House, 1974), 9.

117   "Lee's army will be my objective": Grant, *Personal Memoirs*, 276.

118   "I don't see how": Isaac N. Arnold, *The Life of Abraham Lincoln* (Chicago: Jansen, McClurg & Company, 1901), 371.

119   "Well, Grant has never met": Grant, *Personal Memoirs, 298.*

119   "was calculated to give him": Ibid.

119   "The natural disposition of most people": Ibid., 129.

120   "Oh, I am heartily tired": Walter Gaston Shotwell, *The Civil War in America,* vol. 2 (New York: Longmans, Green, and Co., 1923), 228.

120   "as desperate fighting": Grant, *Personal Memoirs,* 183.

121   "Mr. President, I have a personal word for you": Henry Ebeneser Wing, *When Lincoln Kissed Me: A Story of the Wilderness Campaign* (New York: Eaton & Mains, 1913), 37.

121   "What is it?": Ibid., 38.

121   "Now, Mr. Secretary, you know": Edmonds, *Ulysses S. Grant,* 218.

122   "Oh, yes! I see that": Grant, *Personal Memoirs,* 426.

122   "in a country in which every stream": Ibid., 453.

123   "That camp life at City Point": Adam Badeau et al., *Reminiscences of Ulysses S. Grant: First-hand Accounts of the General, the President, and the Man from Those Who Knew Him* (Portland, OR: Wetware Media LLC, 2012), 34.

123   "General Grant's courage": (Anonymous officer), "Personal Recollections of General Grant's Life in the Field," *National Magazine* (June 1903).

124   "never rose to the grand problem": Smith, *Lee and Grant,* 225.

124   "We cannot have free government": "Lincoln on the 1864 Election," Lincoln Home, National Historic Site Illinois, https://www.nps.gov/liho/index.htm.

125   "They can't do it!": John C. Waugh, *Reelecting Lincoln: The Battle for the 1864 Presidency* (Boston: Da Capo Press, 1997), 292.

125   "I do not know": Ibid., 35.

126   "The Constitution as it is": Ibid., 28.

126   "already broken eggs": Abraham Lincoln, letter to August Belmont, July 31, 1862, in *The Writings of Abraham Lincoln,* vol. 6, *1862–1863* (New York: G. P. Putnam's Sons, 1906).

127   "If the dumb cattle": Waugh, *Reelecting Lincoln,* 290.

128   "I expected something to happen": Flood, *Grant and Sherman,* 256.

128   "When it was announced": P. C. Headley, *The Life and Deeds of General U. S. Grant* (Boston: B. B. Russell & Co., 1885), 517.

128   "It may be of some consolation": Ibid., 518.

129   "We keep hammering": Sherman, *Memoirs,* 359.

129   "I have deemed it": Ibid., 371.

130   "If the people raise a howl": Ibid., 365.

130   "had accomplished nothing": Badeau, *Grant in Peace,* 190.

130   "No one would be more pleased": Simpson and Berlin, *Sherman's Civil War,* 806.

130   "I am a damned sight smarter": James Harrison Wilson, *Under the Old Flag: Recollections of Military Operations in the War for the Union, the*

Spanish War, the Boxer Rebellion, etc., vol. 2 (New York: Appleton and Company, 1912), 17.

131   "It is a little singular": Waugh, *Reelecting Lincoln*, 371.

131   "What business has the turkey": Ibid., 372.

132   "I am thankful to God": Ibid., 379.

133   "We cannot change the hearts": General William T. Sherman, letter to Major General Ulysses S. Grant, October 4, 1862, in Charles Bracelen Flood, *Grant and Sherman*, 133.

133   "But what next?": Simpson and Berlin, *Sherman's Civil War*, 772.

Chapter 6: Surrender

134   "With malice toward none": Abraham Lincoln, "Second Inaugural Speech," March 4, 1865, Abraham Lincoln Online: Speeches and Writings, http://abrahamlincolnonline.org/lincoln/speeches/inaug2.htm.

135   "Can you not visit City Point": Porter, *Campaigning with Grant*, 479.

135   "Their encounter was more like": Ibid., 496.

136   "an informal interchange of views": Ibid., 502.

136   "Mr. President . . . there is no possible way": Admiral David D. Porter, *Incidents and Anecdotes of the Civil War* (New York: D. Appleton, 1885), 314–15.

137   "Let them all surrender": Ibid.

137   "I merely told him what I had done": Young, *Around the World with General Grant*, 356.

138   "As the train was about to depart": Porter, *Campaigning with Grant*, 505.

138   "He was a great man": Young, *Around the World with General Grant*, 354.

138   "He is the only man": W. H. Crook, *Through Five Administrations: Inside the White House with Presidents Lincoln, Johnson, Grant, Hayes, and Garfield* (New York: Harper & Brothers Publishers, 1910), 77.

139   "You're not hurt a bit!": Porter, *Campaigning with Grant*, 518.

140   "I think it is absolutely necessary": "The War of the Rebellion: A Compilation of Official Records of the Union and Confederate Armies," United States War Department 1880–1901, p. 1378, https://www.loc.gov/item/03003452.

140   "The result of the last week": Grant, *Personal Memoirs*, 254.

141   "Not yet": Smith, *Lee and Grant*, 250.

141   "GENERAL: I have received your note": Grant, *Personal Memoirs*, 255.

141   "Your note of last evening": Ibid.

142   "In mine of yesterday": Ibid.

142   "the troops of our broken columns": Longstreet, *From Manassas to Appomattox*, 620.

143   "He was dressed in a suit": Ibid., 453.

143   "I asked if the bloody sacrifice": Ibid., 454.

144   "The pain in my head": Porter, *Campaigning with Grant*, 555.

144   "How are you, Sheridan?": Ibid., 557.

144   "Grant, restrained in victory": Edmonds, *Ulysses S. Grant*, 270.

145   "This will have a very happy effect": Porter, *Campaigning with Grant*, 565.

146   "I did not want his sword": Porter, *Campaigning with Grant*, 563.

147   "The rebels are our countrymen": Ibid., 575.

147   "Are you one of Aunt Rachel's": Richardson, *A Personal History*, 488.

148   "gallantry and persistence": Young, *Around the World with General Grant*, 463.

148   "Pete, let's have another game": "Confederate General James Longstreet Discusses His Friendship with Grant," *New York Times*, July 24, 1885.

149   "Hush, Julia": Grant, *Personal Memoirs of Julia Dent Grant*, 153.

149   "Unless you accept": Badeau, *Grant in Peace*, 362.

150   "Crook, do you know": Crook, *Through Five Administrations*, 66.

150   "The President was assassinated": Laver, *A General Who Will Fight*, 153.

150   "Is there anything the matter": Grant, *Personal Memoirs of Julia Dent Grant*, 164.

150   "The President was inclined": Ibid.

151   "man rode past us": Ibid.

151   "Grant always regretted leaving": Geoffrey Perret, *Ulysses S. Grant: Soldier and President* (New York: Random House, 1997), 396.

152   "O Captain, My Captain": The poem, published November 4, 1865, is available at the Walt Whitman Archive, https://whitmanarchive.org/published/LG/1891/poems/194.

153   "Show me the man": Robert W. Winston, *Andrew Johnson: Plebian and Patriot* (New York: H. Holt and Company, 1928).

154   "I find my duties": Grant, *My Dearest Julia*, 178.

155   "Tell the world": Foote, *The Civil War*, 1060.

Chapter 7: Chaos

160   "I'm afraid my poor": Flood, *Grant and Sherman*, 383.

161   "They gave the appearance": Grant, *Personal Memoirs*, 549.

162   "I believe it was the happiest": Flood, *Grant and Sherman*, 389.

162   "What a defiant and angry": Grant, *Personal Memoirs of Julia Dent Grant*, 159.

162   "I recall the enthusiasm": Grant, *In the Days of My Father*, 44.

163   "GENERAL, THE SIDEWALK IS BUILT": Richardson, *A Personal History*, 514.

164   "Johnson, it will be remembered": John Eaton, *Grant, Lincoln, and the Freedmen: Reminiscences of the Civil War* (New York: Longmans, Green and Co., 1907), 59.

165   "The president of the United States": David Priess, *How to Get Rid of a President: History's Guide to Removing Unpopular, Unable, or Unfit Chief Executives* (New York: Public Affairs, 2018).

165   "A state half slave and half free": Grant, *Personal Memoirs*, 273.

165   "Slavery was an institution": Ibid.

166   "Prior to the time": Ibid.

167   "When can these men be tried?": Garland, *Ulysses S. Grant*, 332.

168   "Upon the rock": Ibid., 333.

168   "found a will more stubborn": Badeau, *Grant in Peace*, 26.

168   "I fought that man": Brooks D. Simpson, "Grant's Tour of the South Revisited," *Journal of Southern History* 54, no. 3 (August 1988): 425–48.

168   "I honor all Confederate soldiers": Simon, "The Paradox of Ulysses S. Grant," 374.

169   "The mass of thinking men": Simpson, "Grant's Tour of the South Revisited," 439.

170   "their slave instead of their being mine": Transcript of meeting between President Andrew Johnson and a delegation of African Americans, the White House, February 7, 1866, available at House Divided: The Civil War Research Engine at Dickinson College, http://hd.housedivided.dickinson.edu/node/45142.

171   "Andrew Johnson, one of the ablest": Young, *Around the World with General Grant*, 362.

172   "the spirit of caste": Frederick Douglass, speaking at a civil rights mass meeting, October 22, 1883, https://udspace.udel.edu/handle/19716/21266.

172   "This was the condition": Henry Clay Bruce, *The New Man: Twenty-Nine Years a Slave, Twenty-Nine Years a Free Man* (York, PA: P. Anstadt & Sons, 1895), 116.

174   "I am a soldier": Badeau, *Grant in Peace*.

175   "Mr. Attorney General": Ibid.

175   "I can answer that question": Ibid.

176   "serious quarrel": Simpson and Berlin, *Sherman's Civil War*, 571.

176   "Well, Stanton was hectoring": Grant, *Personal Memoirs of Julia Dent Grant*, 174.

177   "worked himself up": Ibid., 175.

177   "He believed ends justified": Joseph Wheelan, *Terrible Swift Sword: The Life of General Philip Sheridan* (Boston: Da Capo Press, 2012), xxiii.

178   "was that of a traitor": Crook, *Through Five Administrations*, 121.

179   "Unable to conceal": John F. Kennedy, *Profiles in Courage* (New York: Harper & Brothers, 1956), 116.

179   "being the Presidential Candidate": Garland, *Ulysses S. Grant*, 346.

180   "I should not have liked": Grant and Young, *Conversations with General Grant*, 359.

180   "The square straight brow": *New York Tribune*, February 25, 1867.

181   "There was something about him": Perret, *Ulysses S. Grant*, 411.

181   "No matter how close": Bandeau, *Grant in Peace*.

181   "Always father seemed in consultation": Grant, *In the Days of My Father*, 49.

181   "Ulys, do you wish to be President": Grant, *Personal Memoirs of Julia Dent Grant*, 197.

182   "I have come to tell you": William B. Hesseltine, *Ulysses S. Grant: Politician* (New York: Dodd, Mead & Company, 1935), 120.

182   "There was no shade": Badeau, *Grant in Peace*, 144.

183   "Gentlemen, being entirely unaccustomed": Hesseltine, *Ulysses S. Grant: Politician*, 120.

183   "Let us have peace": Ulysses S. Grant, letter to Joseph R. Hawley, president of the National Union Republican Convention, accepting the nomination for president, May 29, 1868, in David Nelson Camp, *The American Year-Book and Register from 1869*, vol. 1 (reissued Kessington Publishing, 2008), 266.

183   "General Grant is my Admiral Crichton": Grant, *Personal Memoirs of Julia Dent Grant*, 196.

184   "This is a White Man's Country": https://digitalcollections.nypl.org/items/62a9d0e6-4fc9-dbce-e040-e00a18064a66.

184   "Peace—a settled, just": Brooks D. Simpson, *Let Us Have Peace: Ulysses S. Grant and the Politics of War and Reconstruction, 1861–1868* (Chapel Hill: University of North Carolina Press, 1991).

184   "my impressions of [Seymour]": Grant, *In the Days of My Father*, 56.

185   "It is not too much": Henry Whitney Cleveland, *General Grant's Military Abilities* (*Magazine of American History*, 1885).

185   "I am afraid I am elected": Ross, *The General's Wife*.

185   "The responsibilities of the position": Badeau, *Grant in Peace*, 149.

Chapter 8: The Outlier President

187   "I found nothing here": Crook, *Through Five Administrations*, 147.

187   "During the last two months": Ibid., 145.

187   "I have come back": Ibid., 151.

187   "He was the best hater": Ibid.

187   "appointing commanders": Badeau, *Grant in Peace*, 156.

188   "We are not a demonstrative family": Interview with Hannah Simpson Grant, *New York Graphic*, September 16, 1879, available at Ulysses S. Grant Homepage, https://www.granthomepage.com/inthsgrant.htm.

188   "The responsibilities of the position": Badeau, *Grant in Peace*, 149.

188   "On all leading questions": Ulysses S. Grant, inaugural address, March 4, 1869, available at the American Presidency Project, https://www.presidency.ucsb.edu/documents/inaugural-address-36.

189   "To protect the national honor": Ibid.

189   "The question of suffrage": Ibid.

190   "General Grant had something to say": *New York Times*, March 5, 1869.

190   "The air throughout the entire building": Mary Clemmer Ames, *Ten Years in Washington: Life and Scenes in the National Capital, as a Woman Sees Them* (Hartford, CT: A. D. Worthington & Co., 1874), 192.

190   "he bore himself": Badeau, *Grant in Peace*, 159.

192   "A great soldier might also be": Henry Adams, *The Education of Henry Adams* (self-published, 1907; reprint, Boston: Houghton Mifflin, 1918), 227.

194   "The plain man": Allan Nevins, *Hamilton Fish: The Inner History of the Grant Administration*, vol. 1 (New York: Frederick Ungar Publishing Co., 1957), 567.

195   "No, Sherman must succeed me": Grant, *Personal Memoirs of Julia Dent Grant*, 172.

196   "There was something": Crook, *Through Five Administrations*, 155.

196   "He unconsciously treated his Cabinet": Wilson, *The Life of General John A. Rawlins*, 313.

197   "Grant was in reality": Badeau, *Grant in Peace*, 81.

197   "first and most imperative tasks": Nevins, *Hamilton Fish*, vol. 1, 124.

198   "Make a clean sweep": Crook, *Through Five Administrations*, 162.

198   "Her interest in her domestic household": Ibid., 178.

199   "It warmed us all": Ibid.

199   "The White House lot": Grant, *In the Days of My Father*, 58.

199   "the house is brightened": Ames, *Ten Years in Washington*, 173.

200   "old, gray, irascible": Garland, *Ulysses S. Grant*, 397.

200   "You should take better care": Grant, *In the Days of My Father*, 97.

201   "A correspondent from the Old World": Garland, *Ulysses S. Grant*, 404.

201   "Mrs. Grant's morning receptions": Ames, *Ten Years in Washington*, 176.

202   "You and I, General": Badeau, *Grant in Peace*.

203   "The General says": Grant, *Personal Memoirs of Julia Dent Grant*, 182.

204   "pitted against the keen": Garland, *Ulysses S. Grant*, 443.

204   "In his desire": Ibid.

204   "The proper treatment of the original occupants": Ulysses S. Grant, inaugural address, March 4, 1869.

206   "Those about here": McFeely, *Grant: A Biography*, 317.

206   "For the first time": Arthur Casswell Parker, *The Life of General Ely S. Parker: Last Grand Sachem of the Iroquois and General Grant's Military Secretary* (Buffalo, NY: Buffalo Historical Society, 1919), 138.

207   "a system which looks to the extinction": Ulysses S. Grant, "First Annual Message," December 6, 1869, available at the American Presidency Project, https://www.presidency.ucsb.edu/documents/first-annual-message-11.

207   "all lies": Anne Broache, "Chief Lobbyist: He Made Little Headway with President Grant, but Red Cloud Won over the 19th Century's Greatest Photographers," *Smithsonian* (June 2005).

207   "I am poor": Chief Red Cloud, speech at the Cooper Union, New York City, June 16, 1870.

208   "one who is but a remove": Parker, *The Life of General Ely S. Parker*, 155.

208   "In the end General Parker": Ibid.

Chapter 9: The Battleground of Reconstruction

210 "The people who had been in rebellion": Grant, *Personal Memoirs*, 525.

211 "Appomattox signified much but settled little": William Gillette, *Retreat from Reconstruction, 1896–1879* (Baton Rouge: Louisiana State University Press, 1979), 1.

212 "I suppose not": Smith, *Grant*, 502.

213 "Mr. President, I am an administration man": Charles Sumner, *Charles Sumner: His Complete Works* (Boston: Lee & Shepard, 1900), 172.

213 "We are called to consider": H. W. Brands, *The Man Who Saved the Union: Ulysses Grant in War and Peace* (New York: Doubleday, 2012), 461.

216 "A condition of affairs now exists": Joint Select Committee to Inquire into the Condition of Affairs in the Late Insurrectionary States, report to Congress, February 19, 1872.

217 two incidents in that area: Mark L. Bradley, *The Army and Reconstruction, 1865–1877* (Washington, DC: Center of Military History United States Army, 2015).

217 "a carnival of crime": US Congress Joint Select Committee on the Condition of Affairs in the Late Insurgency State, "Conditions of Affairs in the Southern States, South Carolina Report of Major Merrill," 1872, p. 1601.

218 "The machinery for the execution": Annual Report of the Secretary of War (Washington, DC: US War Department, 1872).

219 "They knew little": Benjamin Perley Poore, *Life of U. S. Grant* (Philadelphia: Hubbard Bros., Publishers, 1885), 60.

220 "With sorrow unspeakable": Sumner, *Charles Sumner: His Complete Works*, 93.

221 "He did have a record": Brands, *The Man Who Saved the Union*, 494.

221 "He was an idealist": Crook, *Through Five Administrations*, 189.

222 "We will carry this state": George W. Childs, *Recollections (of General Grant)* (Philadelphia: J. B. Lippincott & Company, 1890), 75.

223 "Greeley's Presidential campaign": Poore, *Life of U. S. Grant*, 120.

223 "he was killed by ridicule": Crook, *Through Five Administrations*, 192.

223 "The effects of the late civil strife": Ulysses S. Grant, second inaugural address, March 4, 1873, available at the American Presidency Project, https://www.presidency.ucsb.edu/documents/inaugural-address-37.

226 "Governments that could not keep": Mark Wahlgren Summers, *Fear, Paranoia, and the Making of Reconstruction* (Chapel Hill: University of North Carolina Press, 2009), 264.

227 "intestines and putrefied": Jack Beatty, *Age of Betrayal: The Triumph of Money in America, 1865–1900* (New York: Vintage Books, 2013), 135.

228 "the right to operate": Michael A. Ross, "Justice Miller's Reconstruction: The Slaughter-House Cases, Health Codes, and Civil Rights in New

'Orleans, 1861–1873," *Journal of Southern History* 64, no. 4 (November 1998): 671.

229   "O youth and health": The poem, published May 21, 1874, is available at the Walt Whitman Archive, https://whitmanarchive.org/published/periodical /poems/per.00134.

229   "silent, tense, with tears": Grant, *In the Days of My Father*, 176.

230   "We are your true friends": *New York Herald*, February 11, 1876; *New York Sun*, February 12, 1876.

230   "Whereas it has been satisfactorily": Ulysses S. Grant, "Proclamation 220: Law and Order in the State of Louisiana," presidential proclamation, September 15, 1874, available at the American Presidency Project, https://www .presidency.ucsb.edu/documents/proclamation-220-law-and-order-the -state-louisiana.

231   "You have had the most trying": Garland, *Ulysses S. Grant*, 429.

232   "Again the barbarous tyranny": Sumner, *Charles Sumner: His Complete Works*, 217.

232   "Don't let the bill fail": "Civil Rights Act of 1875," United States Senate Historical Office, available at https://www.cop.senate.gov/artandhistory /history/common/image/Civil_Rights_Act_1875.htm.

233   "Of course, his decline": Crook, *Through Five Administrations*, 214.

233   "You ought not have done that": Grant, *Personal Memoirs of Julia Dent Grant*, 187.

235   "Whilst proud of what we have done": U. S. Grant, remarks at the opening of the 1876 Centennial Exhibition, May 10, 1876, available at http://www.sonof thesouth.net/union-generals/ulysses-s-grant/president-grants-philadelphia -speech.htm.

235   "he read sulkily": Roy Morris Jr., *Fraud of the Century: Rutherford B. Hayes, Samuel Tilden, and the Stolen Election of 1876* (New York: Simon & Schuster, 2007), 33.

235   "I have had a wide acquaintance": Poore, *Life of U. S. Grant*, 225.

236   "Grant's legendary photographic memory": Timothy Rives, "Grant, Babcock, and the Whiskey Ring," *Prologue* 32, no. 3 (Fall 2000), National Archives.

237   "I have come": Crook, *Through Five Administrations*, 213–14.

237   "the effect of this decision": "Proceedings of the Senate Sitting for the Trial of William W. Belknap, Late Secretary of War," 44th Cong., 1st sess. (Washington, DC: US Government Printing Office, 1876).

238   "the greatest mistakes in his career": Badeau, *Grant in Peace*, 405.

Chapter 10: The Bitter Divide

241   "The truth is that Grant": Dee Brown, *The Year of the Century 1876* (New York: Scribner, 1966).

242 "I would prefer to go": Charles Richard Williams, ed., *Diary and Letters of Rutherford Birchard Hayes, Nineteenth President of the United States*, vol. 2 (Columbus: Ohio State Archaeological and Historical Society, 1922), 17.

243 "a stunning blow": Ibid., 356.

243 "Hallo Twenty-third": Ibid.

243 "An officer fit for duty": Ibid., 497.

244 "the magnetic man": Morris, *Fraud of the Century*, 62.

248 "it seems something more": Charles Richard Williams, ed., *Diary and Letters of Rutherford Birchard Hayes, Nineteenth President of the United States*, vol. 3, February–June 1876 (Columbus: Ohio State Archaeological and Historical Society, 1922), 326.

248 "Governor Hayes is a good selection": Morris, *Fraud of the Century*, 97.

248 "organized upon a system": Rutherford B. Hayes, "1876 Acceptance Speech," July 8, 1876, available at https://www.rbhayes.org/hayes/1876-acceptance -speech.

248 "In 1876 as in 1860": Hans L. Trefousse, *Rutherford B. Hayes*, American Presidents Series (New York: Times Books/Henry Holt and Company, 2002), 93.

251 "is comprised in one word": Morris, *Fraud of the Century*, 133.

251 "General Grant was one of the truest": Childs, *Recollections*, 70.

252 "I am General Grant": Badeau, *Grant in Peace*, 310.

253 "In the minds of many": Paul Lexand Haworth, *The Hayes-Tilden Disputed Presidential Election of 1876* (Cleveland: Burrows Brothers Company, 1901), 8.

253 "Would it be safe": Ibid., 9.

255 "Month after month": Lloyd Robinson, *The Stolen Election: Hayes Versus Tilden—1876* (New York: Doubleday, 1968), 111.

258 "Even before it begun": Dorothy Sterling, ed., *The Trouble They Seen: The Story of Reconstruction in the Words of African Americans* (Boston: Da Capo Press, 1994), 463–64.

259 "cruel, bloodthirsty, wanton": Ulysses S. Grant, letter to D. H. Chamberlain, governor of South Carolina, July 26, 1876, available at Teaching American History, https://teachingamericanhistory.org/library/document/letter-to-d-h -chamberlain-governor-of-south-carolina.

259 "Insurrection and domestic violence": Presidential Election of 1876, https:// www.google.com/books/edition/Presidential_Election_of_1876/TElDAA AAYAAJ.

259 "There is no use concealing": Mark Antony DeWolfe Howe, ed., *Home Letters of General Sherman* (New York: Kessinger Publishing, 2006), 386.

260 "a four year struggle": Ibid.

260 "And all eyes": Garland, *Ulysses S. Grant*, 445.

260   "*Dies irae*": Trefousse, *Rutherford B. Hayes*, 98.

260   "On the night of": A. M. Gibson, *A Political Crime: The History of the Great Fraud* (New York: William Gottsberger, 1885), 49.

261   "Gentlemen, it looks to me": Childs, *Recollections*, 77.

261   "I think we are defeated": Morris, *Fraud of the Century*, 187.

261   "We escape a heavy responsibility": Trefousse, *Rutherford B. Hayes*, 99.

262   "The Battle Won": Morris, *Fraud of the Century*, 189.

262   "Tilden is Elected": Ibid.

263   "We have come, sir": Jerrell H. Shofner, "Fraud and Intimidation in the Florida Election of 1876," *Florida Historical Quarterly* 42, no. 4 (April 1964): 325.

264   "We can fight": Allan Nevins, ed., *Selected Writings of Abram S. Hewitt* (New York: Columbia University Press, 1937), 155–79.

264   "the wrecking of trains": Hamilton Fish, diary entry (explaining Grant's decision to send a telegram to Sherman), undated diary entry, believed to be November 9, 1876, recorded in John Y. Simon, ed., *The Papers of Ulysses S. Grant*, vol. 28, *November 1, 1876–September 30, 1878* (Carbondale: Southern Illinois University Press, 2005).

265   "Instruct General Augur": Smith, *Grant*, 598. Ulysses S. Grant to General Sherman, November 10–11, 1876.

265   "No man worthy": Brooks D. Simpson. "Ulysses S. Grant and the Electoral Crisis of 1876–77," *Hayes Historical Journal* 11, no. 2 (Winter 1992).

265   "Everything now depends": Ibid.

266   "It is almost impossible": Nevins, *Selected Writings of Abram S. Hewitt*.

Chapter 11: An Election in Doubt

267   "He told me": Hamilton Fish, diary entry, November 14, 1876, recorded in John Y. Simon, ed., *The Papers of Ulysses S. Grant*, vol. 28, *November 1, 1876–September 30, 1878* (Carbondale: Southern Illinois University Press, 2005).

269   "I remonstrate and protest": Allan Nevins, *Hamilton Fish: The Inner History of the Grant Administration*, vol. 2 (New York: Frederick Ungar Publishing Co., 1957), 847.

269   "They are always in trouble": Brands, *The Man Who Saved the Union*, 574.

270   "The army should have nothing to do": Almira Russell Hancock, *Reminiscences of Winfield Scott Hancock* (New York: C. L. Webster & Co., 1887), 153.

271   "Few shrewder and more adroit": Gibson, *A Political Crime*, 249.

271   "thought it rather hard": Nevins, *Selected Writings of Abram S. Hewitt*.

272   By the end of the meeting: Morris, *Fraud of the Century*, 235.

273   "It is lucky": Grant, *Personal Memoirs of Julia Dent Grant*, 218.

274   "Grant wanted to present himself": Brooks D. Simpson, "Ulysses S. Grant and the Electoral Crisis of 1876–77," *Hayes Historical Journal* 11, no. 2 (Winter 1992).

275 "This matter is very complicated": Childs, *Recollections*, 77–78.

275 "I have thought": Ibid., 78.

276 "It was repeatedly stated": James Monroe, "The Hayes-Tilden Electoral Commission: How Congress Settled the Disputed Electoral Count in the Presidential Election of 1876," *Atlantic* (October 1893).

278 "The country is agitated": President Ulysses S. Grant, "January 29, 1877: Message Regarding Presidential Election," available at UVA Miller Center, https://millercenter.org/the-presidency/presidential-speeches/january-29-1877-message-regarding-presidential-election.

Chapter 12: The Presidency Saved

282 "a terror": Anthony Champagne and Dennis Pope, "Joseph P. Bradley: An Aspect of a Judicial Personality," *International Society of Political Psychology* 6, no. 3 (September 1985): 481–93.

282 But there was another unspoken reason: "Secret History of the Disputed Election 1876–77," in Nevins, *Selected Writings of Abram S. Hewitt*, 172–73.

288 "The meeting was entirely informal": *Cincinnati Gazette*, special dispatch to the *New York Times*, February 15, 1878.

289 "if in some discreet way": Theodore Clarke Smith, *The Life and Letters of James Abram Garfield: 1831–1877* (New Haven, CT: Yale University Press, 1925), 625.

289 "What did the South want?": C. Vann Woodward, *Reunion and Reaction: The Compromise of 1877 and the End of Reconstruction* (New York: Oxford University Press, 1966), 51.

289 "curious combination": Ibid., 53.

291 "In answer to your dispatch": Stephen B. Packard to Ulysses S. Grant, and Culver C. Sniffen to Packard, March 1, 1877, recounted in Brooks D. Simpson, "Ulysses S. Grant and the Electoral Crisis of 1876–77."

292 "My nervous system": Nevins, *Selected Writings of Abram S. Hewitt*.

292 "Tilden simply lacked": John D. Bergamini, *The Hundredth Year: The United States in 1876* (New York: G. P. Putnam's Sons, 1976), 335.

293 "With so much fraud": Ibid., 333.

293 "By 1875, it was plain": Summers, *Fear, Paranoia, and the Making of Reconstruction*, 250.

294 "Old Eight to Seven": Vincent de Santis, "American Politics in the Gilded Age," *Review of Politics* (Cambridge University Press) 25, no. 4 (October 1963): 551–61.

294 "I will say just what Buckner": Grant, *Personal Memoirs of Julia Dent Grant*, 196.

295 "To my dismay": Major-General A. W. Greely, USA Retired, *Reminiscences of Adventure and Service: A Record of Sixty-Five Years* (New York: Charles Scribner's Sons, 1927), 234.

296   "Mistakes have been made": President Ulysses S. Grant, final address to
       Congress, December 5, 1876, available at the American Presidency Project,
       https://www.presidency.ucsb.edu/documents/eighth-annual-message-3.

296   "No American has carried": McFeely, *Grant: A Biography*, 449.

Chapter 13: The Search for Purpose

299   "Oh, Ulys": Grant, *Personal Memoirs of Julia Dent Grant*, 197.

299   "the wanderings of Ulysses": Badeau, *Grant in Peace*, 307.

300   "the object of his journey": Young, *Around the World with General Grant*, 3.

300   "I know this reception": Garland, *Ulysses S. Grant*, 452.

301   "But it had to be done": Young, *Around the World with General Grant*, 416.

301   "was that twelve years": Andrew L. Slap, *The Doom of Reconstruction:
       The Liberal Republicans in the Civil War Era* (New York: Fordham Uni-
       versity Press, 2006), 239–40.

302   "We got through": Charles Richard Williams, *The Life of Rutherford
       Birchard Hayes, Nineteenth President of the United States* (Boston: Hough-
       ton Mifflin Co., 1914), 64.

303   "The Presidency was not a thing": Ulysses S. Grant Jr., interview with
       Hamlin Garland, Hamlin Garland Papers, Doheny Library, University of
       Southern California; "Ulysses S. Grant, Jr.," available at Ulysses S. Grant
       Homepage, https://www.granthomepage.com/us_grant_jr.htm.

304   "Do you not desire success?": Grant, *Personal Memoirs of Julia Dent
       Grant*, 321.

304   "There is a rumor": Florence Gratiot Bale, "Galena's Memories of General
       Ulysses S. Grant," *Journal of the Illinois State Historical Society, 1908–
       1984* (University of Illinois Press) 21, no. 3 (1928): 415–16.

305   "And when asked what State": Kenneth D. Ackerman, *Dark Horse: The
       Surprise Election and Political Murder of President James A. Garfield*
       (New York: Carroll & Graf, 2003), 86–87.

305   "As the account": Ulysses S. Grant Jr., interview with Hamlin Garland,
       Hamlin Garland Papers, Doheny Library, University of Southern Cali-
       fornia.

306   "I can't say that I regret": Bale, "Galena's Memories of General Ulysses S.
       Grant," 416.

306   "My knees don't knock": Interview with Ulysses S. Grant, *Chicago Inter
       Ocean*, October 31, 1879.

307   "I sincerely hope": John Y. Simon, ed., *The Papers of Ulysses S. Grant*,
       vol. 30, *October 1, 1880–December 31, 1882* (Carbondale: Southern Illi-
       nois University Press, 2008), 116.

307   "He is a sort of lawyer": Interview with Ulysses S. Grant, *New York World*,
       July 5, 1881.

310   "Oh my. I think": Grant, *Personal Memoirs of Julia Dent Grant*, 353.

Chapter 14: Grant's Own Story

311 "The country looks with so much regret": Robert Underwood Johnson, *Remembered Yesterdays* (Boston: Little, Brown & Company, 1923), 210.

312 "a lonely air": Ibid., 211.

312 "He had been hurt": Ibid.

313 "I couldn't stand the amputations": Ibid., 214–15.

313 "I told him": Ibid., 215.

314 "There came moments": Badeau, *Grant in Peace*, 428.

315 "not only the monumental injustice": Mark Twain, *Mark Twain's Autobiography* (New York: Harper & Brothers, 1924), 59. This is a partial autobiography that was published posthumously.

315 "I had delayed answering": Ulysses S. Grant, letter to Samuel Clemens, January 14, 1881.

316 "Mr. President, I am embarrassed": Richard Goldhurst, *Many Are the Hearts: The Agony and the Triumph of Ulysses S. Grant* (New York: Reader's Digest Press, 1975), 123.

316 "Giving his whole strategic mind": Ibid., 125.

317 "I didn't know whether to cry": Twain, *Mark Twain's Autobiography*, 45.

318 "This was just like": Ibid., 51.

319 "down in my heart": Grant, *Personal Memoirs of Julia Dent Grant*, 355.

319 "wonderful machine": Twain, *Mark Twain's Autobiography*, 60.

319 "with what perseverance": Grant, *Personal Memoirs of Julia Dent Grant*, 355.

319 "arrived . . . hoping to win": McFeely, *Grant: A Biography*, 498.

320 "what molten lead": Childs, *Recollections*, 113.

320 "my great dear father": Ulysses S. Grant Jr., interview with Hamlin Garland, Hamlin Garland Papers, Doheny Library, University of Southern California.

321 "One by hemorrhages": Ulysses S. Grant, note to Dr. John Hancock Douglas, Al Rossiter, "Science Today: The Final Victor[y] of Ulysses S. Grant," UPI, March 11, 1961.

321 "I have been twice": Childs, *Recollections,* 112.

321 "General Buckner said": John R. Procter, "A Blue and Gray Friendship," *Century* 53 (April 1897).

322 "'Grant,' Buckner said": Grant, *Personal Memoirs of Julia Dent Grant*, 330.

322 "We were as brothers": Flood, *Grant and Sherman*, 2.

322 "Why, general": Childs, *Recollections*, 72.

322 "The hand which had seized": *Reminiscence of Ulysses S. Grant*, 68.

323 "I feel that we are on the eve": Grant, *Personal Memoirs*, 590.

324 "Look after our dear children": Ross, *The General's Wife*.

324 "I called to give you": Walter A. Friedman, *Birth of a Salesman: The Transformation of Selling in America* (Cambridge, MA: Harvard University Press, 2004), 60.

325 "Get the prospect seated": Ibid., 299.

Chapter 15: The Meaning of Grant's Life . . . Then and Now

328   "He got the big issues": Chernow, *Grant*, 858.

331   The NAACP reports: NAACP, "History of Lynchings," https://www .naacp.org/history-of-lynchings.

331   "Reconstruction poses a challenge": Eric Foner, "Successes and Failures of Reconstruction Hold Many Lessons," *New York Times*, May 26, 2015.

333   "the universally kind feeling": Grant, *Personal Memoirs*, 567.

INDEX

electoral dispute, 260–66
general election campaign, 254–60
Hamburg massacre of 1876, 257–59
legitimacy issue, 292–96
Republican Party nomination, 244–49
Election of 1880, 303–8
Republican National Convention, 303–6
Election of 1884, 308
Election of 2020, xi–xiii, xv–xvii, 332
Electoral Commission, 275–87
Compromise of 1877, 286–92
Electoral Commission Act of 1877, 278
Emancipation Proclamation, 92–93
Enforcement Acts, 216, 225–26, 329
English, William Hayden, 306
Evarts, William H., 287

"Famous apple tree," 305
Ferry, Thomas W., 277, 279, 292
Fetterman, William, 205
Field, David Dudley, 280–81
Fifteenth Amendment, 214, 215, 232–33, 244, 302, 329
Fifth Massachusetts Cavalry, 256
Filibuster, 285, 286, 287, 290
First Battle of Bull Run, 77–79
Fish, Hamilton, 194, 197, 213, 304
election of 1876, 264, 267–70
Fisk, James, 203
Florida
during the Civil War, 71
election of 1876, 4–5, 257, 261, 262–63, 273, 280–82
Floyd, George, 327
Floyd, John B., 82–83
Foner, Eric, 331
Foote, Andrew, 81, 117
Ford's Theater, 149, 151–52
Forney, John, 212
Fort Laramie, 204–5

Fort Laramie Treaty, 204–5
Fort Phil Kearney, 205
Fort Pickering, 174
Fort Putnam, 25
Fort Vancouver, 53–54, 206
"Forty acres and a mule," 172–73
Foster, Charles, 288–89
Fourteenth Amendment, 173–74, 216–17, 227–28, 302, 329
Fourth US Infantry, 28, 32, 33–34, 35, 51
Freedmen's Bureau, 93–94, 170, 173
"Free soil," 63
Frelinghuysen, Frederick, 282
Fugitive Slave Act of 1850, 166

Galena, Illinois, 58–59, 66, 162–63
Galena Methodist Episcopal Church, 75
Garfield, James, 287–89, 296, 306–8
Garland, Hamlin, 56, 168, 179, 183, 200, 201, 203–4, 260
Georgetown School, 20
Georgia
during the Civil War, 71, 172
Atlanta Campaign, 127–31
election of 1876, 282
Georgia Railroad, 128
German Empire, 301
Gettysburg Address, 104–5
Gibson, A. M., 260–61, 271
Gilder, Richard, 311, 314–15, 317
Gildersleeve, Basil, 92
Gillette, William, 211
Golden Gate Park, toppling of Grant statue in, 326–28
Gold Rush, 51–53, 204
Gold standard, 188–89, 226–27
Goodwin, Doris Kearns, 72
Gould, Jay, 203
Grand Review of the Union Armies, 159–62

ALSO BY BRET BAIER

THREE DAYS AT THE BRINK

A gripping history of the secret meeting that helped win World War II—the now-forgotten Tehran Conference, where Roosevelt, Churchill, and Stalin plotted the war's endgame, including D-Day.

ALSO AVAILABLE
Three Days at the Brink
YOUNG READERS' EDITION

New York Times Bestseller

THREE DAYS IN MOSCOW

The story of how Ronald Reagan fought to end the Cold War, as framed around the 1988 Moscow Summit.

ALSO AVAILABLE
Three Days in Moscow
YOUNG READERS' EDITION

New York Times Bestseller

THREE DAYS IN JANUARY

A portrait of President Dwight Eisenhower that reveals Ike to be a model of the kind of strong yet principled leadership that is much needed in America today.

ALSO AVAILABLE
Three Days in January
YOUNG READERS' EDITION

Available in Hardcover, Paperback, and E-Book Wherever Books Are Sold
DISCOVER GREAT AUTHORS, EXCLUSIVE OFFERS, AND MORE AT HC.COM.